DOWN AND OUT IN CANADA:
Homeless Canadians

Thomas O'Reilly–Fleming

University of Windsor

Canadian Scholars' Press Inc.   Toronto   1993

Down and Out in Canada: Homeless Canadians

First published in 1993 by
Canadian Scholars' Press Inc.
180 Bloor St. W., Ste. 402
Toronto, Ontario
M5S 2V6

6010346 2 c.3

Canadian Cataloguing in Publication Data

O'Reilly-Fleming, Thomas, 1951 - .
Down and Out in Canada: Homeless Canadians

Includes bibliographical references.
ISBN 1-55130-017-6

1. Homeless persons - Canada. I. Title.

HV4509.073 1993 362.5'0971 C93-093975-1

Printed and bound in Canada

Dedication

To my dear mother and father,
Alice and William Fleming

For my beloved wife Patricia
and our beloved children,
Kate, Patrick and Thomas

To Scott Fleming, my brother

To James Fleming who rode the
rails and suffered
at the hands of the 'railway' bulls

To Tom Burgess, my grandfather
who experienced homelessness as a
boy firsthand

Table of Contents

Acknowledgements

No book is a singular accomplishment and this one is certainly no exception. There is a wide variety of individuals, organizations, and others who have made a contribution to its completion and who deserve acknowledgement for their efforts.

In Toronto the staff of several hostels and shelters welcomed my research efforts and provided assistance by arranging for private interview space. They are: Stop 86, Mercury House, Youth Without Shelter, Seaton House, and The Metropolitan Toronto Family Shelter Program. In the latter two cases the assistance of Bernie O'Leary and Boris Rostovik were crucial to the completion of the project and they deserve credit not only for their assistance and the lengthy interviews they permitted me, but also for their caring attitude to their clients. Several other organizations provided information on their services and clientele including Beat the Street, Covenant House, The Daily Bread Foodbank and Streethealth. In Oshawa, I am indebted to Terry Dunn of Hostel Services who opened the doors for me. In Victoria, The Association for Street Kids assisted in identifying hangouts and provided me with statistical information on the homeless children who use their storefront offices. In Vancouver, Sharon O'Leary gave me a walking tour of the areas frequented by the homeless which greatly aided my interview efforts. In Edmonton, my good friends Ian James and Jackie Cormier provided me with a place to stay while I conducted my last few interviews. In Windsor, Jennifer Gates of Trillium Cable donated information on homeless youth in the Windsor-Essex area.

Barry Snodden, a former worker with Beat the Street who in his spare time specializes in finding runaway children and whose dedication was inspiring, took me on a guided tour of Toronto's west end and through High Park which was invaluable in locating interview subjects. Angie Simonitz, a former student of mine, facilitated my interviews with the first of the youth shelters I approached.

Throughout the research process a number of individuals have been supportive in a number of ways and, assisted me as the need arose. My colleagues in the Department of Sociology and Anthropology were extremely supportive of this research especially Max Hedley. Several colleagues deserve special thanks and these are Professor Mahesh Pradhan, Professor Claude Vincent, and Professor Mansell Blair. Professor David Booth was a constant source of insight and direction and I am grateful for his ideas. Professor Mary Lorenz Dietz has been supportive of my research endeavours and made me feel welcome in the criminological section of the department. The Council of Deans graciously granted me a short sabbatical to finish writing this book. Dean Kate McCrone, Faculty of Social Science and former dean, Zbigniev Fallenbuchl, were highly supportive of my efforts and I owe them both a great deal. Several of my colleagues at various universities have provided criticisms of the work and ideas as it was ongoing (whether it was requested or not) and the book has benefitted from their insights. They are Livy Visano, Tullio Caputo, Ken Morrison, Robert S. Ratner, Ron Hinch, Frank Pearce, and Barry Clark. I wish to publicly acknowledge the support of his Eminence Archbishop Emmet Cardinal Carter who has long worked tirelessly on behalf of our underprivileged citizens.

A number of colleagues at Ontario universities provided me with various forms of assistance during the duration of the research for this book. They are: Bill Bateman and Dr. David Nimmo of Woodsworth College in Toronto; John Beattie, past Director, and Richard V. Ericson, Director, of The Centre of Criminology, University of Toronto; Roy Bowles of Trent University; Durham College (Oshawa); Patricia Armstrong, York University; and Ken Morrison, Wilfrid Laurier University.

I owe a special debt to four individuals who have deeply influenced my sociological imagination during the past twenty years. The late Ian D. Currie was a source of inspiration and his death in 1992 was a great loss to the sociological community in this country. The late Peter Kong-Ming New allowed me to tag along as his assistant while I was at University College and supported me throughout my graduate studies. Professor Terrence Morris honed my research skills while I was a graduate student in London, England. Finally, Professor Richard V. Ericson, currently Director of The Centre of Criminology, University of Toronto has been a source of support and inspiration during the many years I have known him.

My family in Toronto made possible much of the research that underpins this book by allowing my family and me to park ourselves in the house while I went out roaming the streets of Toronto. Alice and William Fleming put up with us and we are all grateful for their support. Scott Fleming spent a great deal of his leisure time discussing the material in this book and playing video games with me, and I am sure this book could not have been completed without his unstinting support. Two of my students, Peter Brady and John Cater, acted as research assistants providing me with materials and encouragement.

The three word processing personnel who re-typed endless versions of the manuscript, I am eternally grateful to; many thanks Diane Dupuis, Pat Jolie and Lucia Brown. The office staff of the Department of Sociology and Anthropology protected me from an onslaught of callers and put up with endless printings on our department laser machines. They are Andria Turner, Perry Pittao and Sue McGilveary.

The professional manner in which Tim Wayne, Editor of Canadian Scholars' Press handled this project was a refreshing experience at a difficult time in my life. Pamela Hamilton was efficient and a pleasure to work with.

Finally, my greatest thanks is to those homeless people who took the time to be interviewed by me in my travels. I hope I have done your lives justice, and that this book, in some small measure, prompts those with the power to redress the injustices we inflict upon the homeless in Canada to act, and act quickly.

Introduction

In 1987, on a trip to Wolfville, Nova Scotia I was visiting the local mental hospital when someone related that Maxwell Jones lived in town. Would I like to have lunch with him? Having spent more than a year studying psychopaths at The Henderson Therapeutic Community in Sutton, Surrey in the late 1970s I thought they were joking that the founder of the leading institution in this field, was living in a sleepy east coast town. But Max was indeed there, sequestered in his pristine little bungalow overlooking the Annapolis Valley, now 73, suffering from angina but possessed of the mind of a man at the peak of his powers. We spent a lazy afternoon in a local restaurant reminiscing about his early days as a psychiatrist in postwar London. Our talk drifted to Orwell and the Victoria Embankment, a favourite subject, and Max related the story of how he came to be regarded as one of the leading figures in psychiatry in this century in his modest way. His mind took me on a journey into an era long past, and onto new roads of thinking. "As a young psychiatrist I knew nothing of the lives of the down and outs, the homeless, those who lived by their wits, so I realized I had to listen to their stories. That is how our psychotherapeutic approach evolved. The homeless knew best how to treat one another and I simply went along for the ride."[1] Max, of course, did far more, but it was that synchronous meeting that began to reawaken in me an interest in the lives of those who exist on the margins in our society. Perhaps I was more receptive than I had been in a long time since I had just been fired from my job, and the homeless seemed not so far removed from me.

Over the next few months I began to notice, more and more, the homeless in Edmonton and Toronto. On one trip east, an old friend related the story of a high school acquaintance of my wife

Patricia's who, now in her thirties, had degenerated into a 'bag lady.' One night I was confronted by a spectre of a woman begging for money for food in downtown Toronto and talked with her about how she had arrived on the street. Her image haunted me for a long time, and it still does, and I found myself embarking on a sociological journey that would take over four years to complete. Earlier in my career I had benefited from my association with the late Dr. Peter Kong-Ming New, and it was under his tutelage that I commenced the learning process of becoming a field researcher. One of the first projects I completed was a study of skid row in Toronto, on which I lived for a period of time in order to understand the full meaning of the day-to-day activities of my subjects. I found myself now able to see the homeless whom I had just so recently found invisible. I suspect most of us train ourselves to avoid contact with the homeless. We learn to ignore their existence, viewing them as a nuisance, as lazy, shiftless, or potentially dangerous, and to develop avoidance rituals when we come into contact with them. They are an affront to the work ethic that propels us hurriedly and efficiently from one destination to the next. In this, they harken back to the hippies of the late 1960s whose disdain for the capitalist enterprise evoked considerable recrimination at both the personal and public level. The sociologist Steven Egger has referred to victims of serial murderers, who are drawn from the ranks of prostitutes and ethnic minorities, as the 'less dead' since they are somehow less valuable people in our society.[2] In reworking this model, the homeless for us are at once both less deserving, reflecting our intolerance of those who are idle and threaten to interrupt our daily activities, and frightening, for they remind us of the short distance from homefulness to homelessness.

Our general societal attitude of dehumanizing the homeless or even of outright anger towards them is a phenomenon I have been constantly reminded of during my research for this book. It was common when I explained my work to others to receive comments such as, "Why would you want to waste your time studying hopeless bums?" or "I wouldn't want one of them in my house" or "Don't you find they're all drunks?" or "The homeless can't be helped because they don't want it." But equally, many with whom I conversed on the subject, although somewhat reluctantly after some of these initial reactions, were sensitive to the problems faced by the homeless in our country and genuinely curious about a social group that they knew little about. A sad fact of our growing and centralized modern society is that few of us have any direct experience of many forms of human behaviour. As citizens of Marshall McLuhan's "global village" we are acutely aware of developments on a minute-to-minute basis throughout the world yet remain isolated in our own neighbourhoods. The environs of the city are less an inviting panorama to many than an urban battleground to be navigated as with all due speed and with appropriate evasive manoeuvres. We have come to rely increasingly on the media to fill in our knowledge about the netherworlds in our society.[3] But homelessness is not a topic that most Canadians find palatable. We tend to think of it in terms of a problem that occurs, like epidemic levels of violence, south of our borders.

Homelessness has been the subject of innumerable books and articles in the United States in the past three years as public interest in the subject of what is to be done about the homeless has mounted.[4] Homelessness has become a central topic of debate in North America about how our society cares for or neglects some of its weakest members. Homelessness has been the focus of important movies. In The **The Fisher King**, Robin Williams portrayed a college professor driven to homelessness by the senselessness of the slaughter of his wife by a mass murderer. On the street he is the victim of a brutal beating by thugs who want him to stop 'dirtying up' their neighbourhood. Another movie, **Curly Sue** presents a picture of the 'new' homeless, remnants of ruptured families, nameless victims of political and economic inequities in our society. While the media dramatizations have largely been American, the powerful images and moral issues they raise are relevant in Canada, more so now than at any time in our history. Canadians who live in substandard or overcrowded housing constitute the 'prehomeless' who teeter on the verge of homelessness. In late 1992, estimates on the number of homeless can reasonably be adjusted for the effects of the worst economic recession since the 1930s. More Canadians are unemployed in this country than at any time in history. Some 500 Canadian jobs a day were lost every day for the past three years according to Statistics Canada data released in October 1992.[5] Canadians who always thought their jobs were secure suddenly find themselves without employment, and increasingly these are people who are unemployable, either due to age or lack of appropriate skills. Despite considerable rhetoric governments invest in retraining only a small percentage of the unemployed. As large employers shut their doors for good, and the world's largest real estate company, Canadian-owned Olympia and York declared bankruptcy in May, the full depth of the fiscal crisis began to hit home. Many of you reading this book will know someone personally who has lost their employment recently. Few Canadians feel secure in their employment, and at least as many fear they may lose their life savings when they are made redundant.

Homelessness is neither as invisible nor as far-removed from us as we might have once hoped. The Canadian homeless whom I have interviewed are overwhelmingly average, drawn from all walks of life, all social and economic strata, males and females, singles and families, young children and old, from a wide cross section of ethnic and racial backgrounds. Homelessness is not unique to one region of Canada nor, as a recent study by The Addiction Research Foundation has clearly illustrated, is it an exclusively urban problem.[6] Few of the homeless stand out on our streets. One can pass them by without the slightest idea that they are without shelter for they fit in with the crowd. In a sense, part of their invisibility lies in their unremarkable appearance. Again, our lack of experience with the homeless might lead us to believe that they must necessarily act in some bizarre or untoward manner.

It is often a difficult and emotionally moving experience to talk with homeless people. One young woman, barely sixteen, spent hours describing a life of sexual abuse in her familial home followed by her graphic and non-emotional discussion of life as a street prostitute. Interviews like this deeply moved me, to tears, then anger, and provided a catalyst for my research, and refocused my attention on praxis issues. Throughout the research process I have attempted not only to understand as fully as possible the position of homeless people in our society, but also to appreciate it from their perspective. This has not been a hard task. Almost without exception I have been profoundly impressed not only by the sense of idealism that homeless Canadians express even when their own lives are undergoing dramatic transformations but by the value of each of their lives. Everyone of them has something to contribute to their nation.

This book is written in a direct sociological style so that it will be accessible to the greatest number of readers. It is my contention that university-based researchers and writers have an obligation to present their scholarship to the greatest number of people. In a very real sense this extends the boundaries of the university to include all of those within society who would like to learn. While there are fields in which the argument demands language and form that eludes the average reader, or is directed towards a specialist audience, the issue of homelessness is not one of these. In fact, I contend that the "academatization" of such social issues is what relegates them to the status of unresolvable problems that can only serve as the grist for 'further study'. While I have disagreements with some features of constitutive criminology, the necessity to move the focus away from a continuing dialectic to immediate praxis (from discussion/debate to action) is an approach that I believe readers will agree is warranted after reading this work.[7] Homelessness demands attention from the public, policymakers, researchers, social workers, caregivers, and anyone else who cares about the weak in our society. Social science is now assuming an important function in legal cases in our country as judges grapple with interpretations of individual rights under The Charter of Rights and Freedoms. I would argue that the average Canadian not only deserves to be informed about an issue that costs us countless millions of dollars each year, but that education on homelessness and the corollary questions it raises is long overdue. Academic readers will find that I have left them pathways to follow for future research in reference notes in this book, and in several articles that I have published on the topic of homelessness.

The journey that I took into the world of the homeless took me to countless locations across the country, in back streets, on park benches, in coffee and donut shops, hamburger joints, hostels, shelters, bars and flop houses. The interviews with the homeless which inform the analysis for this book consist of 219 interviews conducted in six Canadian cities over three provinces.[8] I interviewed homeless people from 1987 through to the present in Victoria, Vancouver, Edmonton, Toronto, Oshawa, and Windsor. These included persons in all of the major categories of homeless persons in this country: single men, families, single mothers and fathers, teenagers, single women, senior citizens, refugees, and immigrants. My interviews were conducted wherever the homeless congregated in the street or in shelters and hostels that agreed to let me interview their clients. Two methods of recording interviews were used; where appropriate interviews were tape-recorded with the permission of the homeless person. In other cases, notes were taken either during or as soon as practical following an interview if the subject objected to being tape-recorded. Many homeless people do not feel comfortable with "official" recording of their views fearing intervention by any one of a number of social control agencies. All of the research subjects were granted both anonymity and confidentiality. All of the principal subjects, names were changed to protect their identity and some relevant information has been altered to make them unrecognizable.

The underlying methodology was the depth interview technique supplemented by observation in both shelter and outside settings. The clearest statement of this technique and the process of interpreting social reality are provided by Denzin in his book **Interpretive Interactionism**. Denzin's overview of the perspective draws upon a long tradition of thought and research in the field of qualitative research. It comprises, essentially, the attempt to "make the world of problematic lived experience of ordinary people directly available."[10] Basically the approach has five major strengths:

1. It can help identify different definitions of the problem and the programs being evaluated, for example, how persons interpret the processes of becoming and being a 'homeless' individual. The 'thick descriptions' generated by this form of interview data permit the contrasting of the perspectives of various social actors who are involved in this area of human agency.

2. The assumptions held by various interested parties, social workers, the homeless, housing authorities, innovators, on-line professionals, politicians, and interest groups, can be located and shown to be correct or incorrect.

3. Strategic points of intervention into social situations can be identified. In this way, current approaches to services, and alternatives available to the homeless can be improved and evaluated.

4. It is possible to suggest alternatives from which policies, programs, and the problem can be addressed.

5. The more qualitative, interpretive materials furnished by this approach supplement the areas that statistical data and a statistical approach cannot contribute to.

There are, furthermore, five stages or steps in the interpretive process which are applicable to this research project:

1. The deconstruction and analysis of extant understandings of the problem from existing literature. This comprises a review of literature which pre-dates the formulation of the research questions which underscored the project.

2. The capturing of the phenomenon through interview techniques, and obtaining multiple instances of it.

3. The bracketing of the phenomenon so that its essential structures and features can be uncovered.

4. The act of construction or putting the pieces back together.

5. Contextualization, or locating the phenomenon back in the natural social world.[9]

While I had initially planned to interview in several other major cities I found that this was unnecessary for two reasons. First, many of the homeless are mobile and it soon became apparent that homelessness is a problem that is not situated in one location with features specific to that location. While rates of homelessness may vary from city to city, the lived experiences of the homeless are not bound by these geographical boundaries. Secondly, common themes, experiences, and epiphanies soon emerged in the interviews conducted, so that I found that the data were beginning to become repetitious. While I would not wish to contend that I have documented every form that homelessness takes I believe I have been able to produce representative data on this problem. Generalizations have reasonably been made from the sample collected. I have no doubt that, for example, native Canadians represent a significant number of the homeless population in Winnipeg and Saskatoon. There are obviously problems and experiences that are effected by their location on the prairies. However, I would also contend that not only did I have interview data from homeless native Canadians who had experienced homelessness in these cities, but further I was able to draw upon published material and interviews with front line workers.

I have not, due to the limitation of my own resources, been able to document the experience of rural homelessness. Neither have I been able to fully examine the relationship between homelessness and AIDS, a social problem that has received some attention in the American literature. This is not a study that can accurately tell anyone how many homeless people exist in Canada tonight, but this was not my intention in embarking upon this research. To me, it makes little difference whether there are 10,000 or 100,000 homeless in this country because any number of homeless are **too many** in a country as wealthy as Canada. As foodbank lines grow each month, hundreds of thousands of Canadians, many who are working poor, recognize the depths of the current economic decline in Canada. Foodbank co-ordinators are becoming increasingly aware that the public's capacity for generosity is waning not only because of their own declining resources and fears concerning their ability to survive, but because there is a limit to society's benevolence.[11] Part of what is illustrated in this book is the accelerating movement of all levels of Canadian government out of the provision of safety nets for our most

xviii . . . DOWN AND OUT IN CANADA

vulnerable citizens. As the homelessness crisis has grown in Canada so equally have governments kept pace by withdrawal from programs. This has occurred in the crucial area of affordable housing as well as in other core areas of social welfare.

Unfortunately in this country the homeless have not been able to organize as an effective political voice. Incredibly it was only in the last election that the homeless were permitted to vote due not to government action, but advocacy action on the part of a church group which brought a legal case on behalf of those with no fixed address. Although this denial of the democratic privilege would be scandalous if it had applied to minorities or women, the plight of the homeless had gone virtually unrecognized in this regard.

In the book that follows I have tried to remain true to the visions that homeless people expressed to me in our interviews. This is the first book that provides a national overview on homelessness in Canada, a country that has seen little academic interest in this troubling topic.[12] My intent in writing this book was initially to simply explore the homelessness problem in Canada, but my experience has convinced me that academic books must, in some instances, provide a basis for social action. For the first three years of this project I was unable to convince any public or private agency to contribute funding to enable me to carry out this research. In common with many research projects that examine social ills there is not a great deal of enthusiasm amongst funding agencies to underwrite critical scholarship. I have attempted herein to develop an analysis of the lived experience of the homeless set within the larger framework of a political economy analysis of those forces that both sustain and provide a catalyst to homelessness as a growing social crisis. My extensive review of the existing research literature indicated that not only was there very little work to build upon in the Canadian context, but that there were no studies in the voluminuous writing on homelessness that combined these two levels of analysis.

There is much in this book that will be painful and shocking for readers to experience but that is, in most respects, the condition in which homeless Canadians must live everyday. As you read this book you might ponder the meaning of home to you, and what being without a home would also mean in your life. I hope that those who read about the lives of their fellow Canadians will both individually and collectively make homelessness what Orwell called a "living issue," and that we will find the means to bring homeless women, children, and men back "in" to a decent standard of life. Homelessness has remained a silent national shame for far too long.

CHAPTER ONE
Homelessness in Canada

Introduction

In 1990s Canada, the problem of homelessness remains an enigma. The homeless are largely a social crisis for which there is no audience. There is little political currency to be made in championing the cause of the weakest in our society, those who are without benefit of shelter. They are a disenfranchised and forgotten group who only enjoy the momentary penetration of media attention at a moment of intense, yet arbitrarily selected crisis, and then fade into the netherworlds of our city streets.[1] They are the dispossessed and hidden people of our society, existing on the dark edges of prosperity. The homeless fuel our fears and act as a lesson for many of what happens when one does not adhere to the central dictates of our society. If there is little controversy centring around the homeless **problem** is it any wonder given their marginal existence? They escape public gaze, and largely elude our understanding. Little attention has been paid to their plight. During the United Nations Year of Shelter for the Homeless in 1987 efforts to address the homeless problem in Canada amounted to little more than a token effort.[2]

In the United States, where the homeless have not been passive, lobby, protest and action groups formed during the 1980s have been instrumental in bringing a greater public awareness of their problems at a variety of governmental levels.[3] Their protests, including one during the inauguration of President George Bush, have brought national attention to homelessness, but have not resulted in substantial gains in the services provided for the homeless, or in reaching solutions meant to end the problem altogether. In Canada, the mayors of the sixteen largest cities met recently and cited homelessness as the major problem that most of their respective metropoli must deal with at present. Former Mayor Art Eggleton indicated that Toronto has a homeless population numbering in the tens of thousands. He appealed to citizens in his 1991 New Year speech to help those without shelter in his city.[4] More and more, the issue of homelessness is being propelled out of the darkness and into the centre of a growing, fierce public debate about the nature of our society and the way we will deal with massive social maladies.

Most Canadians know very little concerning homelessness. Their stereotypical images of the homeless are drawn from momentary and often fearful glimpses on downtown streets or random media images. A series of documentaries, television programs and movies have created fleeting pastiches of homelessness based almost totally upon the American experience.[5] So rather than inducing us to think seriously about homelessness in this country these depictions provide a powerful comforting mechanism. We think of people living on the street as a problem that is epidemic in the U.S. but is insignificant in Canada. These images also serve to reinforce mythical images of the homeless in our country that are outdated; the old drunken skid row bum, the bag lady, the teen hooker in her miniskirt waiting for a john. The situation of homeless persons in this country bears some similarities with that of their American counterparts. But as with any socially produced problem there are features of this growing population that are reflections of a unique Canadian environment. While the Canadian public has been the recipient of very little information on the plight of the homeless individual it is arguable that the average citizen's consciousness regarding their plight has received some stimulation. While there is a substantial group in society that would prefer to characterize the problems of the homeless as personal failure or pathology, most would be quick to recognize the larger structural forces; i.e., the economy, unemployment, family breakdown, as influential in sending many literally packing to the street. They understand this at a gut level because of their own precarious existence balancing on the edge of the vast gulf of homelessness that confronts every person. Whether it is the auto worker in Windsor who sees the spectre of unemployment looming in the near future or has already forfeited his/her job, the woman who is being battered and thinking about a way out, or the young teen who has dreams for a life in the big city away from an abusive home, the world of the homeless is so close that it often proves more comforting to think of it in terms of a crisis **somewhere**

else rather than to consider the personal suffering and anguish of the homeless. A Gallop poll conducted in 1990 demonstrated how close the slide into homelessness is for most of us. They found that 20% of Canadians could last between one and three months if they lost their job, but a full 29% would be ruined within a month![6] These are sobering statistics that begin to inform us of the thin line that separates those with a home from those in the street.

We have not seen the development of any strategies for dealing with the elimination of homelessness arise from government. In almost completely ignoring the growing homeless problem in Canada, the federal government has continually cut funding for low cost housing projects even during the during the 1980s and 1990s when recession driven inflation has swelled the number of homeless and near homeless persons to new highs.[7] This has occurred in an era when the cost of housing has risen unbelievably quickly, outpacing the ability of large numbers of Canadians to ever consider home ownership, and for many, to even have a safe roof over their heads. At the provincial level we have seen little initiative to provide affordable housing for the variety of homeless who inhabit our streets. Much of the innovation has come at the grass roots level from homeless organizations, or creative shelter staff who have used their experience to find new solutions to a persistent problem.

Even though there has been very little research on the homeless condition in Canada there are already a considerable number of debates concerning the 'causes' of homelessness and the possible solutions to it. Homelessness by its very nature raises disturbing questions about our vision of ourselves and our society. How can so many Canadians be disenfranchised in a country that is so financially wealthy? What is to be done about homelessness, and why do we have homeless people at all? Why do so many children seek a life on the mean streets where violence, the sale of sex, and drugs are a way of life? Shall we ignore the homeless amongst us, and learn as one woman informed me, 'to step right over their carcasses' on our streets? The role of various levels of government in dealing with the homeless problem is one that is of central concern to this book given the failures that for too long have marked our approach, or lack of it, to the homeless.

We live in a country of great diversity and political contradictions that colour our approach to social woes. At the federal level the conservative government espouses policies in keeping with its American and British counterparts whose countries have served as a dress rehearsal for our future treatment of social ills.[8] Conservatives favour 'free-trade', competitive capitalism, 'trickle down' economics, tax breaks and incentives for the wealthy, and the cutting of social welfare schemes to the bare bones. Universal medical care in Canada, and unemployment insurance have already been cited by American politicians as 'unfair subsidies'. Liberals and New Democrats have a seemingly more humane approach that calls for the shifting of tax burdens, increased support for the most economically oppressed, and a role for the welfare state that is maintained at a reasonable level to accommodate the social ills produced in this country. However, in times of fiscal crisis, these good intentions are likely to, and have been fading rapidly.

Being without shelter is not a new phenomenon in our country. But neither is it a social problem that has been the focus of any considerable amount of public attention. This is a disturbing fact in itself. This book is the first one in this country to deal with the growing problem of homelessness, a problem that by the account of all reasonable sources has reached staggering proportions. Homelessness has become a national crisis that is in need of understanding, public attention and action. A more just society demands that the problems of the homeless become human problems of real people, and are not simply understood as a faceless 'crisis' that exists somewhere out there in the dark reaches of our cities.[9]

The term 'crisis' is one that I use with appropriate caution. It is a word that has been much overused in the media, trotted out when we wish to underscore the urgency and importance of our own beliefs, but I believe the term is warranted, and by the end of your reading of this book, I believe you will also agree with this assertion.

There is still a controversy that exists over the number of homeless people in our country and this problem is addressed in the pages that follow. Whether one agrees with the estimates of social action agencies that the number of Canadian homeless numbers between 100,000 and 250,000[10] or accepts a more conservative reading of the gravity of the situation, there is no doubt given the evidence provided by hostels, emergency shelters, advocacy reports, conferences, and government reports that a number of conditions exist:

1. Homelessness is a problem that has been growing consistently throughout the 1980s and began to spiral in the late 1980s as recession, unemployment, and inflation impacted upon Canadians, recently reaching unprecedented levels in the 1990s;[11]

2. There is a lack of affordable housing in major cities, which is a consistent factor associated with the rise in the homeless population;[12]

3. The composition of the homeless population has been changing over the 1980s and now young men, teenagers, and families with children predominate amongst homeless Canadians.[13]

4. Refugees and minorities are over-represented amongst the homeless.[14]

5. There are a growing number of homeless subpopulations who require not only decent housing but a variety of social support, medical, and counselling services. These include AIDS sufferers, the mentally disordered, substance abusers, and those with chronic medical conditions.

By 1992, as this book is being written, the condition of homelessness is one that cuts a wide swath across the social fabric of our society. We have become a less kinder, less gentler society where the list of persons who have become embroiled in our homeless crisis is long and inclusive. Women, men, and children from all socioeconomic strata; drawn from all racial and ethnic groups; those who are unemployed and those who are underemployed; the old; abused and battered mothers and their children; released prisoners; persons with AIDS; children who are runaways; the mentally infirm; alcoholics; drug users; the sexually abused and the throwaway people of our society: refugees, immigrants, and many who once held a place in the mainstream of society.

What is Homelessness?

Homelessness is a contemporary term that has its roots in the expansion of the numbers of persons without shelter that began to climb during the 1980s in North America.[15] This is not to say that homelessness is a new phenomenon. During the 1930s in Canada thousands of men traversed this country looking for work in the midst of the Great Depression. They literally 'tramped' the streets of their home and native land looking for a stake in society. In British Columbia many were herded into work camps in the northern part of the province to keep them from forming into a collective social force that might have the power to disrupt the current government of the day.[16] The homeless men of this era were viewed in two very distinct ways. Average Canadians saw them as men 'down on their luck' waiting for a brighter day to dawn. Police and government officials often saw them as a potentially destructive political force that had to be closely monitored and controlled.

Throughout history, Western society has had a very low tolerance level for the visibly shelterless. In England, vagrancy laws were enacted as early as 1349 but since that point have been a constant fact of common law and hence our conception of socially acceptable behaviour for the visibly impoverished.[17] Throughout history, since that point, we have witnessed cyclical attempts to control the homeless through both harsh and more humane applications of the law, though the latter are extremely difficult to find and often are of an anecdotal form. The plain fact is that we, as a society, have little tolerance for those who plainly demonstrate in a public place that the great dream of equal opportunity that underlies our work ethic in this country does not deliver for innumerable people.[18] We recognize in municipal by-laws that prohibit loitering, panhandling, begging or sleeping in public places a contempt for the homeless. In denying the questionable pleasure of sleeping on an iron grate in freezing temperatures, law enforcement agencies underscore our interest in business over the rights of the individual.

Panhandling laws are a primary example of the hypocritical attitude that municipal politicians have toward the homeless and poor in our society. It is a municipal offence to panhandle or beg for money in a public street. Persons apprehended engaging in this activity are liable to a considerable fine, generally in excess of $50.[19] This heavy-handed approach of the law punishes persons who have no money by fining them even more money they do not have. What are we protecting by such a law, other than the sensibilities of passersby? What place does such a law have in a just society? Why would we wish to fine the hungry for having the audacity to ask pedestrians to voluntarily give up a small amount of money? The answer is that we are not fining the beggar for his request, but for his presence on the street. Many view the homeless as undeserving of help. Their condition is viewed as pathological, self-induced and self-selected. They are, in effect, living rough because they are lazy, shiftless, bums. The constant request of businesses to remove the homeless from public places since they are 'bad for business,' and their almost certain removal, gives credence to the view that the homeless are seen as having less than full status in our society.[20]

Whatever its roots it is certain that homelessness and poverty are inextricably connected in our society. When all the existing literature on the subject throughout Britain, The United States and

Canada is reviewed the central place of poverty in the creation and maintenance of homeless persons is obvious.[21]

Although a seemingly simply question, the idea of who is a homeless person and what constitutes homelessness, requires some consideration first of all of what constitutes a 'home.'[22] All of us have varying definitions of this term that include, though at a minimum, visions of comfort, peace, and safety. While our ideas might be very different depending upon our socioeconomic ability to purchase or rent living space there is no doubt that some form of relative permanency is involved. Most of us think of our friends and family being close at hand, and we would visualize our furniture, special possessions, food on the table, and warmth in the cold Canadian winter. It is a place where one likes to be that is restful, providing a respite from the demands of life.

When one does not have a 'home' it implies not only a true sense of material deficit but provides a serious blow to our emotional well-being. To find a place within our society requires a place where one can organize resources to look or maintain a job and friendship networks. Think for just a moment what it would be like if you were to be removed from the place you call home tonight with only the clothes you have on your back and the possessions you can carry. Obviously this would be a situation that is not only highly traumatic but that would pose great obstacles in terms of getting things sorted out. Devoid of resources you have become a social threat, someone who must now seek assistance without home, job, and often the support of family and friends. As you wander the city streets, little or no idea of where to find help, all of your actions are visible on the stage of the urban theatre, and your audience is anyone who passes within sight of you. From this place of personal and social degradation, one can begin to understand the meaning of the reality of homelessness.

The term homelessness is as difficult to pin down as are the number of homeless in Canada to count. Homeless has been conceptualized variously as 1. chronic—involving 30 or more days of continuous lack of proper accommodation; 2. sporadic—wherein individuals vary between domiciled and homeless for less than 30 days; or 3. situational—where homelessness is a result of acute life crisis.[23] The term has been the subject of a great deal of debate amongst academics and policymakers, and disturbingly much of the debate revolves fundamentally around who will be the subject of social relief efforts. There is no doubt that there are varying degrees of homelessness from those who are temporarily displaced from their homes to those who are without shelter for periods of from several months to years. There are also a small number of homeless who choose the lifestyle avoiding contact with other people, or simply are content to wander the streets freed of responsibility. Dictionaries printed prior to the 1980s often do not contain any reference to homelessness. One must turn to definitions of the term vagrancy which according to **Cole's Concise English Dictionary** (1979)[24] refers to concepts such as wandering both from place to place and in one's speech, and shiftless or idle wandering without money or work. This linking of the condition of homelessness with laziness as well as criminal and quasi-criminal intent is common throughout not only literature, but in popular images of the homeless.[25]

There are several other connotations that must be considered when constructing a definition of homelessness. Homelessness **implies** that one has been thrown out of work, housing, and appropriate care and support, although as the interviews that inform this book clearly illustrate, the homeless often suffer from either underemployment or unemployment.[26] But there are broader questions that must be addressed in building a definition. Should homelessness also include those who are in imminent danger of losing their shelter? At least peripherally, it is important to realize that there are large numbers of people in this country who are living in substandard conditions, both urban and rural, which include doubling up in living space so that the rent can be paid. Children often are now either not leaving their parents home because of the unaffordability of accommodation, or returning in the twenties and thirties. 'Piggybacking' is another term that refers to the practice of one person renting an apartment and six or seven other individuals moving in to make the cost of accommodation affordable. Overcrowding, which includes large numbers of people co-habiting in a dwelling which is inadequate for the purpose, poses people at the precipice of a homeless state. One report from Windsor had some 40 plus people living in a single-family dwelling in which overcrowding had led to a homicide. We know that jamming large numbers of people into an inadequate space has the effect of increasing violence and socially condemned behaviour.[27]

There are, of course, women who are the victims of domestic violence who may leave their homes for short periods of time over a period of years, and who are therefore temporarily displaced.[28] Alternatively they may find themselves in a period of transition as they seek to re-establish themselves in an independent existence in the community. Runaway kids may either be on the street a short time or be 'serious' about staying long periods of time.[29] One of the problems that seriously hampers efforts to understand the depth and complexity of the current homeless situation is the great variety of definitions that have been used by researchers. There is little agreement about what homelessness is, or who should be included in any study of the problem. Residents of long-term single occupancy hotels and subsidized hostels may or may not be considered homeless. While it is obvious that without these facilities they would certainly be out on the street, it is less clear if they deserve to be classified as homeless. Residents of detoxification centres which dry out chronic alcoholics, released prisoners, former mental patients, and juvenile offenders who are currently living in halfway houses may or may not be defined as homeless.

Two definitions arising out of research in The United States and Britain provide a quite comprehensive definition of homelessness. In 1985, The Ohio Department of Mental Health proposed a definition that would categorize a man, woman or child as homeless if they live or sleep in: (1) limited or no shelter for any length of time; (2) shelters or missions, (3) cheap hotels or motels, or (4) other unique situations which do not fit the above categories but where the intent to stay, or the actual stay, is 45 days or less.[30] All of the definitions advanced so far would exclude some individuals from the condition of homelessness, and thus consideration in terms of social policy and assistance. A preferable definition might be found then in the person-centred definition. It has been the guiding focus of the interviews conducted for this book that the only person who is in a position to judge whether they are homeless or not, and need shelter or not, is the individual who sees themselves in this way.[31] The homeless should also be seen to include those who judge that the accommodation that they currently have is inadequate for reasons which make sense to the person.[32] While the majority of life stories you will read about in the pages to follow come from people whose condition is centrally within most competing definitions of homelessness, there are many who exist in substandard accommodation who prove extremely difficult to locate for the enterprising researcher. However, there is ample evidence to underscore not only their existence as homeless persons but also the inadequacy of their current living arrangements. This is not a matter of degree either. It is not simply that a person is living in accommodation that does not suit them; it implies places where lack of heat, the presence of drug abusers in the halls, filth and insect infestation, violence and human misery surround the residents. It may include released mental patients huddled four in a room in boarding houses, paying rents which mean impoverishment and under-nourishment. It raises the spectre of single mothers living on welfare, trapped in a cycle of poverty listening at night to the violence and inhumanity to which their children must be exposed. All of these people are part of the crisis of homelessness which exists in our country.

In the end, the research question of exactly who is homeless must come to rely not upon a definition developed by middle-class researchers but rather from the perspective of those who are living the experience they deem to be 'homelessness'. Research is often guided by concerns which have little to do with, and accomplish less in terms of, challenging the problem of homelessness.[33] Whatever the definition which evolves, homelessness must refer consistently not to some absolute condition but to calculations of the degree to which the current living standards, or lack of them entirely, varies from housing considered to be standard in the adjoining community. Other factors include the temporary or unstable nature of the living arrangements, and the time period for which these conditions must be endured. Additional relevant factors include the social isolation and material deprivation of the individual(s) and these must inform the construction of a meaningful definition.[34] To translate this into real world experience, would the young couple and their child who have endured in one room that is devoid of windows under a tavern fit into this definition? Camping parks have had a continual battle in recent years with homeless families and singles who pitch their tents and live in recreational facilities for the entire summer. One elderly couple, both alcoholics, were living in mid-town Toronto in their automobile, a common choice of homeless persons for shelter. Is a car a home?

In a very real sense questions regarding who shall be called homeless and how many homeless there are out there are somewhat pointless. We require no more evidence that the problem is gravely serious as you shall read in the pages to come. We have had that information for several years now but little, and less, is being done to address the myriad of problems that accompany homelessness. Like our native Canadians, homeless people cannot await the outcome of endless inquiries into their condition. In comparing their condition to that of persons suffering from AIDS, homeless people suffer from the same frustrations of being unable to get governments to respond in any effective way to their predicament. While one would not wish to make such a simple comparison, it is important to remember that many of the homeless who are not helped will not be here to receive help, when and if it is ever offered.

The Legions of Homeless Canadians

One of the great difficulties which confronts any attempt to deal with and analyse the problem of homelessness in Canadian society is the lack of consistent and reliable data on both the number and composition of the homeless population. The inherent problems in simply counting the number of homeless arise from the dynamic and very fluid characteristics of a nomadic population. The ranks of the homeless rise and fall slightly almost constantly although the sheer number of homeless is almost staggering and certainly unbelievable to the average Canadian. Statistics that we read on crime are somewhat similar and can provide us with clues to understanding the complexity of this seemingly simple problem. Figures on crime that we are constantly assailed with in the media reveal only recorded acts of crime, that is, those reported to authorities. Criminologists reliably know that a great deal of crime is never reported for a variety of reasons, some perfectly understandable, and some that arise out of perceptions about our criminal justice system. Victims of sexual assault, for example, very commonly refrain from officially reporting their victimization out of embarrassment, fear of reprisals by the assailant, or through lack of belief in the efficiency of the police and other agents of social control to deliver justice to them. This difference between crimes committed and crimes reported is termed 'the dark figure of crime.'[35] With the homeless the so-called dark figure which refers to the hidden homeless amongst us must be assumed to be significant. Interviews with front line workers in the field of homelessness quickly reveal that there are significant numbers of homeless who avoid any unnecessary identification by social service agencies. At an Oshawa hostel, some men and women will come to the nightly free dinner, receiving it either in a takeaway bag or sitting quietly avoiding interaction with others. They seek anonymity and shun social control personnel who might class them as mentally ill or otherwise in need of professional intervention and perhaps institutionalization. This researcher, in traversing the streets of several large and small Canadian cities, had no difficulty in locating homeless people to interview, and in larger urban settings, like Vancouver and Toronto, the problem was more one of not having the ability to interview the numerous homeless I would encounter.

Several factors impact strongly upon the estimates developed of our homeless people. First, there is the evolving nature of the population in question. New members join the ranks of the homeless every day of the year in Canada, others may leave permanently or for a short period of time. Some homeless will spend a few days in jail, a mental hospital (despite being sane) or with a friend, only to rejoin those on the street. Second, there is a marked reluctance, as already noted, for many homeless people to seek out assistance from 'official' agencies, so many exist in the shadows almost totally elusive to the researcher or social worker. Attempts to enumerate the homeless for the recent American census required workers to travel through abandoned factories, dark alleys, remote areas of parks and to areas of the city which rarely see even the most stalwart and seasoned of police personnel to seek out homeless people. In the 1991 census, Canada attempted for the first time to count the homeless, but again, their counts are likely to fall far short of the actual number of homeless due to the reporting problems noted above. Still more homeless elude counting efforts evidencing fear, apathy, avoidance, and anger. Finally, the use of fictitious names by the homeless who seek medical and social assistance is commonplace, so for anyone consulting records from various facilities it is difficult to construct an accurate picture.

There are a number of problems associated with attempts to collect accurate statistics on the the incidence of homelessness in Canada. Existing statistical data may be characterized as well intentioned, yet haphazard, a situation whose problems can be traced to the limitations of methods of collecting data. A brief review of the ways of counting the homeless illustrates the difficulties facing researchers. First, one might count the number of homeless on any given night in various Canadian cities enlisting the help of social service agencies, street workers, religious help groups, soup kitchens, police, shelters and hostels. While this would present a somewhat more accurate count than anything that has ever been tried in this nation, there are a number of variables which would intervene in the collection process including double-counting of persons, the reluctance of some homeless to be counted and the limitations of the abilities of researchers to find the homeless in the many resting places they inhabit. Many homeless cannot be identified because they blend with persons who inhabit the nightstreets of our cities in the early morning hours. There are a small number of homeless who do not wish to be identified in any way, and there are obviously some who will not co-operate with any study.

A second approach could be to count the number of homeless over a specific period of time, for example, for one year those homeless who seek all forms of shelter accommodation, but again, this would not take into account those who do not use such facilities. It would not, as with the first approach, be able to identify those who might fit into a broader definition of homelessness, as discussed earlier in this chapter, who are simply not on the street.

Finally, we often fall back upon crude statistics that are collected by hostels and shelters to make estimates of the homeless population. These figures are subject to a great degree of variation given that no uniform way of generating the statistics has been developed and accepted by these helping agencies though undoubtedly they would in all likelihood welcome the construction of such a survey instrument.

No one agency has been delegated the task of collecting data on the homeless in our midst so that efforts in this area have been rather piecemeal. But neither would we want to construct a ministry for homelessness with its attendant functions of more pervasive social control. There is no doubt that such contributions are of value but we are forced to rely for information on inconsistent and unco-ordinated efforts by a great many organizations whose intent is good, but whose techniques may leave a great deal to be desired. Helping agencies such as shelters, hostels, halfway houses, church groups, medical treatment facilities and the police provide us with a great deal of information. Collectively, the impression is clear from the observations and figures developed by these various sources. This is a social phenomenon of growing proportions that is outstripping the ability of the networks currently in place to deal effectively with its many manifestations. The human tragedy and suffering have reached levels that disturb even the most callous of workers. Facilities are overburdened and underfunded, unable to provide the kind of real support needed to move the homeless away from the welfare go-round. Solutions are temporary, responding to emergencies and having little capacity to effect long-term change. The homeless are increasingly drawn from groups that are new to the street.

Media sources are of particular relevance for coming to an initial understanding of the homeless situation that confronts us. Journalistic accounts provide the most numerous accounts of the homeless problem. While they are important they are fraught with the problems which plague media reporting. There is a tendency to focus upon the tragic and in many cases unrepresentative scenarios of street life. While sensationalistic reporting can serve to raise public concern and consciousness, it may also reinforce certain negative stereotypes that harden the average citizen in their viewpoints. The public attention generated by the media is short-lived. Soon there is another pressing social problem, usually the next day, and very little is done to address the issues which have been raised. Homeless people are left feeling 'burnt', they have been used to sell a paper or raise the ratings, or make us feel grateful during festive occasions, temporarily paraded before us as symbols of the fate that can befall us. We may feel momentarily concerned, but the images that fill our television screens usually only serve to underscore widely accepted myths about the undeserving nature of the homeless. The lazy wino, the welfare recipient, the 'dirty' teen hookers all are not worthy of our efforts. One American writer has said that for us, the homeless are, in fact, shit.[36] We do not want them to come near, we do not want to see them, they are like so much human trash that we want something done about. The police should move them on, the shelters should take them in (as long as they do not locate in my neighbourhood), anything which will remove them from view, so we do not have to think about them. We pay little attention to the wider ills of society that have brought them to the street. We pay little attention to the thousands of men who use throwaway teens to satisfy themselves sexually every day and night of the week. It is in reality far more reassuring simply to assign blame to the homeless for their condition.

The media's presentation of the homeless crisis is predicated not upon proposing any alleviation or removal of the ills created by homelessness or even upon engendering deeper understandings of the problem, but rather upon sales and viewer attention. Thus we are stuck with periodic crisis reporting.[37] The homeless have a brief place on the stage on the screens of the nation filtered through the evening news. Canada's third world is glimpsed only rarely by its citizens lest we become too upset in the realization that so many with promise, ability, and willingness to work have been cut out of the Canadian dream.

Let us now turn to the efforts so far in Canada to count the homeless. As I already indicated, in 1991 the Canadian government for the first time in history attempted to count the homeless during the census. Their efforts are likely to bring results similar to their attempts to enumerate natives living on reserve settings, that is, they will draw a partial picture that does not accurately reflect the diversity of the homeless population. In 1987, Mallin made an examination of emergency shelter and soup kitchen use and put the number of homeless at between 20,000 and 40,000 individuals.[38] However there are consistent data that place the number of homeless Canadians at a level between 100,000 and 250,000 people. This figure has been developed by The Canadian Council on Social Development whose advisers across Canada have collectively amassed a great wealth of experience in working with, and on behalf of the homeless. Cardinal Carter, the Archbishop of Toronto recognized the gravity of the situation as early as 1987 when he called upon 208 parishes in Toronto to assist the homeless in finding suitable housing.[39] If we were to argue that the figures above are inflated some ten times, we would still, nonetheless, be faced with a social malady which may arguably be the most serious which will confront Canada now and in the immediate future. In consideration of the fact that these estimates were made during the late 1980s, and that economic conditions have deteriorated markedly since then, these may be viewed as quite conservative.

As early as 1984, The Canadian Council on Social Development estimated that there were 992,000 families and 1,025,000 unattached individuals who were living in poverty. Of these groups, 98,000 family members and 422,000 individuals were elderly. Overall, this represented 4,544,000 persons who lived below the poverty line. McLaughlin's one night count of persons using shelters on January 22, 1987 yielded the following enlightening statistics: 7,751 persons sought shelter on that night; 61% were men, 27.5% were women, and fully 11.5% **were children under 15 years of age!**[40] Shelters for battered women, in other words, held 1,271 mothers and their children. General shelters in Ontario were running at 101.5% capacity. This meant that people had to be turned away because of lack of bedspace even on the coldest nights of the winter! There are many people who perish on our streets each year in tragic circumstances, having frozen to death for want of a bed. Nationally, McLaughlin found that shelters were at 77% capacity, but this reflected uneven usage, including shelters that were overflowing as well as some working below capacity due to their policies of turning away persons who are violent or ill, who are drunk or disorderly, whom they feel may be disruptive or difficult to accommodate. By 1987 Canada had 472 facilities which were capable of sheltering some **13,797** individuals nightly.[41]

The most surprising development, perhaps, concerning home-lessness in the 1980s was the growing diversity of the sub-groups which researchers were to discover. McLaughlin found that the 7,751 persons seeking shelter could be sub-divided as follows, giving clear indication of the variety of persons who find themselves without a place to call home:

1. 54.7% were unemployed, underscoring the fact that not all homeless are without resources but that many live in conditions of poverty or underemployment;

2. 51.5% of persons were receiving social assistance of some kind;

3. 33.3% fit the categorization for alcohol abuse devised by McLaughlan;
4. 20.1% were current or former psychiatric patients;
5. 15% could be classed as drug abusers;
6. 9.4% had been evicted, and
7. 3.1% were physically handicapped.

This latter group composed of persons who have either naturally occurring or employment related handicaps were individuals who popped up with surprising frequency in my discussions with homeless persons. It was not uncommon for a person to indicate that the reason they were now unemployed was due to a work-related injury that had rendered them unsuitable for certain forms of employment. The results of McLaughlan's survey, which constituted the Canadian effort for the United Nations International Year of Shelter, found that .5% of the Canadian population use shelters, and concluded that ". . . an estimated range of 130,00 to 250,000 homeless people during the year remains **conservative**."

When we examine the estimates available from some of the major cities in Canada regarding the number of homeless in our country it underscores the enormity of the problem that is gripping the nation. By 1990 the coalition of social service agencies that services the downtown area of Toronto, and which meets on a monthly basis to exchange information and ideas, reliably estimated that 10,000 or more young people between the ages of 16 and 24 are homeless in Toronto on any given day.[42] Research by Livy Visano, a sociologist at York University, found that many of the children who arrive on the street fall through cracks in the social fabric eventually to become embroiled in street networks. His book, **This Idle Trade**, a study of male street prostitution, provides us with a chilling vision of wasted lives involving the sale of sex by young boys to anyone willing to pay the cost. His book sends a clear signal that homelessness is not merely displacement to the margins of society, but often involves induction into the netherworld of drug use, deviant sexuality, and criminal as well as quasi-criminal pursuits as a means of day-to-day survival.[43] The wide ranging social implications of this contribution were again reflected in Marlene Webber's recent contribution **Street Kids: The Tragedy of Canada's Runaways**, which involved interviews with twenty-nine street kids in several major Canadian cities.[44] Both of these works provide compelling evidence that the societal implications of ignoring this process, of literally letting children be used and abused in this way, will result in crime, social and health problems of enormous impact. In the end delinquency of this sort may in the future no longer be a symptom of urban decay but rather a direct cause of it.[45]

Although the homeless population is not only larger, and hence more visible, in Toronto than in any other Canadian urban centre due simply to the sheer size of its population and its severe problems with housing affordability and supply, one should not assume that other cities are immune from the growing homeless groups within Canadian society. Montreal was reported by 1987 to have homeless numbering in the thousands by the late 1980s.[46] In a 1986 newspaper article, 5,000 women alone were reported to be homeless and living on the streets of the city. Similarly, reports in the daily press from Halifax, Edmonton, Ottawa, Winnipeg, and Victoria[47] serve to reconfirm the growing size and diversity of the homeless population amongst us.

Homelessness is often created by forces outside the control of its victims as I have already argued. In fact, the actions of supposedly responsible governments can have a direct hand in adding significant numbers to our homeless rolls. The hypocritical attitude of governments, who often publicly bemoan the plight of our homeless while on the other hand doing nothing, or as little as possible, to alleviate the suffering, is best evidenced by the actions of the British Columbia government. In preparation for Expo, landlords were permitted to evict 791 persons from hotel rooms that they had occupied on a long-term basis, and in total some 3,500 low income housing units to provide accommodation for visitors to the fair.[48] Some governments, as I have argued, not content to do nothing, take an active approach to creating homelessness! Similarly, the comments of Albert Ross, the former chairman of the Metropolitan Housing Authority, underscored this apathy by policymakers when he stated that optimism amongst applicants for low cost housing was unwarranted given that, "little has changed in the 40 years he has been involved in public housing."

In summary the number of homeless people in Canada is significant, and numbers **well over** 100,000 nationwide given current knowledge on the subject. Although the data sources are not complete, nor in many cases the source of first choice, they do provide clear and compelling evidence of a major social problem, which it will be demonstrated throughout this book is both increasing and diversifying.

Who are the Homeless?

If there is one fact that is irrefutable concerning homeless people in Canada, it is their sheer numbers. To this may be added the growing diversity of the people who find themselves abandoned by society. Mallin conducted research into the use of shelters in Canada and found that reports from all servicing agencies reiterate the conclusion that the ranks of the homeless are now filled by women, children and men, and in numbers that are greater than at any time since the Great Depression.[49] I would argue that these numbers may indeed be far greater and reflective of greater social ills since women and children, who were largely strangers to the streets until the 1980s, now comprise a significant and escalating number of our homeless. Moreover the demographics of the groups are not only changing rapidly, but are coming to represent a wide spectrum of Canadian society. In shattering comforting myths concerning the undeserving homeless, researchers across North America have shown that a great variety of sub-groups, as I have already argued, are represented amongst our homeless peoples.

One study of men using the Salvation Army hostel in Ottawa found that 47% of the men surveyed were under 30 years of age, and only 5% were over the age of 65.[50] In a survey of 29 American cities, the United States Conference of Mayors in 1987 found that 34% of the homeless were families.[51] These figures not only presage the future of the homelessness problem but point to disturbing trends in the composition of the urban poor.

The gravity of the homelessness problem when understood in terms of human suffering is overwhelming given the case histories reported in The United States Mayors' report. Children suffer in innumerable ways, reminiscent of the most disturbing of Dicken's and Engel's well known accounts of the sufferings of the poor in Victorian England.[52] Families are usually separated both in the United States and in Canada when they become homeless. In some instances this is because a battered spouse seeks refuge with her children from her husband or partner. When a mother, father and children become homeless it is generally impossible to put the entire family in one facility. It is standard practice to separate the husband into a shelter for men while the mother and children are housed in a women's shelter.[53] This arrangement not only places an additional stress upon the family unit but makes regrouping much more difficult. Hostels for women unfortunately, as we shall explore in a later chapter in greater detail, are not set up specifically for family groups, so that moms with children often share common kitchen and bathroom areas with women who are mentally ill, drug or alcohol abusers, or are themselves prone to disruptive behaviours. Again, children are the most vulnerable victims.

Many shelters across North America have 'policies' or 'rules' that do not allow families or singles to stay in the shelter during the day. This means that they must wander the streets with no resources, prone to the dangers that inhabit the downtown core where the majority of shelters/hostels are located in large cities. This reflects an attitude that the homeless must not be permitted to be 'lazy' and 'lie around the shelter all day', a sentiment echoed often by both staff and residents of shelters interviewed by this researcher.[54] Shelters and hostels generally assume a role far more encompassing than simply providing a bed, food and some meagre resources. They believe they must discipline the homeless, provide social training if you will, getting them up and out the door, looking for work. Idleness is a luxury of the wealthy in our society, and so there is a consistent attempt made to 'get them going.' Children experiencing these conditions have no sense of security, are constantly associating with frightening strangers, may be subject to removal from their parents and placement into care, do not receive proper nutrition, and suffer in terms of educational achievement and self development. Their self-esteem is assailed on a daily basis as they suffer the brunt of society's refusal to provide properly for their needs. Children are the silent victims of homelessness. They have no advocates, no one to speak on their behalf, to say how much pain they must endure. They become strangers in their own society forced to move from place to place, devoid of security, watching their parents tortured efforts to construct a reasonable life for them. Their faces and the depth of pain in their eyes tell the story but few in our society have heard it so far.

In 1986 a Task Force to examine rooming arrangements, boarding and lodging was struck in Ontario by the Ministry of Housing.[55] They developed what they referred to at that time as 'brutal statistics' concerning the plight of low-income persons seeking accommodations. They were concerned in their report centrally with the question of why the number of homeless was rising in Ontario at such an alarming rate. The current backlog of persons waiting for public housing in Ontario is so great that many applicants had by the late 1980s ceased to believe that there was any point in applying. On March 25, 1991, **The Toronto Star** in a front page story reported that more than 500 people a week in Toronto alone were joining the waiting list for subsidized housing. By this date The Metro Toronto Housing Authority had 12,310 families and individuals waiting for accommodation which was reported to be the highest figure in 15 years. Barbara Watson, tenant placement co-ordinator for the housing authority, commented on how grave the situation is, "It means there are an awful lot of people out there who need affordable housing and they can't find it anywhere else."Much of the new demand has been created by legislative changes which now permit refugees who were previously barred from applying for subsidized housing to add their names to the waiting list. Fully 25% percent of applicants are refugees according to Andrew Duffy who wrote the article and this number can be expected to increase given that there are 80,000 refugee claimants currently in Ontario alone. Duffy also reports that many families have been on the waiting list for three years.

In 1986 the Task Force found that Ontario welfare recipients paid 64% of their benefits towards their rent each month leaving virtually nothing for the other necessities of life. In December 1988, a protest outside the Ontario legislature by welfare recipients (who numbered some 500,000 in Ontario) graphically demonstrated the plight of those individuals who are forced to feed their children endlessly on macaroni as fresh fruit, vegetables and meat exist as simply memories or infrequent luxuries. This group, the poor and impoverished, skirt the edge of the ever-thinning line between the accommodated and the homeless. They represent the potential, given growing economic pressures, for a social disaster in the making, a virtual hidden army of homeless who might, and give every indication of being poised to, pour onto our streets.

In some Canadian cities, reflecting the trends in American jurisdictions, homelessness has an ethnic character, that has been referred to by some writers as racial in nature. Refugees and new immigrants are certainly not the only groups affected, although their numbers are growing as a percentage of all homeless. Some studies have argued that young native people predominate as the homeless in prairie cities like Winnipeg, Regina and Saskatoon.[56] One author concluded that these young people are at a dead end already with virtually no hope of finding employment or housing, the victims of racist discrimination against Canada's native peoples. In this sense they suffer from the double stigma of not only being homeless but native. Their homeless status only serves to reinforce racist stereotypes that predominate in these communities amongst the members of the dominant culture. It also serves to illuminate the rural genesis of this specific group who have lived in the social isolation of Canada's reserve system with its arguably over-documented problems of alcoholism, poor medical services, and lives of frustration, boredom and defeat.[57]

'They're all Bums or They Want to be There':
Myths Concerning the Homeless

Despite, or in spite of, media attention that is short-lived, public ideas about, and attitudes towards the homeless, suffer from a general lack of knowledge. There is some question about whether people lack information or 'do not want to know about it.' Behaviours which are labelled deviant, that is, which bend or break the norms of our society often involve behaviours of persons with whom the vast majority of citizens have no contact. In the absence of good information, cultural myths are perpetuated, and similarly, the lack of political organization and power on the part of the homeless leads to an ongoing misunderstanding of the basic nature of the problem. The public's attitude is inconsistent, responding to well-publicized crises in an often haphazard fashion. Moral indignation over the death of a homeless person who has needlessly frozen to death can excite a call for 'something to be done' but in reality the complexity of the situation precludes knee jerk responses from accomplishing lasting results.[58] Thus very little of this public outcry results in basic reforms in the area of provision of housing or services that are crucial to the homeless person.

Various researchers have confirmed that myths concerning who comprise the homeless have prevailed that have long ago lost their usefulness and social relevance. The publics' perceptions are seen to divide the homeless into several distinct groups none of whom are deserving of help. First, some portion of the homeless are seen as representing the independent and eccentric of society, who prefer to live by their wits, eschewing contact with wider society and their fellows. Second, it is assumed there is a large group of lazy, degenerate bums who will simply not work. This is an attitude that often is expressed concerning welfare recipients, and its discriminatory view of moral character has been reflected in 'workfare' programs in which welfare recipients are forced to work to receive their payments. A third group commonly identified by the public as those who inhabit the street are individuals who are crazy or dangerous and who deserve to be, or should be, forced into institutions. The public here demonstrates a view contrary to many healing professionals in the mental health field who have argued that the community should form the centre of care for the mentally ill rather than placing them in institutional settings for long periods of time.[59] A variety of laws in this country reflect this general view and prohibit behaviours that are disturbing, irritating or that provoke fear (whether this reflects the sensitivities and intolerance of the complainant or not). The public both fears and finds distasteful the

homeless individual according to the leading research in this field.[60]
Their attitudes often focus upon the alleged capacity of the desolate
for unprovoked violence.

Struggling for Survival on Mean Streets

Life on the street is the world of the immediate, the world of
survival. For the homeless person the pressing concerns of finding
both food and shelter, whether it is in the form of state provided
shelter, or any safe place to sleep is an activity that occupies most of
their day. From the beginning of the day, when those who sleep in the
crevices of our urban landscape begin to rise, cramped, damp, and
cold from the park benches, grates, dumpsters, and stairways, the day
becomes a constant slow trek with little purpose other than getting
through another day. The constant miles of walking necessitated by
the widely dispersed soup kitchens, shelters and other services, which
are not located for the convenience of the homeless, mean that they
are forever walking.

One of the places where homeless people gather is at the local
McDonald's restaurants which open their doors at 6:30 and whether it
is Halifax, Vancouver or Edmonton they can be seen lining up long
before the doors are open. Devoid of access to taken-for-granted
amenities of life, such as running water, toilet facilities, cooking
apparatus, they are virtually unable to groom themselves for the day
ahead. The perceived unhygienic appearance of the homeless is
associated primarily with those who are suffering from severe mental
conditions, or individuals who are caught in the throes of alcohol or
drug abuse. The overwhelming majority of the homeless are
extremely creative and resilient in presenting as 'normalized' an
appearance as possible. So effective are they at this, that aside from
some minor clues to their status, i.e., their presence in public places at
unusual times, or the condition of their shoes which wear at an
incredibly quick rate, they are indistinguishable from any number of
average citizens in our society. It is perhaps their enforced idleness,
born of lack of money and committments that separates the homeless
most tellingly from those citizens who are rushing to another time-
bound activity ever mindful of 'the time'. For the homeless time is a
concept with little meaning. Time is the morning, afternoon, evening
or night as I learned when I tried to arrange for interviews with street
people. If I was to say, "I'll meet you at two tomorrow," I found that
the person would beg off meeting me. "I can't make it then...too
busy..." A wise street worker clued me into this saying, "Try telling
people you'll meet them in the afternoon, that way people will show
up, say mid-afternoon. You'll have to wait but they are usually pretty

reliable." What was required then was to adjust one's perception of the importance of time. The view of the homeless person like many of us on holidays is very flexible when it comes to time and committments.

Homeless persons first arriving on the street often have little information about the services available to them. In 1990 it was suggested that information booths be set up in bus stations and parks frequented by the homeless to provide information on shelters, hostels, foodbanks, soup kitchens, medical services, and other forms of community help. It was not uncommon for persons interviewed for this book to mention their initial naiveté concerning street life. One young man who had slept in doorways and on firestairs for several weeks told me that it took him all this time to discover the existence of hostels: "Shit, if I'd know about this kind of place I wouldn't a been sleeping in doorways. Its only because I met a guy and told him what I was doing and he told me about this place that I'm here. I never heard the word 'hostel' before I hit the streets." It is this lack of co-ordination of information that often disadvantages the recently homeless at a time when help is most needed, and arguably could be most effective in preventing a lapse into longer term homelessness.

The medical problems of the homeless are numerous and largely reflect the lifestyle they lead. Their lot is one of degradation and the sapping of human dignity. The will to fight out of this cycle of despair is an ability which most of us assume we have.[61] But this is certainly because we are not under the constant assault of the street. Homeless people are constantly on the move during their waking hours and are baked by the sun in summer and frozen in the unforgiving Canadian winters. Their clothes, often donations given to shelters and thrift shops, are generally out of fashion, often ill-fitting, and contribute to a presentation of self that can suggest a careless attitude. Moreover homeless persons are often not properly clothed for the season, so that flimsy unseasonal dress is common in winter, and winter clothes are frequently sighted in summer, due to the tendency of donations to be related to persons giving up old clothes after a season of wear. Many on the street report good overall health but medical research on the homeless indicates a myriad of medical conditions that occur in this population. Ulcerated legs and blistered, swollen feet are epidemic in the homeless; wounds that do not heal and that are filled with dirt are often noticed by health officials when treating the homeless; skin infestations such as lice, severe dental problems, upper respiratory infections, conditions of the hands, hypothermia as well as low grade depression and signs of stress-related disorders are frequently found among the homeless. Alcohol and drug use that provide perhaps a dulling of the humiliations and violence of street existence lead to a number of medically related problems both physical and psychological.[62] One of the central debates underlying attempts to understand the homeless revolves around the issue of the prevalence of mental illness amongst the homeless. This is the subject that occupies the discussion in the final section of this chapter.

Mental Illness and Homelessness: Deinstitutionalization as Marginalization

The arrival of large numbers of the released mentally ill on the streets of North America heralded the beginning of the deinstitutionalization movement and attempts to empty mental hospitals of all but the most severe cases. Deinstitutionalization is a term coined to describe the mass release of patients from mental hospitals when social service budgets are in crisis. Resuscitating the image on the **Gemeinschaaft** village, the community responsible for the locking away of the mentally troubled was transformed virtually overnight into the community of care. Hospitalized individuals would benefit from exposure to the 'therapy' of community life, and so critics of long term commitment would realize the goal of reintegration of the ex-patient. In Canada, the closing of one large psychiatric facility, The Lakeshore Hospital, meant that virtually overnight large numbers of mentally ill persons were released into the Toronto community. More specifically they emptied into the Parkdale region of Toronto, a lower class neighbourhood adjacent to the hospital where like their American counterparts they became ghettoized in large boarding houses. Private entrepreneurs realizing the potential for exploiting marginal and ofttimes ill individuals functioned as mini-asylums dispensing ripoff rents rather than therapeutic benevolence. These deplorable conditions became widely known and the existence of large numbers of visibly disordered persons in the area led to both stigmatization and isolation. As Scull has demonstrated, the transferring of the mentally ill into the community often does not attain the ends favoured by its humanitarian advocates. Community treatment schemes for the released mentally ill do not materialize as legislators fail to transfer institutional funds into street front facilities for the now often homeless mentally ill. Deinstitutionalization came to represent economic saving and community neglect.[63]

Homelessness in itself is a difficult and highly defeating condition for the human spirit; madness only compounds the problems faced by the wandering street people of Canadian society.

Baxter and Hopper[64] reflecting current street philosophy in the United States inform us these individuals are referred to as 'space cases'. Scull[65] uses the highly evocative term, 'human trash'. Both phrases reflect the extremely marginal position of the homeless mentally ill in the political and economic spheres of society. There is no doubt, considering the volume of research in this area, that deinstitutionalization is a national disgrace in both Canada and The United States[66] and has been for over two decades.[67] Treatment for those homeless who suffer from, or develop, forms of mental illness is really a secondary consideration. Mere survival supersedes it in importance as every available piece of literature amply illustrates.

The Homeless Mentally Ill or the Mentally Ill Homeless?

The current levels of mental illness among the homeless are a difficult issue to resolve. First, there has been little concerted effort to identify the nature of illnesses which present among these populations. The central research question revolves around whether mental illness is a causative factor in the drift into, and sustaining of, the homeless condition or whether mental illness manifests as a result of the homeless state of the individual. It certainly must be hypothesized that depressive and stress-related conditions must emerge from the overwhelming strains placed upon homeless persons in their daily round of survival activities. Care must be taken however to separate the homeless into distinct groupings: adult men, single women, married women and/or couples with children, adolescents, and lone children, as research results are not normally generalizable across the various categories of homeless.[68]

The existing research evidence is both contradictory and confusing, and estimates of the occurrence of mental illness in homeless populations range wildly from very little evidence of mental disturbance to characterizations of the homeless as overwhelmingly deranged. In a study of the Keener Shelter in New York it was asserted that 84% of the 240 residents suffered from some form of mental illness, and eighteen of these cases were deemed to be in need of immediate hospitalization. Arguing in a 1985 article, Dr. Charles Krauthammer[69] asserted that 90% of homeless Americans could be classified as mentally ill. Insisting that homeless persons either cannot or will not seek assistance, Krauthammer concluded that these individuals should be forcibly institutionalized for their own good. His conclusions demonstrate the substantial flaws that fuel public myths concerning the homeless. His policy recommendations are based on a study conducted by Bassuk, Rubin and Lauriat (1984) of homeless persons seeking refuge in one Boston shelter. The researchers found that 40% of those studied suffered from psychoses, 28% were chronic alcoholics, and 21% had personality disorders. The study had a severely limited sample size, and was characterized by the authors as only moderately in-depth. A further problem that hinders research efforts in this area is the disagreement within psychiatric circles over the basis of diagnosis, particularly poignant in studies where untrained personnel are asked to evaluate the psychiatric history and present condition of the respondent.

Hope and Young's research relied upon the reports of practitioners in the field. They found that estimates of front line workers put the number of mentally ill homeless at between 30% and 60% of their clients.[71] This figure includes both alcoholics and drug abusers. It is both a wide ranging figure and one which is difficult to interpret, given the inclusion of substance abusers in the overall figures. The Ohio Department of Mental Health found that 30.8% of their sample had psychiatric problems and 64.2% said they had been drinking some or a lot in the last month.[72] Since over 90% of Canadians regularly consume alcoholic beverages this is scarcely an astonishing finding. The National Institute of Mental Health has provided estimates that up to 50% of the homeless may suffer from some form of mental disorder. Finally, The American Psychiatric Association estimates that the number of mentally ill among the homeless fluctuates between 20% and 50%. The so-called HUD study found that half the persons currently using shelter accommodation could be classified as mentally ill, including all forms of substance abuse.[73]

Within the Canadian context, McLaughlin (1987) found that 20.1% of her sample of persons seeking shelter were current or ex-psychiatric patients, 33.3% were alcohol abusers, and 15% were drug abusers. These categories have a considerable overlap but they do raise the possibility, although not conclusively, of a somewhat lower prevalence of mental illness among the Canadian homeless population. Visano's research among street youth in Toronto raises the issue of whether underlying psychiatric problems are discernible in street populations particularly those individuals who do not seek or are forced into psychiatric intervention.[74] An overriding concern is that the classification of homeless persons as mentally ill is not abused given the vulnerability associated with powerless social status. Again, some minor forms of mental illness are arguably 'normal' when considered in relation to the ofttimes overwhelming gravity of the homeless individual's or family's situation.

'Holes in the System': The Self-Selected Sample

Arguably the appeal of medicalizing the problem of homelessness lies in the explanatory label and antecedent characteristics that can flow from this reassuring concept. The homeless are either mad or bad, i.e., mentally ill, substance abusers, or engage in crimes of survival. Homelessness, therefore, is not conceptualized as a condition linked to larger structural forces (economy, family dissolution, the shortcomings of the welfare state) but is rather a symptom of personal pathology. For many, despite understandings forged over the course of this century on the nature of addictions in the scientific community, addictions are self-selected by the sufferer. Mental illness remains the broken mind that cannot be healed. Crimes of survival warrant the intrusion of social control apparatus and personnel and the criminalization of the homeless.[75] All of these explanations and attitudes reflect not only a fractionated sense of homeless populations, but also inconclusive or otherwise limited research data.

More current research on the incidence of mental illness among the homeless has yielded much more conservative and convincing results. They show a greater degree of correspondence with existing Canadian research results. This does not mean however that there has been any subsiding of the controversy surrounding this issue. Snow et al. sought in their research to dissipate the myth of pervasive mental illness in the homeless.[76] The researchers interviewed a sample of 184 homeless persons who sought treatment at both local and state mental health facilities in Texas. They concluded that the rate of mental illness in their respondents hovered at between 10% and 15% a figure far lower than that discovered in previous investigations reviewed in this article. Much of this rate was based upon alcohol abuse rather than simply reflecting psychiatric problems of the sample.

Wright (1988) was critical of the findings of the above research study.[77] First, it ignores those persons who do not seek assistance from the formal mental health system, or those whose records are faulty for some reason. In a society which has adopted a policy of transinstitutionalization of marginal populations, from institutions to agency to street, back and across control boundaries, it is crucial to note that, "Every care system has holes through which some people fall."[78] The size, number and width of these holes is of course, a question of considerable importance. Many homeless, fearing the threat of involuntary commitment as mentally ill persons, either actively avoid or seek to minimize any contact with official agents or agencies, or refuse shelter when a psychiatric clearance is required before a bed will be issued. Some American hostels require a psychiatric interview before admitting clients for shelter. In New York, women are routinely referred to Bellevue which is a considerable distance from most shelters. Fearing they will be classed as 'crazy' or simply due to fatigue and frustration many simply leave. Canadian shelters routinely require an admittance examination which includes information on the person's medical background. For this reason, many homeless persons avoid shelters that insist upon collecting other than routine personal information. Students of the history of psychiatry are well aware that not only is there little agreement over basic diagnostic criteria (Wright, 1988)[79] but that such criteria are often applied to the certifiably sane who foolishly allow themselves to be evaluated.[80] Ropers further argues that the problems associated with street survival may be difficult to distinguish from seemingly chronic psychiatric symptoms.[81] Thus Wright's criticisms as well as the tactics of the homeless in avoiding medicalization of their problems, and hence deviantization of their condition, are well founded.

Snow et al. utilized a criterion for the evaluation of the presence of mental illness that is questionable at best and demonstrates some of the inadequacies of existing research efforts.[82] Respondents were assessed as to whether they met the following criteria: 1. prior psychiatric institutionalization; 2. designated mentally ill by other homeless people; 3. conduct so bizarre or situationally inappropriate that most observers would be likely to perceive them to be disordered. To be classed as mentally ill the behaviour of the sample members had to fit two or more of the above categories. As Wright has pointed out, aside from debates concerning what does or does not constitute a cognation of mental imbalance, the assessments in the third category were carried out by field workers with no clinical experience whatsoever.[83] Mentally ill people might well fit only one of the criteria, and so the estimate must be correctly interpreted only as being only a 'lower boundary.' Finally, most of the mentally ill homeless who fall within the age range of 20 to 39 years of age are unlikely to have ever been institutionalized and the never institutionalized now predominate amongst homeless persons.[84]

Towards Comprehensive Data Collection

Wright et al. and Wright have recently begun to report on data from their study of homelessness in 19 major U.S. cities.[85] This sample addresses many of the methodological problems associated with earlier studies. In the first year of data collection 25,000 clients were interviewed; more than 11,000 adults were seen more than once. The study is broad ranging in collecting data from a number of key urban areas, and avoids some of the pitfalls of non-generalizability that characterize single-city studies. Trained mental health professionals carry out the interviews. However, one criticism that Wright himself has noted is that the sample members self-select to seek attention from project teams.

Wright (1988) has reported that current data indicate that some 19.4% of adult clients show distinct signs of emotional problems or psychiatric impairment. Despite the quantity of Wright's data and the quality of the interviews, certain problems still present. It is difficult to determine whether the form of mental illness or emotional difficulty is transient, a situational or episodic emotional crisis, or chronic psychiatric disease. Also, there still remains the complex question of weighting the effects of homelessness upon the presenting mental condition.

Directions for Canadian Research

The pressing need for exploratory research on the relationship between homelessness and mental illness is evident within the Canadian context. However overreliance on a medical model that focusses upon individual characteristics of homeless persons such as mental illness or substance abuse is seemingly not warranted by more recent and far ranging research results within the American context. Canadian research efforts can benefit from attention to the development of universal criteria for key variables and terms which have eluded efforts so far making comparison of data problematic at best.

The problem of homelessness is significant within the Canadian context and is likely to escalate within the near future. A 1990 Geneva report concluded that Toronto was "the most expensive (city) in North America."[87] Given the current crisis in the political economy which has prompted rising interest rates, plant slowdowns and shutdowns, and a general downturn in the business cycle, the spectre of increasing numbers of homeless in Canada seems likely.[88] What directions can then be established for Canadian research efforts?

First, it is evident that a national study of homelessness in Canada which is of a cross-disciplinary nature is in order. At present, writing about the problem of homelessness in Canadian society is a difficult process since we have no reliable figures concerning the composition of the general population or sub-populations. This study must explore not only the relationships between mental illness and homelessness, but also the contexts in which such maladies arise. This implies a research approach which goes beyond the 'self-selected' sample and is able to investigate homelessness at the ground level. In essence, I would argue that the clinical interview that characterizes much of the American research effort must be used in conjunction with or supplanted by depth interviewing of subjects in the field.

Stein, in reviewing the dress-rehearsal enumeration for the United States Bureau of the Census, cites both the 'public environment' of homelessness and the appropriateness and advantages intrinsic to qualitative methods as evidence for their value in researching this area of human behaviour. The 'extraordinary contingencies' which this group must face and problems of 'defining, identify and locating' make the use of qualitative approaches necessary.[89] Without them the 'understandings' our data generate are suspect at best. The data which should be produced in Canada will inform us through 'thick description' of the processes underlying, contributing to or sustaining mental illness amongst those homeless who display such problems.[90]

However, it is also important to eschew uni-dimensional research approaches for those that consider the broader contexts in which homelessness arises; i.e., the structural forces of politics and economy which impinge upon the lives of those who eventually drift, or are forced into a homeless status. A fully informed analysis must also address the interaction between social control agents and the homeless in the production of mental problems. It is only through analysis at a variety of empirical levels that we can achieve a full understanding of the problem which addresses the unique social, economic and political formations that underlie this country.

Canadian researchers are in a unique position to benefit from the experience of our American colleagues in this difficult area of human behaviour. It is incumbent upon us to provide understandings that permit the amelioration and hopefully the eradication of this grave social problem.

The central dilemma that presents itself for homeless people is the need to nurture the will to survive and to overcome the conditions that can rob a person of human status. The often overwhelming personal, social and economic misfortunes that lead to the street can leave victims dazed for long periods of time. Crime victims often suffer great emotional and psychological trauma for years after their victimization. Why should we expect persons who are disenfranchised, often with great rapidity, to suffer any less than other victims? To lose one's place in society, to be thrown out of full status, to be in the position of asking for help leaves people traumatized and often unable to act. They may be in need of a period of time to regroup their resources, to rebound from despair, for their battle will be one that must come in the few moments in the day when survival is not a completely overriding concern. Those moments are fleeting and few, and therefore we should not be surprised that the homeless may take long periods of time to re-establish themselves in the mainstream of society.

In the chapters to follow we will explore the reality of homelessness in Canada by examining the paths to homelessness and the lives of the people who we call homeless. Life on the streets and the lure of sex, drugs and escape will be discussed as well as the interaction of people on the streets. The causes of homelessness at both personal and societal levels will be analysed to provide an integrated analysis of the homeless problem. Finally we shall explore policies for ending homelessness through the organization and empowering of homeless persons and the creation of viable alternatives to the present systems of social assistance.

CHAPTER TWO
Drifting Into Despair

Roads to Homelessness

In Canada, the spectre of homelessness is not one that most of its citizens have to regularly contemplate. However, the forces that propel persons to a homeless existence are perhaps closer than most of us care to imagine. Indeed, the question may be, what keeps us from the street? Canadians have recently reported that their ability to live on their current resources would allow them, on average, to survive for a period of only one to three months. Many could not ward off the loss of their accommodation for more than a month. There are two broad categories of forces which create homelessness; the first are political and economic forces in larger society that manufacture the conditions that give rise to wide-scale homelessness. The second group of factors that lead to homelessness involve a variety of social, personal, and societal factors that together are the catalyst for this drift into despair.

Political and Economic Factors

Let us begin this chapter with an examination of the political and economic forces that have a direct impact on this social problem. During the 1980s, successive Canadian governments at both the Federal and Provincial levels have allocated few resources to the creation of low cost housing. This occurred in an era when supplies of affordable housing, particularly in large metropolitan areas, shrank at an alarming rate. The process called gentrification, that is, the renovation of older houses in urban areas, had a two-fold effect that impacted most forcefully upon the economically weak in our midst. First, the large stock of single-room boarding accommodation dried up during the 1980s displacing large numbers of skid row residents, boarders, and those requiring cheap shelter. Second, new forms of housing did not emerge to fill this gap, as incentives to investors to create this form of housing were absent from government policy initiatives. Some landlords recognized the profit to be made even from those who are most economically disadvantaged and offered cramped and substandard accommodation to those on the lower end of the economic scale. There was however little attempt to develop low cost housing that was really affordable for those who subsist on welfare, disability, limited pensions or other forms of social assistance.

The 1980s may also be characterized as an era in which the gap between rich and poor accelerated in Canada. Not only do we discover the poor caught within a cycle of welfare entrapment wherein they are unable to develop sufficient resources to escape their impoverished condition, but the emergence of new forms of charity signal clearly the abdication of social responsibilities by all levels of government. This involves the reliance of government on private or society sponsored charity as a basis for ameliorating conditions of poverty. Consider that the Canadian Senate reported this year that over one million Canadian children are poor.[1] Realize that this means that one in six children in our country lives in poverty. Fully half of these children would starve if it were not for food banks. Food banks supply them with their basic nutritional needs. Is this the same Canada that Senator Keith Spicer recently referred to in terms of a poetry of spirit? Spirit is a luxury of the rich and well-fed. The government's refusal to acknowledge and address need in a meaningful way, that is, through the provision of food for Canadian children, impacts across their lives. It affects their performance in school and ultimately limits their life chances. It means that they have less stake in a society that has not made provision for them. Finally, it means that we require an urgent restructuring of our priorities in spending by governments.

When you think that almost 30% of children in Metropolitan Toronto go to school hungry every day, and the number across Canada that are similarly undernourished, it gives one a gauge of the enormity of the problem.[2] Indeed, Canada, according to Carolyn Jack, president of Comic Relief, an organization which raises money to alleviate the suffering caused by poverty, has written that Canada is second only to the United States in the rate of child poverty among all industrialized nations.[3] This is nothing less than a national disgrace, and that it continues, and grows, is a shame to this nation and its people who have done little to alleviate this problem. When one also considers that there are over 1,100 food banks across this country and only 625 Mcdonald's outlets the reality of the grip of poverty has some measure.[4]

Governments, federally, provincially and municipally, have been content to let private organizations set up food banks to keep up with the ever-increasing demand for food. Users of food banks span every part of the lower socioeconomic scale from those who are entirely without income to those who find that government supplements, welfare, disability, mother's allowance, or unemployment benefits fall short in meeting their basic living expenses. Many food bank users are employed individuals who find that their paycheques, like those of their 'dependent' neighbours, do not allow for eating.

The question (among many) that this raises is, "Why are governments in Canada willing to let hundreds of thousands of our citizens rely on charity to eat?" Why indeed should any of us allow this situation to continue and grow? One of the paradoxes that paints this clearly as a matter of political will is the obvious surplus of money available to endlessly promote a "Yes" vote in the Canadian referendum in the form of media advertisements, pamphlets and personal appearances by politicians whereas no money can be found to end this cycle of dependency. The evidence which is steadily mounting is that the public has reached, and now moved beyond, its greatest capacity for limitless charity. This reflects a diminishing ability for Canadians to assist others in such a fashion when record levels of unemployment are being recorded, and individual citizens feel insecure about their present and future economic condition. In every arena of social and community work the effects of "the great depression of '92" have meant that budgets have been frozen and that they are increasingly unable to assist deserving potential recipients. The limits of benevolence seem to have been reached or we are balanced precariously near the edge of this state of affairs.

Throughout the 1980s Canada also experienced growing unemployment that is now running at historically record levels. The free trade agreement heralded by the Mulroney Conservatives as the economic inducement to prosperity has proven to be the economic undoing of Canada. Sociologist Gordon Laxer has referred to Canada as a resource rich country that is 'open for business,' that is, to economic exploitation from other countries.[5] Under 'free trade' a misnomer for the potential exploitation of the Canadian worker, the removal of sundry labour rights, medical schemes and social welfare entitlements, the rates of unemployment have risen astronomically.

Canadian business bankruptcies are at an all time high, as many businesses are simply folding up and heading for the cheap labour havens of the United States. Little is, or seems to be, or can be, done to protect Canadian jobs.

This downturn has naturally had an effect upon the lives of a large number of Canadians. In Windsor, Ontario, the centre of automobile manufacture in Canada, unemployment had reached almost 30% by May of 1991, and the welfare role estimated by municipal officials reached almost 6,000 by mid-summer.[6] Increasingly, Canadians also find it difficult to rise above the poverty line due to inadequate pay levels. Many of the highly paid manufacturing jobs are rapidly disappearing with the advent of new technologies and the flow of plants to the United States, and soon to Mexico in the wake of trilateral free trade agreements. These are being replaced with jobs that are in the low paid service sector, the kind of jobs that pay minimum wage or near to it. Examples of this type of job include work in the hotel industry, security guard positions, restaurant staff, clerking jobs, and sales jobs in many retail industries. This form of employment does not constitute a 'living wage' for many who must provide their own accommodation as the analysis presented later in this book clearly demonstrates. Although one can survive on this wage if living with parents or other relatives, or if the wage is simply a second income, this form of underemployment is insidious in its effects. It was common in interviewing persons for this book to find men and women who were working supposedly 'full-time' jobs in the industries mentioned above and other related jobs, who could not afford to rent reasonable accommodation and so found themselves living in shelter or hostel accommodation. Research conducted by The Social Planning Council of Metropolitan Toronto confirms this problem. The rate of poverty for young families has risen since the mid-1970s from 25% to 47%, and the rate has also risen dramatically in other sectors of the population.[7]

Social, Personal and Societal Factors

The more micro processes that lead to homelessness involve a variety of social, personal and societal factors that have not been thoroughly examined by contemporary researchers in Canada. Little is known, if we examine research by academics, about the kinds of contingencies that cause a person to slip into homelessness.[8] Is it the case that the individual who becomes homeless chooses the wrong path in the road, or is it a series of miscalculations, poor choices, and personal tragedies that propel one on into homelessness? Let us briefly examine the general areas that have been identified by homeless persons themselves as important in causing their present state of affairs. One of the central arguments of this book is that homeless people have not only been largely ignored by researchers, but that even when they are researched it is often in the third person, that is, not by allowing them to relate their own life experiences but by seeing them simply as victims of various systems of social control and exclusionary practices. In contrast, at critical junctures throughout this book the voices of homeless persons are heard. They are able to relate their life experiences in words and images that make sense to them, and which convey the starkness of their condition. Let us now briefly explore some of these key factors.

1. Family Structure and Pressures on the Nuclear Family

Traditionally, the family has been thought of as a haven from a violent and unforgiving world that is constantly assailing its members. The family nurtures individuals in this vision of domestic life providing members with love, care, and attention, all essential elements of a healthy life. In actual fact, academic research has demonstrated that far from being a haven from a violent society, the home is the centre of violence in our country. Women, for example, are at far greater risk of assault in the home than on our streets as criminological research has consistently shown.[9] Children and the elderly have been recognized in the past two decades to be victims of physical, sexual and emotional abuse in the home as we have come as a society to recognize behaviours that have previously not been spoken about or hidden behind closed doors. The Ontario government recently recognized the wide extent of this problem, which some have called an epidemic, in allocating millions more dollars to the building of shelter facilities for battered wives and their children.

Many of the teenagers that come to our streets, in fact the overwhelming majority, have been the victims of both physical and sexual abuse. They seek the streets as a relief to a constant backdrop of abuse and violence that has become intolerable in their teen years. The pressures on the family unit in our society also lead to family breakdown and dissolution at an increasingly frequent rate. Since the introduction of more liberal divorce laws in 1983, the number of marriages that end in divorce has increased exponentially in comparison to the pre-1983 era. The traditional nuclear family, of a male and female and two children, has succumbed largely to the pressures of a society which hypocritically lauds the value of the family on one hand, particularly when it can bring political gain, while constantly either undermining the ability of parents to support children or accomplishing the same end through sheer inaction. Tax systems do not assist the family in helping their children. Day care, recognized as a necessity for two decades has not been a government priority and so many mothers are forced to remain in the home, and/or take low paid part-time work because they cannot find, or often times finance, adequate, quality day care. Although many politicians are quick to cite the importance of the family to Canada's future, few take this beyond posing for publicity photos or making public statements to this effect. Politicians, not surprisingly, often make use of their own families in publicity photos to instil in the voters the sense that this is a person in touch with family people, responsible and caring, but this has not translated into action on behalf of families or family members.

We see increasingly families that do not fit the traditional mold, and this may be a positive step. Blended families consisting of partners from previous marriages and respective children, single parent families, single sex parenting families, and father headed households, are collectively far more common in our society than traditional family forms.[10]

Women, children and the elderly are often rendered homeless or come to the street to escape the violence of family life. This was a theme repeated throughout the interviews conducted for this book and one that is common to front line workers who attempt to assist these people. Whatever the dynamics it is clear that for many thousands of Canadians, most especially women and children, families have become dysfunctional, unable to supply the nurturing and support that we have come to associate with this institution. For them, as you shall learn, homelessness seems a preferable condition.

2. Personal Troubles

One of the most perplexing things for persons who are not homeless to understand is why homeless people wind up on the street. We have already ascertained that there are both wider societal pressures that contribute to this problem, as well as difficulties associated with family structures. There are a number of personal contingencies that also impact on the production of homelessness, and they are worth understanding at a more general level before we move our attention to the specific or individual dimensions of this phenomenon.

In attempting to understand these processes I have identified several 'themes' that permeate the explanations offered by the homeless on the forces that propelled them to wander the streets. Many of these contain elements that straddle the twin dimensions of the personal and the public. They are often difficult to separate or categorize due to this overlapping. This having been said, I have tried to address the key issues which consistently arose in conversation with homeless persons. These may be summarized in the following way:

3. Unemployment

The loss of a job may precipitate homelessness. Many are not prepared for the closure of a plant or forced retirement at an age when re-employment, especially for the low skilled worker, is unlikely. Those who have been employed in low paid jobs are less likely to have the financial resources to survive long, or the ability or aptitude to commence retraining (if this is available at all). Similarly, the loss of work has been associated with alcohol and drug abuse and can precipitate family violence and breakdown.[4]

4. Alcohol and Drug Abuse

The misuse of drugs and alcohol is a constant theme of street life. In some cases alcohol and drug abuse precipitates the drift into homelessness. For a majority of street kids, drug and alcohol abuse commence after arrival on the street as they both try to avoid the reality of their existence in a world characterized by violence, mistrust and degrading activities and seek to acculturate to their peer group.[11]

5. Mental Illness

Approximately twenty percent of the homeless have been found through various studies to suffer from some form of mental illness. One must be cautious when examining these figures. Is the mental illness the condition which contributed to their status as homeless or have they developed a form of mental instability since their movement into the world of the homeless? This seemingly simple question is one that is difficult for researchers to cope with, for not only is there substantial disagreement over the diagnosis of what constitutes mental illness amongst psychiatrists and those who observe the mental health system,[12] but it is exceedingly difficult to determine the effect of homelessness on one's mental condition. If you think about the stresses that you must face, try to imagine facing the stresses associated with attempting to survive on a daily basis on the street with no shelter, no money, and no food. Medical authorities have long been aware of the effects of stress on one's physical and mental well-being. Little wonder that a disproportionate number of the homeless shown signs of mental illness. The release of substantial numbers of the mentally ill into the community occurred during the 1970s and 1980s when the reigning philosophy of the mental health movement was that confinement in a mental hospital was not humane. The community, in this scheme, would help to heal the walking wounded as governments poured more resources into community help schemes. Unfortunately, the development of

DAMAGE NOTED

community facilities was grossly inadequate and released mental patients simply became the prey of eager slum landlords in places like the Parkdale district of Toronto.

6. Legal Troubles

The presence of a criminal career is a factor in the creation of homelessness amongst a small proportion of persons who find their way into hostels across Canada. Released prisoners, as The John Howard Society has graphically demonstrated, suffer from an overriding stigma. For prisoners perhaps the most difficult period of their confinement begins with their release from prison. It is at this point that they are the most vulnerable and the most in need of assistance. However, for many, limited financial and personal resources mean that they wind up occupying a bed-space in a hostel for men, if one can be found, and competing with others for a job in a time when our number of unemployed is at an historical high. With a criminal record their chances of success are severely limited when even those with good work records find it hard to break out of the cycle of homelessness.

7. Castoffs

Amongst seniors, the spectre of homelessness has generally not been with them during their adult years. Although there are some seniors who have been living on the streets for many years, these regulars are the exception rather than the rule. Increasingly seniors are finding themselves falling through the social welfare net, which we assume protects us. As families become increasingly caught up in processes of inflation, unemployment, and marital dissolution, senior members of families often become a redundant hardship that families are either unwilling or unable to shoulder. In the United States, a disturbing trend is the abandonment of unwanted seniors and Alzheimer's patients in hospital emergency rooms. Women seniors may find themselves considerably financially weakened after the death of their spouse, and indeed, widows account for an alarming number of the poor in this country. We simply do not make proper provision for women at many levels of our society throughout the life course.

8. Problems in Cultural Adjustment

Several of the women and men interviewed for this book were either recent immigrants or refugees in this country. One of the supervisory staff of Seaton House shelter commented that, "Immigration officials give these people maps of Toronto at the border with a big red circle marked around our shelter. That's because they know we can't turn anyone down." A common theme in the story of homeless immigrant women is that they came to Canada on the advice of a relative but following a brief stay they were no longer welcome in their accommodation. So a life of homelessness, often characterized by drifting from one city to another, in an alien country began.

9. Running out of Resources

Like most of us, those who eventually become homeless have some form of familial resources they can call on to keep them from going to the street. However, it may be that homeless people possess slightly or appreciably fewer personal resources whether in the form of accommodating relatives, finances or friends to impose upon for shelter to 'get up on their feet,' than those who do not become homeless. This is a theme that will be explored throughout this chapter and in the remainder of the book.

"No Matter How Bad it is at Home Its Worse on the Street"

In Metropolitan Toronto, as we have already learned, there are over 10,000 young people who are homeless. Although under Canadian law teenagers graduate into adult status at the age of 18, accommodations under social service guidelines extend this age of societal protection to 24. While it is rare to see or hear of children under the age of sixteen on the streets, there are numerous sixteen, and seventeen-year-olds who inhabit the netherworld of the downtown core of our cities.[13] The Yonge Street 'strip' in Toronto is a collection of strip taverns, movie houses, pornographic book stores, electronic stores, video game arcades, record stores and restaurants that stretches from Bloor Street in the north to Dundas in the south. Homeless teens walk a track that also extends this area to periphery areas along adjoining Wellesley and Jarvis streets cutting through the 'pink ghetto', an area of gay-oriented business and accommodation running along Wellesley. In the heat of summer nights gathering places serve the function of an old city meeting square where hundreds of gay men crowd the streets or loiter on the steps of the local coffee shops.

Yonge street is where the teens 'hang out' throughout the day and night. Unlike conventional citizens who must live by a watch, homeless teens unless they have acquired shelter that has an imposed curfew, spend the days and most of the nights engaged in a variety of activities that are a futile attempt to ward off boredom. This is the type of boredom generated by a lack of financial resources so that the vast majority of pursuits we regularly enjoy, and which generally rely upon money, are not open to the homeless teens. A great deal of time is spent in conversation with other homeless teens in the parks and parkettes that line or lie a block from Yonge. Alternatively, teens seek money or connections for drug 'scores' so that they can find escape from sheer boredom through chemical comforts. This forced idleness is degrading and teens often feel the pressure of societal condemnation. Passersby will resort to remarks about their laziness or appearance and concerned business people have shown a tendency to telephone the police to roust young transients. Canadians, in common with their British and American counterparts, have shown a very limited capacity for tolerance of loitering behaviours both historically and in contemporary society. Alan Borovoy, the Chief Legal Counsel of the Canadian Civil Liberties Association contends that this characteristic makes it difficult for people to engage in behaviours that are very legal, but simply irritating to specific segments of the population who will resort to the police to 'hassle' young people, and other visibly homeless persons.[14]

Police officers have an ambivalent attitude towards homeless teens. For those who are obviously young or new to the street the police have a policy of resorting to scare tactics to get the teen to leave the street scene. They are painfully aware of the rapid decline of young people, and their maturation into adult vices when exposed to street networks. The police tend to view many homeless kids as a nuisance that they are called upon to deal with in the absence of sufficient social work intervention. Despite the existence of organizations that send workers, often ex-street people themselves, on a nightly basis to counsel and assist teens to get off the street, there are simply not enough resources or bodies to do an adequate job. Police are frustrated by their innate instinct to help on one hand, and the problems which street kids often present in terms of their own desires to stay on the street.

When teens arrive on the street it is for a variety of reasons that we have already discussed. Far and away, however, two reasons predominate in their drift into streetlife. First, and overwhelmingly foremost, is a prolonged history of physical and sexual abuse in the home. Secondly, and relatedly, family troubles characterized by remarriage situations that do not work out figure prominently in the stories of many street kids.[15]

Once on the street the teen has few of the resources needed for mere survival. They quickly assess their financial situation and realize that they are unable to stay on the street without money. As they 'hang out' on the street corners they become recognizable to street regulars who have regular haunts where they 'hang' with their friends. These street friends are seen as a form of family that will protect them in situations where they are personally threatened. On the other hand, this trust does not extend to concerns of money or drugs where the rule of the street is to trust no one. New recruits can often contribute financially in their first few days on the street with money for food, cigarettes, drugs and alcohol, and in some cases perhaps temporary shelter. However, when their resources dwindle they are faced with a realization that either they must secure a job in a low paid occupation (most frequently in a burger restaurant or a pornographic bookstore) or turn to prostitution to stay alive. Although many readers might ask why they do not take advantage of shelters, hostels, welfare and other assistance the answer is quite simple; many do not realize that such services exist or they do not wish to deal with bureaucracy. In fleeing the abuse of adults they have no wish to place themselves under the control and whim of another group of adult helpers whom they may initially regard as just as abusive as those they have just shed.

Prostitution offers a form of seeming freedom for runaway teens. In selling their bodies both girls and boys are able to exert what they consider to be a form of control over what they are doing. Although it may sound odd, they can decide which 'john' or customers to go with, and which may be refused. They are able to barter for the price of their services. Finally, they claim to be able to make large sums of money from prostitution that are not available in other forms of work given their age, lack of education and lack of experience. They are also free from the perceived restrictions of punching a time clock or listening to the boss give orders. Many of their references are to restrictions of time interestingly enough, and this is of importance given their disdain and ignoring of time, once homeless. These 'freedoms' often referred to by street youth are short-lived. The black shadow of drug use invades their world as they turn to cocaine, the favoured drug of young hookers to dull the senses of a degrading existence. They work impossibly long hours using drugs to keep them awake as they search for johns, drugs, food and shelter, often staying awake for periods of several days. The degree of their needs will quickly dictate whom they will perform sexual services for and at what price. It was often surprising to initially hear of the sums of money made by young teens as they sold their bodies in the headlight glare of cruising johns, cars. Figures of $200 or $500 per night are not uncommon depending upon the age, desirability and negotiating skills of the prostitute.[16] Obviously the rule of thumb which permeates street sales of sex favours the youngest of prostitutes. Youth, whether on the street, in magazine ads or in most of the commercial exchanges in our society motivates middle-aged male buyers who are overwhelmingly the customers of teen prostitutes (and purchasers of pornography).

In their search for a release from misery and despair homeless youth often find a life marred by hopelessness, sexual degradation, drug use, and transitory acquaintanceships. For all the bravado that street youth demonstrate in yelling to one another from the doors of arcades, in leading a kind of circus of the street, their grim reality only becomes illuminated in the dead of night. As the bars, strip joints and burger places close their doors after midnight, the world of the homeless teen who finds himself or herself without shelter, either by choice or because their are no beds or they have worn out their welcome at the agencies, begins the night wanderings that characterize life for homeless youth. Those that are 'lucky' may get an offer for a place to stay with a 'john' in exchange for sex either at their home or in their car.[17] Many wind up resting fitfully on park benches, curled up on the heat grates or shivering in the cold as the iron grates impress a pattern in their backs. Some gather in the all-night restaurants where they chat, smoke and drink coffee, nodding off on the hard stools waiting for daybreak and the opening of the first burger place.

From lives of sexual, physical and mental abuse they have moved to a world of violence, unforgiving and quick to age them. For some, they are a lost generation, joining those children who subsist on food bank donations and who have little stake in a society that they perceive as having turned its back on them. Few have any idea anymore about what having a 'home' is. It is like some distant shore that they have never seen, an ideal that can never be realized. "Home" said one young man, "Home is where someone else lives."

"Life Has Not Always Been Kind"

She calls out to the man on the street,
Sir, can you help me?
It's cold and I've nowhere to sleep,
Is there somewhere you can tell me?

He walks on, doesn't look back,
He pretends he can't hear her,
Starts to whistle as he crosses the street,
Seems embarrassed to be there.[18]

A teenager, 16 years of age sits on the pavement at Yonge and Wellesley. He is wearing jeans, a t-shirt and a summer jacket. The temperature is well below zero. He holds up a sign that reads, "Would rather beg than steal." Few stop to throw money into the cardboard box at his feet.

On Yonge at St. Clair it is Sunday morning. A man of twenty crouches against a lampost. A sign is wedged in front of him, "Will work for food."

A deaf woman tries to stop pedestrians to ask for spare change. She is pushed unceremoniously out of the way or avoided physically.

These are all faces of homelessness that have become familiar on Canadian streets in the past decade. Scenes of despair and hopelessness that are repeated daily in ever increasing numbers.

It is winter in Toronto and the temperature has fallen well below the freezing mark. Christmas is only a few days away. On fashionable Bloor Street a jewellry store displays watches in its windows that are priced at $10,000. A few yards away a woman stands trying to find shelter from the stark and chilling wind. She is around 50 years old, but there is no way to tell accurately for the street ages people well before their time. Her clothes consist of a worn ski jacket whose colour has faded with overuse and lack of cleaning, a pair of leisure slacks, ill-fitting, suited to summer wear, and a red woolen toque drawn low across her ears. Beside her a restaurant, warm food and warmth beckoning to passersby. She holds a sign in her shaking hands that few bother to read. The sign says simply, "Life has not always been kind, can you help?" Few stop to give her some change, she is left to freeze in the howling winter winds, a woman, ignored by her fellows, invisible in her despair.

There is a sense in which people feel that the homeless will somehow drag them literally away from their lives, that perhaps it will as one homeless woman expressed it, "rub off". Perceptions of the homeless as derelicts, alcoholics, or mentally ill and hence unpredictably violent individuals pervade pedestrians' views of the homeless. This is nowhere more amply illustrated than in the case of homeless women who seem to engender a greater wrath than that visited on their male counterparts. As in most areas of human interaction, women find themselves the object of intense scrutiny, anger and violence. Exposed on the street, women bear a form of double stigma, that is, they are seen as having failed in the roles ascribed to women as caregivers and nurturers of life, and secondly, they have failed to stay off the street. This additional burden colours the views many hold of women on the street. There is an assumption that the women are sexually available due to their disenfranchised status. This is particularly true of young women on the street. Homeless women present two extremes of street life if we wish to consider the stereotypes which persist in our visions of the homeless. Young women quickly become the objects of intense efforts to move them into a career of prostitution or they move towards this role because of the need to survive. Older women are seen as 'bag ladies' a term which has developed due to their habit of carrying their personal possessions with them in numerous plastic shopping bags. Our vision is quite myopic; we see individuals who fit these roles, and they in turn reaffirm our conceptions as accurate. Although I would not want to argue that these two types of women do not exist amongst the homeless, it is naive to assume that most, or many, 'fit' into these limited categories.

One Canadian researcher, sociologist Lesley D. Harman, conducted an in-depth study of women using a Toronto women's shelter. She found that homeless women are both "visible" and "devalued" in our urban centres. Harman argues that the anomalous nature of homelessness for women is contextualized with normative prescriptions regarding the "normal" roles allocated to women in patriarchal social relations. Women's homelessness is thus unnatural within this taken-for-granted ideology which permeates male-female relationships and perpetuates mens' ability to exercise dominance. While a woman's place remains stuck within the domestic home both literally and figuratively (despite outside employment) then visibly poor homeless women contravene this cultural stereotype. Moreover, moving beyond Harman's argument one can argue that homeless women's presence in 'deviant' spheres mounts a direct challenge to this established hierarchy. This is what Harman describes as "the unexpected appearance of women in the public world."[19]

Men have long been a central feature of homeless life in North America as I have already argued. "Hobos" for example, have been glorified in song and story, and are thus "normal" in the world of street life. Women homeless are newcomers and our cultural vocabulary has struggled to fit, or more accurately to exclude, them from popular images which are informed by reality. As Harman argues, the sight of poor, alone, destitute, cold and hungry women literally embarrasses and disgusts us because of its eradication of the image of women as mother, homemaker, and anchor of family life. Further, we are likely to resort to concocting understandings which are likely to frame the woman within a model of personal pathology. We resolve our confusion in interpreting the presence of an abandoned and degraded woman by "blaming the victim," arguably the most expedient and least socially challenging route. The message of Phil Collin's Grammy award winning song, the most popular tune of 1990, underscores the patriarchal relation evident in women's homelessness as well as bringing recognition of the plight of homeless women to the forefront of our consciousness:

> She calls out to the man on the street,
> He can see she's been cryin;
> She's got blisters on the soles of her feet,
> She can't walk but she's tryin'.
>
> You can tell from the lines on her face,
> You can see that she's been there,
> Probably been moved on from every place,
> Cause she didn't fit in there.[20]

A Teenaged 'Woman' on the Street

Lisa is seventeen, and left home after her father moved in a new girlfriend. Lisa and the girlfriend didn't get along. After weeks of constant fighting she left her Mississauga middle-class home and hit the streets. She is getting ready to go out to the streets for a night of 'carousing' as I interview her in a women's hostel. She is well-dressed in an expensive black blouse with matching mini-skirt. Lisa has long dark hair to her waist and is very attractive. 'Everyone says I'm beautiful' she laughs. She is lacing up her full-sized Dr. Martin boots as we talk.

Lisa is typical of a portion of the young women who have begun to appear on the streets of our cities. She is not from a lower socio-economic class background. She is not heavily involved in the drug scene, 'only a bit of grass for recreation', and she is street smart enough to avoid the pitfalls of drifting into or being propelled toward prostitution as a way of survival. "Oh yah, I'm asked all the time if I'll do it with someone, but there's no way. I've got boyfriends who'll buy me stuff if I want it, but there's no way I'm going to sell my ass." For Lisa, homelessness is a transitory state. She has left the parental home with few resources. She has a high school education, but is cogniscent that this will not get her far in terms of employment. "Look, I slept out on the street the first few days out, but it was just a kick. I met some good buddies, good people, and they help me out if I need it. I got in here, and now I'm going to get some job training and get a place of my own."

Lisa has a job placement interview in a few days from our discussion. At that time she seemed confident of getting a job soon and leaving the hostel. The hostel, which services women only, has a three month stay policy, after that she must move on, if not to her own accommodation then to another of the hostels that service young women only. At the end of the summer, a month after the interview, I meet Lisa in front of the City TV studios on Queen street in Toronto. She is standing near the windows trying to peer in at the shows which are taped a few feet away. She has not been successful in getting a job, and is still a resident of the hostel. Although she insists she has not given up hope she is 'wasting' her days listlessly standing near the television station hoping that she will 'meet a star who'll like me.' Her fantasy is far removed from the world of the women's hostel where she beds down each night, and from the middle-class home in suburbia that she abandoned three months ago.

Women and Homelessness

A growing proportion of women who find themselves abandoned to the world of the street are driven by marriages that have failed or relationships that have disintegrated. Spouse battering or domestic violence has become a significant phenomenon in our society. Over the past two decades with the progression of the womens' movement coupled with increasing academic and popular interest in the area of violence against women, we have come to recognize the widespread nature of this form of social abuse. Throughout Canada, hostels specifically designed for women and their children escaping violence have been set up. The number of these hostels has grown over the last decade as officials from all levels of government have begun to acknowledge the unacceptability of violence towards women. Bob Rae's NDP government in Ontario recently set aside some $3 million dollars for initiatives in both housing and research to tackle this social problem.

Battered women represent a special category of homeless person. Often they have emerged from a long-term relationship that has been characterized by increasing violence directed towards them. They often struggle for long periods of time before deciding to leave their partner. The decision, as are all decisions effecting relationships of significance, has inevitably been difficult to make. Battered women are often embarrassed to publicly seek help for a problem that they may wrongly believe is somehow 'their' fault. In cases of long-term abuse they may suffer from low self-esteem which makes it painful to reach out for help. In many instances, the spouse may threaten to come after them and inflict more harm, possibly promising to kill the person and/or their children as a way of forcing them to return. Many women who become homeless in this group suffer from a lack of skills to support themselves. This can include educational deficits, lengthy periods of time away from the workforce, and problems with childcare which would permit them to earn a living.

'Safe' houses for battered women are located in most urban centres and are places where they can regroup and begin the process of reconstructing their lives. This is a tough battle for most. They must escape from the mental prison that has held them in abusive relationships, and seek ways of establishing connections to wider society. It is a period of transformation of 'self' and the building of a new identity. For most, homelessness is a temporary state lasting several weeks to several months. The 'permanent' accommodation that they often find, though, may be substandard and inadequate for their needs. Escaping revenging husbands who become fixated on intruding constantly into their lives becomes an horrendous burden to bear. Most must face it over several years, for although they have recourse to the police and other agencies, they prove singularly ineffective when a determined abuser is intent on harassing his ex-partner. For him, 'ex' is a relative term.

Besides familial violence, the ending of a living relationship that is relatively positive can still result in a woman falling into the trap of homelessness. How many women in Canada are involved in relationships where they are financially quite dependent on the male they are residing with? Even when a woman is working her salary is, on average, likely to be far less than that of her male counterpart. Despite best intentions, and legislative intent, pay equity has not been realized by the majority of our female working force. When a relationship ends abruptly, as they often do, a woman may find herself without the resources to set up a home again. In large metropolitan areas like Halifax, Toronto, Montreal or Vancouver, the price of rental accommodation often outstrips the ability of women to pay for space, that is, if space is even available! With availability rates hovering at less than 1% in many cities, and the costs associated with setting up residence, many women find themselves quickly ensconced within substandard accommodation. Consider the factors that must be accounted for: moving expenses, first and last months rent, deposits (whether legal or illegal) and cleaning, let alone the cost of furnishings, and one has some sense of the enormity of this transformation which can often cost in the realm of three thousand dollars or more. In large cities perspective tenants may be forced to pay an illegal "finder's fee" to the superintendant.

Single women are particularly vulnerable to becoming homeless when they are laid off or fired from employment. Since women earn on average some 60% of what their male counterparts are able to demand, they are less likely to have accumulated personal assets and savings that will see them through job crises. As I have already argued, it has been demonstrated that few Canadians report assets sufficient to survive for more than a few months time. Women who live on their own, I would assert, are more vulnerable than couples or single males. When you consider that 56% of single parent families in Canada are headed by women, and 64.7% of poor children reside in such families, and that the family members live below the poverty line, some gauge of the enormity of the problem is readily apparent.[21]

Age is also a significant factor in the drift into a homeless status. Fully 59% of all the aged poor in this country are women.[22] Prevented by education and a patriarchal, male-dominated society from taking their proper place within work spheres many senior women in our country were not able to accumulate savings during their life time. As they were not employees of a company they are not eligible for private pension benefits, which often mean the difference between living in poverty and living well in old age. For many of our senior women the problem is also one of having been denied participation in financial decisions during their lifetimes, so that on the death of their spouse they are not accustomed to budgeting their funds, or preparing for their future. Those who may live relatively stable financial lives while their husbands are alive and bringing in a secondary company pension as well as their own Canada Pension benefits find that life on a single old age pension is unmanageable. If they are without assets, namely a house whose mortgage has been burnt, they may soon find themselves downgrading into cheaper accommodation, and possibly soon unable to afford reasonable accommodation. All of us are familiar with senior women in foodstores purchasing small amounts of food, or even pet foods for personal consumption, emaciated, ailing, alone, and unable to cope financially. It does not take an expert in financial management to realize that even when one has a 'good' pension plan that inflation can rob it of much of its value over a period of a few years. If one assumes an annual inflation rate of even 4% (it is currently 6.3%) the buying power of our pension payment is reduced substantially over a five year period, particularly if it is not indexed to inflation!

In the end these figures lead us to two disturbing conclusions. First, those who are taking the brunt of the economic pressures on the poor in this country are women and children. Secondly, single women, single parent families that are headed by women, and senior women all are the objects of considerable social apathy and disregard.

Mental illness also has a part to play in bringing women into the sphere of a homeless existence. Women have, since the development of psychiatry as a scientific discipline, been the main objects of psychiatric interventions. Their problems have been subject to medicalization rather than directing our efforts towards the structural causes of their illnesses. The history of the treatment of women under psychiatry is a long and sordid history of subjugation and abuse that is not simply a long forgotten episode in the treatment of women. In fact, a simple reading of the voluminous research literature in the United States can lead to only one conclusion, that the study of homeless persons in general is largely set within a medical framework attempting to determine the type and degree of the mental illness they are suffering from.[23] Those who have traversed our busy downtown streets are aware of the seemingly obviously mentally ill. The woman screaming at the top of her lungs to passersby. The streetman mouthing obscenities above the din of the cruising traffic. These are familiar yet misleading examples, which again serve to reinforce our images of homeless people, and particularly those we might suspect suffer from mental maladies.

Yet many who are apparently suffering from mental disorder are merely displaying the signs of normality in a street existence that demands much of those who must survive on a daily basis. Ask yourself how you might act if you spent the night sleeping on a park bench with strangers constantly passing by you. It is not uncommon for people to approach at three or four in the morning and ask for a cigarette. If you are lucky the police will not roust you from your bench. After fitfully sleeping, you must stiffly rise and begin walking, looking for food, perhaps begging. If you have the energy you might make one more attempt to hassle with the people at welfare or some other social service agency. Another long walk in the heat of summer or the cold of winter and you may be able to see if there will be any space for you tonight at one of the few womens' hostels in town, that is, if you did not act out so much last time that they have banned you from the premises. Under these circumstances how might you behave? Would your behaviour seem rational or insane, clear-headed or disordered? Might you not protest verbally at the madness of it all?

We might also remember that the initial assessment of whether you are disordered will be conducted by police officers. They are responsible for the apprehension of persons who are a public nuisance or are acting in a manner that suggests they are suffering from some form of mental disorder. This is most pressing when the person is presenting a danger to themselves or others. Obviously if a person is holding a weapon and threatening to do injuries to others, or is making clear suicidal gestures, the police have a legal obligation to remove the person to a treatment facility. But often senior women who have no obvious presenting mental illness are brought to mental health facilities because of a lack of beds for women at city hostels/shelters and the reluctance of shelter staff to accept women who are troublesome, unhygienic, or difficult to manage in any way.

A growing number of homeless women are also being drawn, according to a variety of sources, from the ranks of refugees. The waiting list for subsidized housing in Toronto during May 1991 included a substantial portion of immigrants, both male and female. Refugees often arrive in this country with few resources either financial or personal. Often they are faced with both language barriers and cultural differences that place them in a vulnerable position. They find it difficult to obtain employment other than in sectors of the economy where work is undervalued, and the remuneration is not sufficient to 'start' a life in their adopted homeland.

Lesley: A Homeless Refugee

Lesley's experiences since her arrival in Canada illustrate some of the typical problems experienced by young women refugees in Canada. She was raised in a family of nine in her native Jamaica. Recently her father died leaving the mother with insufficient resources to care for the family. Lesley is in her early 20s and has a sister who lives in Montreal. At the encouragement of her sister she came to Canada and applied for refugee status after a prolonged stay in the country. Life in Canada seemed much better to her at first. She shared an apartment with her sister and the sister's boyfriend. This arrangement worked out for a couple of months until one afternoon the boyfriend took advantage of Lesley's sister being at work. He said, "C'mon now girl, you better be good to me." "He wanted to have sex with me. He said if I didn't do it he'd tell my sister I was botherin' him." I told him, "No, no way will I have sex." She found herself uncomfortable in the home, and after her refusal to have sex with the boyfriend he began to make life miserable for her. He finally presented the sister with an ultimatum, and since her sister was financially reliant upon the boyfriend, Lesley was forced to leave.

Lacking resources and a job she was able to get a place to stay in a hostel run by a church group in Ottawa. She stayed there for a few weeks but found the conditions difficult. The sleeping arrangements were dormitory style, and mixed 'normal' women, with the mentally disordered as well as alcohol and drug abusers. Her sleep was constantly disrupted by the moaning or screams of other women. "Women would be moanin' and groanin' all night long. They would steal your shoes if you didn't leave them on. A lot were sick, sick in their head and would act strange. Oh and the smell was so bad from some." She decided after a few weeks to travel to Toronto. She was able to hitch a ride and considered herself lucky to get a low paid job in a restaurant the day she arrived. She was also able to find a very cheap apartment and moved in with no furniture.

The apartment was in a small building that she soon discovered was frequented by drug dealers and their clients. The signs of drug use littered the halls; old syringes, modified pop tins used for smoking crack, and other refuse of lives of addiction. She met a young man who moved in with her, a move that she thought would help her out. Like many women she thought that partnering would help them both to achieve stability. "I was thinkin' and so was he that together we can work and get it together, like two is stronger than one. Only, he was like a lot of men; I was supposed to do the workin' and he would do the spendin.'" This relationship lasted a few months and she was able to accumulate a few possessions and some meagre savings. Her boyfriend, however, met someone else, and one night when she returned home from work her apartment had been emptied along with her bank account which she had co-signed with her boyfriend. He had also not paid the rent, pocketing the money.

As Lesley was a refugee and afraid of police she did not report the incident. She was evicted the next day, and made her way to the hostel in which I interviewed her. She still has her job as restaurant help and is saving to find another place to live.

Men on the Street

Aside from the period of the Great Depression in the 1930s when hundreds of thousands of men were thrown out of work in North America and began to 'ride the rails' to try to find work, young men have not formed a significant number of the homeless population. Since the 1980s however, the average age of men on the street has been consistently moving downwards. By 1990, the mean age of street men in this country was 29 years. These are men who cannot be written off as hopeless derelicts or as lazy, shiftless non-contributing members of our society. While a small percentage of homeless men suffer from problems of mental disturbance, and or alcohol/drug abuse, the vast majority, approximately 80% or more, are fit and able-bodied.[24] It is noteworthy also to contemplate that problems with alcohol and drug abuse often constitute the 'mental' affliction of a significant proportion of the number of homeless who suffer from mental illness as such behaviour is often classified as a form of mental sickness by psychiatric authorities and social control agents.

There are numerous factors that have played a part in the production of this disturbing figure. First and foremost, perhaps, is the impact of increasing unemployment in our country. While poverty and lack of educational attainment can play a key role in disenfranchising men, it is lack of reasonable employment that caused many of the men interviewed for this book to be homeless. Outside of Seaton House in Toronto, I sat and talked with a man from Newfoundland.

Seaton House is the largest facility for homeless men in North America. It can accommodate some 700 men within its walls. Greg is 26 years old and dressed in neat pressed jeans, a plaid short sleeve shirt, and clean running shoes. He is well groomed and would fit in unnoticed on any college campus in the country. He is a bright, interesting conversationalist and was eager to talk with me. He had been living in Seaton House for a month when we talked. However he has 'made the rounds' of the shelter and hostel accommodation for two years. For him, the experience of homelessness is similar to that of many other young men. He is bitter that there is little that seems to be done in terms of providing employment for men in his position. It is incredibly hard to find work in the economic downturn even though he has a high school education. During his stay in Toronto he has applied for some 200 jobs. He has 'been close, a couple of times' but has never received a job offer.

Greg finds it difficult to even apply for jobs. On top of the depression which comes with each turndown, there is the added burden of constantly seeking a new place to stay, which takes considerable time and effort. The ordinary tasks of life that make many of us cringe take inordinate amounts of time and ingenuity to complete for a homeless man like Greg. First, he must find paper, pen, envelopes, and postage to apply for jobs. There has to be a place to write out the application, so this means a walk to the library, the local McDonalds, (The 'McOffice' of many homeless) or to 'Beat the Street' a storefront agency which provides coffee, sandwiches, access to daily papers, free local telephone calls, and a place to sit down and write an application out. These are precious resources for homeless people, but it is often difficult to keep applying for jobs. "A lot of guys just give up, accept it like because you just get so frustrated, you know, there's just so much a guy can take." Greg also finds that prospective employers are often positive about his application but react negatively when they see his address, which must be listed as Seaton House. "I've had people say to me, 'Well you're just a bum living in a rat-hole like that. We don't want you.'" His spirits have not diminished completely. He has recently met a young woman who has a subsidized apartment. "If things work out, we'll move in together. It'll give me a start. That's all I want."

There are many lost dreams in the stories of the homeless. Young men who emigrate to the big cities of Canada: Toronto, Montreal, Vancouver, Halifax, looking for a new and exciting life, a chance at success that they have just dreamed about, or seen on a television set. They come from small towns across Canada, the rural heartland that is dying a slow and painful death under the onslaught of high interest rates and the encroachment of large corporate resource users. David, a goodlooking 20-year-old has come to Vancouver looking for a job. He had been living with a family who were friends of his mother after the divorce of his parents, and the arrival of his mother's boyfriend left him 'odd man out.' He wanted to come to the city to make a fresh start, hoping to get a job and settle in. He rented a bachelor apartment in the downtown core with most of his savings and set about looking for a job. After several weeks of fruitless search he had also found his nights disturbed by the antics of the landlord's brother who lived upstairs from him. "The brother spent his nights listening to heavy metal music at mega-volume and imbibing as many drugs and forms of alcohol as he could stand." One evening when he was out the brother 'borrowed' the master key for his flat and removed all of his valuables, including his life savings, which as meagre as they were, he had not bothered to deposit in the bank. That night he complained to the landlord who told him 'to get the fuck out'. David did not complain to the police, a route that he thought would prove fruitless. So, David found himself without a place to stay, with his dreams in ruins.

When I talked with David he had been in the hostel system for three months. He found himself unable to go out to look for work. Demoralized, victimized, and too embarrassed to go to his family for assistance he found himself 'dreaming' his days away walking in the downtown areas of Vancouver. Although he still has hopes of recognizing his dreams he finds himself unable to work towards them at the present. In this, he is no different than many of his contemporaries who were interviewed for this study. The 'drift' into homelessness is a time of relative frenzy while a person tries to use every resource at their disposal to 'stay afloat.' This activity occupies the days of the pre-homeless. However, when an individual finally finds themselves on the street, they experience a shock not dissimilar to that reported by victims of personal crimes. David described it like this, "When I walked across the threshold of the shelter it was like someone had just hit me in the guts. I felt sick to my stomach. I'd read about homeless people but they were different, bums, and that wasn't me. Now, here I was just like them, one of them, a bum. It was a shock that has left me numb ever since." This precipitous fall from "fully human status" to that of street person leaves the individual traumatized. As David noted, "You know you're at rock bottom but you just can't shake it. You're homeless, a homeless person, that's your identity now, everything else just drops away. It's like the rest of your life never happened." Hostel life has become comfortable for him. It requires no decisions. A bed, food, a car ticket, perhaps a dollar or two of spending money is provided and this seems to sustain David as he regroups emotionally. "It'll probably take me months more to get out of this rut. I know I will, but it gets harder every day, you get used to it."

"Troubles" of many varieties also bring men to the street. Crime and criminal acts are a source of homelessness for many men. Released criminals often find themselves in facilities for the homeless as they are without resources following their stay in prison. Shelters and hostels represent a dubious launching point into full civilian life after varying periods of institutionalization. Those who have lost jobs may also find their way to the streets. One man in his late fifties begging for change on Jasper Avenue in downtown Edmonton had spent most of his adult life working at a local hotel. They had provided him with a minimum wage and a place to sleep and eat during several decades of service. In 1990 he was suddenly informed that the hotel could no longer employ him. His family had long since passed away, and he found himself without work, friends, family or resources after a lifetime of work. The shock had been immense for him as a man possessed of low intelligence. This had led to severe mental problems for him. He imagined that his mother was still alive somewhere in the city where he had grown up, and he began to look for her. "She's on a bench with me as a baby. She's crying and I must find her, only I can't remember where the bench is." Upset and alone, he wanders throughout the city looking for a world that has long since disappeared, a victim of a world that did not care for his pain.

Old men wander our streets, abandoned, irrelevant, cast as nuisances, people to be avoided, 'things' of little value for whom little or nothing can be done. These social castoffs are men who have been made 'redundant' in our society. There are many who have served their country in times of strife, veterans who now find themselves the objects of ridicule and scorn. It is educational to watch pedestrians do their best to avoid the most obviously homeless. People will steer a path several feet clear of homeless people to avoid having to look at them directly, and to free themselves of the responsibility of responding to their requests for a bit of spare change. The elderly homeless are painful to observe, often dressed in clothing that is completely inappropriate for the season. Today, in Windsor, it is 28C and I encountered several homeless men wearing extremely dirty winter parkas walking the downtown streets. I am uncomfortably hot in this extremely humid of Canadian cities with only shorts and a t-shirt on. One can only imagine what this senior citizen must be feeling like as he half falls and half faints against a convenient light standard. He is ignored by those on the street. "Another stupid drunk" laughs a young man loud enough to be heard by the senior as he walks by. His attitude openly reflects what is felt by many of the other people who pass him on the street.

No Life for Families

When families join the ranks of the homeless it is not only a more serious situation because it may involve children, but one that is more difficult for our existing assistance network to deal with. The spectre that haunted American newspapers, a picture of two sisters barely more than seven years old holding a sign reading, 'will work for food' is becoming commonplace in Canada. The sheer number of families who are homeless is staggering. Families come to the street in many of the same ways that other single persons finally become homeless—under the onslaught of inflation, rising costs, and increasing unemployment.

Families are often lauded as a centre of safe haven but as research into wife and child abuse in this country clearly demonstrates violence is not only commonplace in family life but abusers are drawn from all socio-economic strata. Every year, for instance, some hundreds of thousands of Canadian women are assaulted by their partners, and these are only the number which are reported to authorities.[25] Abuse of children still suffers from social taboos surrounding the reporting of violence or sexual behaviour against children to the authorities. One in ten women in Canada will be the victims of physical abuse this year. Violence, far from emanating from the street, is more common in households across this country, and can assume many forms from physical beatings, to psychological abuse, to neglect.

The demand for our small stock of shelter space that can assist battered women gives some indication of the severity of the problem being generated by violence in our society. In 1985 in this country 110,000 children and their mothers sought refuge in public shelters. In 86,000 cases shelter was being sought because of violent actions by a male partner. They had to compete for space in the 230 shelters that existed at that time. Recently,[26] the Ontario government, responding to this problem, set aside millions of dollars for the creation of an enlarged network of shelters for the victims of violence against women that will begin to have an impact in the coming years.

Reports that emanate from a variety of social work contact points that deal with battered women also indicate that many of the children who reside with a battered mother have also been abused. This abuse can take the form of assaults upon the emotions of children, physical and sexual abuse. These forms of abuse are the most common feature of the movement of teens onto the street to escape the violent family unit.

Families who become homeless together find that another bodyblow awaits them. There is little provision made across Canada to accommodate families under one roof, and so the separation of the male parent into a men's shelter is generally required. This makes planning a path out of their homeless crisis more difficult and places an incredible burden on the female parent who must now try to cope in a shelter with family problems as well as the tensions and stresses that homelessness produces. She is often in the position also of having to protect her children from the violence and madness of other residents of the shelter. Our society, both within shelters and in the wider public realm, displays a great deal of contempt towards children. Terrified children in shelters, displaced from their homes and possessions, separated from their fathers, find it difficult to sleep, or 'settle down'. Mothers are faced with the impossible task of trying to take care of their children in cramped and difficult circumstances that defy our imagination. In the chapters to follow we will explore the street world of the homeless and the impact of shelter life on men, women and children who must seek shelter from the storms of life.

CHAPTER THREE

Down and Out in Canada

Once I lived the life of a millionaire,
Spent all my money didn't have any care,
Took all my friends out for a mighty good time,
We bought bootleg liquor, champagne and wine.

Then I began to fall so low,
Lost all my good friends,
And had nowhere to go,
If I get my hands on a dollar again,
I'll hang on till that old eagle grin.

Cause, nobody loves you,
when you're down and out.

In your pocket not one penny,
And as for friends,
You don't have any.[1]

"Living on Dreams and Little Else"

The street life of the homeless in this country is an experience that the average Canadian has little knowledge of. Homelessness, contrary to stereotypical images that have pervaded our views on these persons do not underscore the fact that homelessness is more than simply a material condition. Far more than this, it is a condition that saturates the life of those subject to it. To say that the street is 'hard' does not convey the stark realities which the homeless must confront on a daily basis. While we live in a society in which we have been socialized, more or less through norms of behaviour, a process Foucault has termed the production of docile bodies,[2] many of the homeless quickly become detached from this reality. The regulations, conventions and rules that govern our lives and circumscribe our behaviour become irrelevant for the disenfranchised. Middle-class standards of behaviour and ideas concerning acceptable behaviour represent a source of resentment, scorn and bafflement for the homeless. These rules which appear at the sites where the homeless must look for assistance are only a source of further alienation. Homelessness is not a right in society, it is rather the subject for the ministrations of charity, and the object of intense control efforts.

This implies an element of pathology in the behaviour of the individual. Although larger political and economic forces may provide a convenient backdrop for the presenting problems of the homeless, explanations of their current condition are almost exclusively phrased within the personal pathology model by social control agents and agencies. Put another way, the question which this begs is, "What problem in **your** behaviour has resulted in **your** current condition of homelessness?" Solutions then are seen to arise not by addressing structural issues that contribute to increasing numbers of homeless, but in seeking to find resolution through changing the behaviour of the individual, i.e., seeking employment, dealing with personal problems, finding more permanent forms of shelter. In other words, solutions which clearly put the onus back upon the individual to "do something" about their condition. However, the inadequacy of this solution is reflected in the high rate of readmittance to shelters, and histories of long-term involvement with the shelter system on the part of substantial numbers of homeless.

This chapter examines the street life of homeless Canadians. Specifically we will explore several representative descriptive and analytical sketches of homeless existence in Canadian cities.

Sex, Drugs and the Street

Youth Without Shelter is a hostel for teens who find themselves without a place to stay and who want a break from the intensity of downtown Toronto streetlife. Located in the far northwest suburbs of the city it requires some measure of stamina and determination for street kids to reach the facility on public transport, hitching or walking. The cul-de-sac street that houses YWS is lined with halfway houses for a variety of societal child misfits, prostitutes, the criminal and the mentally ill. It is on the park benches that straddle the outside of the house that I interviewed Cindy. Cindy has just recently reached her sixteenth birthday. That was the day she left home for good. Although she is sixteen, she gives the appearance of a much younger, more immature girl and this is reflected throughout in her conversation. Her voice is high-pitched and childlike. She is full-faced and is dressed in jeans and a second-hand top that she picked up at another shelter. After only a few months as a homeless person, she is already a veteran of shelter life and knowledgeable about the hostel facilities available to assist her.

Cindy: From Abuse to Abuse

Cindy had suffered through a childhood filled with many of the problems common to street kids. Her mother and father were physically abusive and negligent when it came to her care. She was a latch key kid from an early age and the focus of constant beatings. "My father used to belt me all around the house, and my mother too. Nothing I did was right." Cindy suffered through the abuse for years and her performance at school was "poor". She failed several times and felt she had few friends. Then began the abuse that would cause her to leave home. Her father entered her room one night,"He had this funny kind of look on his face. He told me to shut up or else he'd hit me...anyway he raped me." The incest continued for several months; "He kept coming into my room late at night. He told me if I told mom he'd kill me." When Cindy finally did approach her mother with the story her mother turned on her; "She started yellin' and screamin' 'You're a tramp, you liar, you're always telling lies.'" Her mother physically assaulted her once again, and it was at this point, with no support for her and the prospect of future sexual assaults now ensured, that she decided to leave home.

When she 'hit the streets' she soon discovered that there were no jobs available for unskilled and ill-educated sixteen-year-olds, especially one that looked all of thirteen. But it only took a few days before a 'friend turned (her) on to hooking.' Within two weeks of leaving home Cindy was turning tricks on College Street in downtown Toronto. "The first time I didn't know what to do but the guy was okay. Pretty soon it got easy, and when I got into drugs it was easier." On Hooker's Row Cindy dressed to find clientele and they certainly found her; "I wear a really tight dress with high heels and a top with a real low cut so that johns can see my tits cause they're big. I'm kinda fat but my tits are really good so that gets them in. Most of them think

I'm twelve or thirteen and I guess its kinda like being with their daughter, isn't it?"

Cindy is eager in the interview to demonstrate her knowledge of prostitution, "Well, most of the men you just do them in the car, a straight blow job for $50 or more if you can get it. If they want you to go to their house or hotel or something to fuck its $100. I don't do any of the kinky stuff like up the ass or anything like that, but most of them ask."[3] Cindy has been 'roughed up' by johns but not seriously physically hurt. Although she is afraid of the prospect of violent johns who might cause her serious damage she also finds a hooker's life to have a very immediate form of attraction. "You're out on the street with everybody at night. There's the lights and action, cars, kids all over the place. You're out till 2 or 3 when business slows down. There's a lot of freedom in that."

On the other side of a life in prostitution is the spectre of heavy drug use. The predominant drug of street hookers is cocaine, which keeps the kids awake, and detaches them from their immediate pain. The price of cocaine is one of the factors that ensures, despite claims of making large sums of money on a nightly basis, that hookers never accumulate any savings. As Cindy explained, "Like you get blow whenever you can. Do a trick, get some blow, and on and on." When cocaine is not available or money is short, hookers will turn to marijuana and alcohol. All of those interviewed for this book saw the drugs as a way of dulling the chilling reality of degrading themselves, in a sense repeating their own various victimizations while viewing hooking as 'freedom.'

The freedom of the street, most are astute enough to realize, is short-lived and largely illusory. Money made is soon spent on drugs, short frenzies of spending on expensive hotel accommodation and food, the need for new clothing almost constantly due to a lack of laundry facilities, and the need to appear attractive to customers. As Cindy had already concluded after a relatively short period of time, "spending my nights in the front seat of a car with my mouth on the dicks of all these married guys," that the freedom was bought at the expense and the sacrifice of much of her remaining dignity and self-respect. Her story, like increasing numbers of those who live on the street often results in their early death as the victims of drug overdose, murder, or exposure, or A.I.D.S.[4]

"Boys Town"

Its hard to run when a coat hanger
beats you on the thighs,
Pedro dreams of being older and
killing the old man,
but that's a slim chance he's going
to the boulevard ...
Pedro sits there dreaming,
He's found a book on magic in a
garbage can.
He looks at the pictures and stares
at the cracked ceiling.
"At the count of three" he says,
"I hope I can disappear.
And fly, fly away...."

L. Reed, 1991.

In every major city in Canada there is a gathering place for prostitutes that is less well known than the 'track' where female hookers sell their bodies to an endless stream of slowly cruising cars. In Toronto, it's 'Boys Town,' a cruel euphemism drawn from a home for orphans known for its religious affiliations and for a popular movie of the 1940s. Edmonton has 'the hill,' Vancouver 'the meat strip,' as do all other cities where boys gather to sell sex. All of these human flesh exchanges are the juncture at which hard reality closes in on rhetoric in our society. These are places little talked about and less well researched. The existence of male prostitution elicits a strong negative response in our society ranging from public ignorance, through academic inattention, to political apathy. Homosexuality, in general, is not a subject with which society feels comfortable; in fact, violence against gay men has been a source of considerable protest and action within the gay communities of large urban centres in Canada. Symptomatic of this unrealistic and unfounded fear of gay persons or 'homophobia,' are gaybashings or queerbashings perpetrated by groups of young males as a hollow expression of masculinity.

For a large proportion of homeless youth and men, prostitution is the only avenue for financial survival open to them. Newcomers to the street find their meagre savings, if they have any at all, last only a few days before they are broke. Most kids on the street bring little in the way of social or educational skills with them. They are escaping a world of adult control or mayhem in which they have not fared well.

Most teens interviewed for this study had little or no awareness of their eligibility for social assistance payments or of the shelters for their first few weeks as a homeless drifter. One young man commented about this lack of knowledge, "I was like livin' in the doorways up and down the street. I slept on the fire escapes, up on the roof or in the gutter. Shit, you can't get any sleep like that. The cops roust me all the time. So finally, a friend clued me in; he said, 'Why don't you check out the hostel brother?' I said, 'What you talkin' about?' So he told me about it. I never heard the word before. There's no one to tell you about this stuff."

For a large number of young people contact with social services or other social control agencies such as the police, welfare, or Children's Aid is avoided religiously. Their attitude towards adult caregivers has been formed from the violence, neglect and pain of dysfunctional and abusing families. Their flight to the street is born of anger and desperation largely attributable to adults. Therefore, few seek to embroil themselves in a social control interlude with any official agents of the state. Those who are alone on the street under the age of 16 must seek more drastic means to escape discovery by agents of the state. The law requires that such individuals hold underage runaways for the police so that they may be taken under the care of the Children's Aid.

Young males who are without money are easy to spot for seasoned veterans of the sexual trade. Just as violent criminals develop an intuitive sense that guides their selection of potential victims, so the veteran players become sensitized to the point at which boys are malleable, 'open' to the option of selling sex. Professor Livy Visano of York University has conducted the most thorough and probing study of young male prostitutes in Canada. His research involved following the daily round of activities of his subjects as a witness to their lifestyles. From his extensive research emerges the description of this process of conversion into a deviant career. Boys without money appear at the periphery of the staging area where hookers conduct their business, joining them in conversation over endless coffees and cigarettes. Lounging in the fast food restaurants that are their offices, hookers take needed breaks from sexual exchanges. Here they spin tales of bravado and daring, aggrandizing their interactions with johns retrospectively. Whether they claim to have received far more for the sex act performed than it was worth, have robbed, beaten or verbally humiliated the client, they spin their tales of excitement and adventure. Ultimately they emerge in a self-portrait triumphant in the midst of their own tragedy. The johns are suckers and they are in charge.

Sociologist Walter Miller would argue they share at least four of the five classic characteristics of working class culture that he developed in his theory.[5] The hookers value toughness, excitement, autonomy, trouble and smartness in the street sense. Free to improvise since the only witnesses to the tricks they turn are themselves, degradation becomes reconstructed as power over the john. For potential new recruits, the lifestyle becomes synonymous with freedom, control of one's fate, and power over adults. The moment-to-moment life of hooking, fraught with danger and excitement in these accounts, becomes equated with that of rock stars or celebrities. As one young man patiently explained to the researcher, "Hey, I work when I want, sleep all day, up all night, just like Jon Bon Jovi. Plenty of the three C's; cash, coke and chicks. How many dudes live that life?"

Despite engaging in sex with several men on an almost nightly basis most male prostitutes adamantly maintain that they are heterosexuals. Their male-to-male exchanges are characterized as 'situational' sex like that experienced by prisoners subject to a same sex environment who revert to heterosexuality upon release. Hookers claim that when their street days are over they will resume heterosexual liaisons, although the incidence of A.I.D.S. in prostitutes, often cited as a crossover point for transmission of the deadly disease, makes assertions about a future life of marital bliss seem highly unrealistic. Surprisingly, many claim to have 'girlfriends.' While young women do hang around with them in the all-night joints, few confirmed that they accept this status. Any encountered by this researcher were either hookers themselves or indicated they were simply platonic friends who enjoyed being near to the seamy side of life. None confirmed the assertions of the male hustlers. Similarly, there was no indication the boys were interested in any kind of sexual liaison . "Joey gets blown or screwed all night by his johns. He's got no time for sex with anyone else." "Besides," she added, "I don't need A.I.D.S. from those queers (johns)." In fact, we know very little about the post deviant lives of former hookers who leave the trade.

As young males soon discover prostitution represents a bleak and desperate form of bare survival despite its seeming promise of excitement and freedom. Mike, a 17-year-old with two years of street experience described the dark side of hooking as we talked in a men's shelter, "No one gives a shit when you're hustlin' your ass, no one really watches your back, you're on your own. You go with some guy in a car, he blows you, you suck him, maybe, and you're out. But you never know when a trick will go bad, get violent. You use drugs or booze to get high, eat garbage, feel sick a lot...If the cops aren't hasslin' your butt, then some other guy is on your case." Despite two years of prostituting Johnny is living in a homeless youth shelter with no money. He dreams of going to the country and escaping the street. Still he is aware that his behaviour may bring disaster; "I get tested for A.I.D.S. every three months. I figure one time my number will be up cause sometimes you don't make the guy wear a "safe," either cause you're too high to give a shit or he's paying for the privilege." His situation reflects the contradictions inherent in one form of homeless life where despite earning a substantial amount of non-taxable income prostitutes still remain trapped in a cycle of transient homelessness and personal degradation.

Tracks and Trannies

Another group of homeless persons who reside in the sexual periphery of Canadian city life are the transvestites and transsexuals who are familiar figures on late night downtown streets. They form a colourful part of what author John Rechy has termed 'the city of night,' a world which the average citizen is not aware of, or has only glimpsed the periphery of. Transvestites are males who derive sexual gratification from dressing in women's attire. Transsexuals are distinguished from this former group as men who are 'trapped' within the wrong gender body according to Canadian sociologist Robert Stebbins.[6] Significant numbers of transsexuals undergo a series of surgical interventions that result in their conversion to 'females,' that is, surgically constructed women. This involves the removal of the penis and the construction of a vagina, as well as breast implantation and numerous forms of plastic surgeries to develop a female presentation of physical self. While in the 1960s the first of these transformations was considered experimental and bizarre, such surgery is now commonplace.[7] In order to qualify for surgery perspective patients must live as women for a two-year period before the difficult and painful procedure can be performed. It is during this time, while living as pre-operative transsexuals in a state of temporary transvestism, that most fall prey to the problems of homelessness.

In downtown streets wedged between the 'gay ghetto' and the local cruises, transvestites and transsexuals join in a nightly parade starting roughly at eleven o'clock. Obviously their appearance at late hours in locations off but close to main drags is neither random nor frivolous. During the 'parade' several dozen "T and Ts" strut in full female dress on designated streets. To the undiscerning they may appear to simply be prostitutes, yet further observation quickly reveals that they exhibit as Stebbins has pointed out, overly feminine attributes accentuating their movements, wearing heavy makeup, and speaking inappropriately loudly (a common practice among most street groupings). The veil of night provides cover for the deviant behaviours they will feel free to engage in unconstrained by incessant interruptions by uninformed 'day trippers.' Both of these groups survive by offering sexual services since their choice to 'live the life' means that their chances of obtaining and holding most jobs are quite low.

The need to 'cross-dress' in the clothes of the opposite gender also creates substantial problems in terms of their housing choices. Few landlords are tolerant of sexual diversity when it is transparently visible, and the financial and employment problems of both groups make them poor risks as tenants. They form part of the economically underprivileged and socially marginal subculture that often band together for a temporary escape from homelessness. A common practice of 'trannies' is to rent an apartment, and immediately move four or five other 'girls' in to share costs. Apartments act as a convenient location to entertain customers for quick sex. This practice is akin to that of welfare recipients who piggyback numerous others into their subsidized housing.

Small enclaves of "T and Ts" can be found living in the larger parkland areas of Canadian cities. In Toronto's High Park I observed, and was able to later interview, several who camp out in secluded areas, living rough in the undergrowth. Barry Snodden, a teacher and former streetworker who volunteers much of his spare time to finding runaway kids, was a knowledgeable guide to the hiding places of the homeless. "I knew one young kid who was 17. His father kicked him out of the house after he came out and told him he was a transvestite. The father wouldn't have anymore to do with him, cut him off completely, and told him he never wanted to see his face again. I found him cold and shivering in the rain down here under the bushes with a little dog huddled up against him, the two of them shivering together. He was dressed in womens' clothes and hadn't eaten in three or four days."

Many who live in the forested valleys of city parklands create small cubby holes made of twigs, papers and discarded plastic under the shelter of bushes or trees. One usually has to crawl in under bushes through a entrance only big enough to accommodate the body into an inner sanctuary. Abandoned living areas display the trappings of homeless life; remnants of fires to ward off the chill of the night, old food containers, bottles, and discarded pieces of womens' clothing. The number of these scattered throughout the park when Barry and I investigated and the presence of several homeless 'campers' indicated that several groups were regularly bedding down in the park. A regular figure in the park for many years, Barry led me through the world of those who are marginal even in the world of the homeless. For many of the transvestites and transexuals the world of homelessness persists throughout the transformation process, and after. Trapped in a body that is neither male nor female they are denied access to full legitimate status within our society rendering them outsiders who have little hope of acceptance in wider society. They share a marginality with other homeless subcultures that effectively stigmatizes their behaviour, leaving them outsiders in our culture.

Street Families

For city dwellers the sight of small groups of street kids hanging out in the city centre in parkettes, on benches, in fact in any convenient resting place, is a familiar motif. Homeless youth, as we have already learned, almost universally share a background characterized by some form of familial abuse. Fleeing neglect and abuse they are in the initial stages of their adaptations to street life, solitary and guarded, avoiding much human contact except that which is necessary to survival. For many, the family is a symbol of violence and maltreatment, a maelstrom of hurt, anger and depression that they are relieved to have escaped. For most, this has been a long process of decision-making as they struggle to come to terms with the fact that in a society that continually makes reference to the family unit as the pillar of our society they have been caught within the seeming abnormality of a severely dysfunctional family. Having extricated themselves from the restrictions of adult interventions, their first experiences of the street often are exhilarating and washed with the colours of freedom. The suffocation they have felt within the ruptured family is replaced with a sense of rebirth. Jody described it in this way: "It was so good not to have anyone telling me what to do for once. My first couple of nights out I was just high, super high on the street, no drugs, just the feeling of being away from all that control."

Before their entry into homelessness young homeless people knew little of what the life would entail. Most had no idea of the harshness, violence and brutality that awaited them. For many escape from their home environment and entrance into a homeless existence represented the only alternative that was open to them. Wayne, a sixteen-year-old put it this way: "My old man got a new wife. So they said, 'Hey there's no room for you here now' and I had to pack my things and get out." Others flee sexual abuse that can only stop when they leave the home of their assailant and seek freedom from violence.

The street dwellers they meet validate their feelings of hostility towards traditional families as they are quickly socialized into a new way of viewing society. Here, abusive families are the norm and they quickly find kindred spirits in the late night coffee bars of the downtown who share stories of their own troubled backgrounds. Soon they recognize that survival on the street is also linked to an ability to gather useful information and to ward off serious trouble. The predominant method of accomplishing these goals was discovered during the course of my many interviews. There are a significant though inestimable number of homeless who do not seek the company of other street dwellers. Essentially these individuals fall into three groups. First, there are the chronically or sporadically mentally ill who avoid interaction with other homeless as well as the rest of society out of a sense of mistrust, paranoia, or inability to communicate. Their mistrust may be a natural consequence of numerous unhappy hospital experiences and the realization that those who often seek to help may actually inflict suffering on the recipients of their ministrations. One such individual, a man in his 40s, wandered through a park late one evening as I interviewed a homeless woman. His voice was raised in a high pitched wail, an obvious reflection of deep inner turmoil akin to that of someone in mourning. Wendy, my interview subject, called out to him, "Norman, Norman, what's wrong?" But he continued walking past us and continued to wail. Wendy was moved to comment, "He's a victim of the mental hospitals. Its all the suffering they put him through so some nights he walks around like this."

Aside from the walking wounded there are those homeless who simply are independent, whose lifestyle is one that does not include socializing with others except in the most limited of terms. At a men's shelter the director pointed out a man sitting in the corner during free meal time. "That's old Harry. He comes in here everyday for lunch and dinner. Never says anything to anyone, although he has spoken with me the odd time. He won't tell us where he lives, and no one has been able to find out. Some of the guys say he sleeps under a bridge somewhere but your guess is as good as mine." Many of the elderly homeless are afraid of involving themselves with others and for good reason. Many, if not most, have fallen prey to street people who have befriended them only to rob, beat, assault or threaten them. The elderly homeless have little recourse to the law. They do not have the resources to call for assistance, and often their physical appearance is one that dissuades passersby from viewing them as worthy of attention. As Grant put it, "I got robbed by this young fella and I'm lying on the street beggin' people to help me. You know what they said, 'Get up old man. You stinkin' drunk.' That's what they think, if you're old, you're a bum, a skid row type."

Physically infirm and perceived of as dependent and helpless by most social service and social control agencies, the elderly often fear that contact will bring attempts at institutionalization. Like the mentally ill they have come in many instances to fear the 'helpers' that our society has invested with the task of dealing with its errant members. Although being homeless is not a crime there are many in society who view the condition of the homeless as being not only self-selected but also indicative of a deviant character. The condition of homelessness in itself seems to give many a licence to degrade, insult and ridicule those who are already suffering personal hardship. This process, referred to as victim blaming ties a present social condition to a presumed pathology within the individual, i.e., this person is homeless because there is something wrong with them, something that they can do something about, **if they wanted to**. It is of course the very presumption that the homeless are able to simply walk away from their life condition that ensures that they will often seek ties amongst those whom they view as trustworthy, that is, other homeless souls.

Finally, there are those individuals who do not wish to be a part of society as they are either escaping some past they do not wish uncovered or because they are simply solitary people who seek a life unencumbered by responsibility. It is however a misconception to view the homeless as those who shirk responsibility, as the choice of this lifestyle really means a change simply to a different set of priorities and responsibilities. Many of these are much more immediate and direct. The need for food and shelter predominates in the lives of the homeless, a theme reflected earlier in the work of writer Henry Miller.[8]

A Bed for the Night

When I'm back on my feet again,
I'll walk proud down this street again,
And they'll all look at me again,
And they'll see that I'm strong . . .

And I'm not gonna crawl again,
I will learn to stand tall again,
No I'm not gonna fall again,
Cos I'll learn to be strong.

D. Warren[9]

The problems of the homeless are, in a very practical sense, immediate. The pressing needs for food and shelter make considerations of **getting out** of homelessness seem distant and meaningless. The longer people remain on the street the further escape from homelessness seems to retreat into an unreachable horizon. Soon dreams of a 'normal' life disappear for many. The taken-for-granted reality that we assume everyone shares fades. As Colin, a shelter resident for several years, explained, it is a transformative experience. "People on the street aren't really refugees of society; they're just themselves. . . . they're moving through the world but they're just not attached to it." As time frames begin to distort and become largely irrelevant in a life dominated by enforced idleness, the homeless drift away from the concerns which preoccupy what one street person calls 'joe citizen.' So as much as the homeless are 'invisible' for us whether they are indistinguishable through appearance or we simply choose to ignore them, the rest of society is just as phantom-like for many homeless Canadians.

In this state basic necessities begin to predominate thought and actions, and primary amongst these is the acquisition of daily shelter. Failure to secure lodging for the night means that the homeless must face a night on the streets, a dangerous and foolhardy exercise. As most shelter stays are short term, i.e., two or three weeks or less, the homeless must constantly plan ahead for the next shelter that they will approach. This constant eviction of shelter residents is intended to reinforce in a very meaningful and cruel way the dependency of the homeless person, and to attempt to reinforce the notion that this is simply a temporary state. It is meant to function as a catalyst for the homeless person to get their lives on course. Welfare, they must be constantly reminded, requires that persons demonstrate at least some intention of rehabilitating themselves.

There are a variety of shelter types in Canadian cities, some set within a traditional framework of large institutions that deal with indigent males, and others that provide more innovative forms of shelter. First, consider the variety of shelters that are available in Canadian cities, although not on a universal basis, and which fall into two categories for the purposes of our discussion; traditional and alternative types:

Traditional Shelter Types

1. Large institutions for the indigent generally built following the Second World War and serving up to 700 plus men.

2. Shelters for men associated with religious groups.

3. Shelters and hostels for women age 16-24.

4. Co-operative shelters for teens aged 16-24.

5. Shelters and hostels for women (and in some cases children) in a mixed environment.

Alternative Shelter Types

1. Shelters for battered or abused women and their children.

2. Long stay residential apartments for homeless men.

3. Motel conversions for homeless families with children.

4. Single-room motel accommodation for families with children.

5. Shelters for native Canadians.

6. Warehouse conversion into divided living units.

Traditional shelters typically have a flexible system of entry and stay. Persons may stay for a night to two weeks. Near the end of the two-week period a person may be assessed as to their suitability for a continued stay. Generally three rules predominate across shelters; drunkenness that is disruptive, drug use leading to the necessity for staff intervention, or assaults will result in the person's immediate dismissal from the shelter. In some cases it may also result in a banning period of roughly one month. There is considerable discretion given to admitting staff in these matters. As one shelter supervisor commented, "Look if its a freezing cold night out, wind howling and twenty below we can let a guy in to sleep even if he has committed a serious attack in the past on someone. We give him a bed in the corner and say, 'Look you stay there and don't move.' If he does cause trouble he has to go." There are also a large number of men who may move into long-term residence in institutions making it their home for a period of from many months to twenty years. These men may suffer from drug/alcohol related problems of a chronic nature, may have become dependent on the institution, or can have a disability, whether mental or physical that makes them difficult to place in accommodations that are more comfortable. The conditions which these men live in are discussed later in this chapter.

Shelters for teens generally have a short-term stay policy reflecting an approach that emphasizes the fact that teens are somehow more salvageable, that is less embedded in the shelter/hostel system. The fortnightly ejection of the teens appears to have no other purpose than to shock them constantly, reminding them of their homeless condition. The idea, reinforced by shelter workers was not to let the kids get 'too comfortable.' However this policy has the net result of ensuring that homeless teens have little chance of securing long-term accommodation as they are constantly concerning themselves with the two-week mark of their stay when they will have to move. After only a few days into their stay they are already on the telephone looking for their next bed. This approach does nothing more but reinforce the dependency of the teens and engender long-term dependency, the very state of affairs that it is intended to short circuit.

Shelters and hostels for women and children in a mixed environment are facilities where children may be exposed to a variety of inappropriate or bizarre behaviours. Some of these shelters, which are hopefully to disappear in the near future, mix women who have minor to severe forms of mental illness, drug, alcohol and hygiene problems with women who are quite 'normal.' Many of the women interviewed for this book made comparisons between various shelters in terms of the quality of the staff, accommodation, food and assistance offered, but more centrally in terms of the clientele housed within. While 'beggars' cannot often be choosers, they can be critics despite the oft-expressed sentiment that they should be silent, and above all else, grateful. Most had experienced shelter accommodation that was unsuitable, considered 'dangerous' or that placed troublesome clientele. They spoke of these problems expressing a great deal of anger, "Why do they have to put us in with bag ladies who haven't had a bath in ten years? _____'s hostel there were women walking around stinking, yelling at the top of their lungs, whatever, and you have to share space with them. Can't they figure out that you need two kinds of shelters, one for ordinary women who are just having a bit of trouble, and those other ones that really need help of some kind?" In context, their experiences underscore the necessity for the provision of various forms of shelter for women that can provide flexibility in response. Certainly forcing women who have a temporary crisis in housing need into interaction with those who compromise the walking wounded in our society, those with extreme behavioural problems, seems unnecessary and detrimental to their attempts to re-establish themselves in the mainstream.

There are several forms of alternative shelter that have emerged in the 1980s as either responses to specific forms of social problems, rehabilitative efforts which attempt to empower the homeless, options that address long-term housing needs, or more inclusive shelter that can look after families with children. Shelters for battered women represent a response to increased interest by womens' groups and the state in addressing the needs of women as victims of violence. Recent work by sociologists Walter DeKeseredy and Ron Hinch and others has underscored the centrality of enlightened response in the form of shelters for dealing with the aftermath of woman assault. Battered womens' shelters provide shelter and accommodation centred around the provision of safe haven for their clients, and are medium stay facilities that women can use as a basis to reorganize their lives. They serve women and children from all socio-economic classes as woman abuse is not restricted to only those who are poor or ill-educated in Canada.

A second form of alternative shelter is that represented by the mens' shelter in Oshawa, Ontario. Here, the second floor of a short-stay hostel has been converted into a series of bachelor apartments for long-term homeless men. This program has enjoyed considerable success according to the director of the program, Terry Dunn. The men who reside in the apartments had long histories of homelessness and many suffered with alcohol problems. Having now found a place of their own, they have also correspondingly developed lifeskills. They shop, cook and clean for themselves and several have given up drinking over a significant period. They are not only proud of their 'homes' but it appears that having been given an opportunity to develop independence under more flexible support systems, most have responded positively.

The use of public motels as a means of housing families has recently assumed a significant role in our response to the homeless in Canada. Although this trend has been been long entrenched in the American welfare system where hotels are converted for the use of the homeless the approach has only emerged during the 1980s in Canada as the number of homeless families seeking assistance has expanded substantially. Factors that have produced this increasing number of homeless families include unemployment, spiralling accommodation costs in urban centres, the influx of refugee and immigrant families without accommodation, and the increasing number of marriage dissolutions resulting in one-parent families in Canada. These motel units were observed by the writer and do not represent suitable accommodations for families, or families with children. The motels are used frequently by prostitutes and those using and selling drugs. On my first visit to one of these areas I had barely emerged from my car before being accosted by a prostitute who has just emerged from a nearby room.

This form of motel accommodation may be favoured by two interest groups; motel owners and the government. For many motel owners accommodating the homeless represents a significant portion of the income on otherwise difficult-to-rent units. These subsidies are guaranteed on a per diem basis. Prostitutes and their customers who rent rooms in blocks of half an hour or less increase income exponentially. But the placement of homeless persons in these units, while arising out of a lack of proper accommodation, underscores the lack of investment by the provincial and federal governments and builders, in low cost housing. Surely, the cost of constructing low-cost permanent housing which provides a greater chance at self-sufficiency for residents must prove less costly than subsidizing the motel industry through per diem grants, not to mention quality of accommodation. Longer-term-stay residences for families with children represent a much more humane and acceptable response.

Shelters for native Canadians are a new development that reflects an increasing concern by native peoples for the welfare of their fellows. In several metropolitan areas including Toronto, Winnipeg, Saskatoon, and Regina there are short-term-stay shelters exclusively for the use of native peoples. These facilities offer not only a bed but counselling from a traditional native perspective, and assistance in picking up the pieces.

Finally, one of the more innovative attempts to bolster the self-esteem of the homeless and provide an innovative form of shelter is that represented by 'Cityscape' in Toronto. In a leased former warehouse homeless persons have renovated the interior of the structure and built small living units partitioned by plywood. This home structure is a subculture of homeless people who live in, and supervise, the activities of residents.

In order to more fully appreciate the quality of life within shelters in Canada the following section will provide an in-depth sketch of life within three types of accommodation; the large institution; the teen shelter, and long-term motel accommodations for homeless families. This will provide coverage of three groups who now figure significantly in the composition of those who seek shelter in Canada.

Mammoth Institutions – Seaton House

Toronto's Seaton House is the largest mens' shelter in North America. Situated on George Street in the central core of the city, it is surrounded by dilapidated rooming houses, provincial court buildings, and streets that provide tracks for hookers. Abandoned houses awaiting demolition line the adjoining streets where drugs and sex are openly trafficked. The main building of Seaton House is an imposing grey concrete structure which is decades old. It has the appearance of most of the other government buildings in the immediate area. This facade is cracked when during the afternoon dozens of homeless men, some dishevelled, some under the influence of alcohol, many giving the impression of office workers out on a break, begin to gather on the front lawn and steps. Some lie on the grass attempting to sleep. They are engaged in waiting for the four o'clock entry time at the shelter. When, in the summer, large numbers of men lounge on the grass close to entry time a staff is posted outside of the entrance to supervise activities. The individual doing this on my first day at Seaton House presented himself in the manner of a police officer and was hostile to the men, treating them in a demeaning manner. He persisted in shouting at the men when he wanted their attention, and despite three introductions to the writer kept referring to me as "Hey you". In keeping with the spirit of the work ethic which pervades the institutional approach to the homeless, men are not permitted to stay in the facility during the day. At roughly seven o'clock after two shifts of men have eaten breakfast and have taken their bag lunch, they are ushered out onto the street both winter and summer. As an intake worker at **another** facility observed, "They've got to show some effort at helping themselves. That's the whole principle of welfare. You can't just keep expecting a handout so we want them to look for work."

It is a requirement of most shelters that clients actively look for work. Residents for admission must fill out job search forms and continue to do so during their stay, that list all of the job applications and/or interviews they have completed. Although the intent of this form is to ensure compliance with the transformation of the homeless into productive citizens, its function is largely symbolic and frivolous for many: "For a lot of guys who come through, they've got a problem that they're not ready to deal with yet whether its alcohol, drugs or something else, nothing much can be done."

Men enter Seaton House primarily by applying for a blue card through the intake office during the week, while on the weekends overnight pink slips are issued by staff. The waiting room is a familiar site to many welfare applicants with a dozen vinyl chairs for clients. On the several occasions I conducted interviews the room was always filled with men waiting their turn to receive an intake interview. Men sit or lie on the floor in a room which reeks of stale body odour, waiting to be called into the office that can only be accessed through a locked door, a precaution against hostile applicants. Initially they experience a cursory interview through one of the two intake 'holes' which resemble bank tellers' windows but only the top half of the worker is visible to the homeless person. If they have been admitted previously their file is retrieved and they are interviewed by a caseworker after their file has been studied. Privacy is not a primary concern of the workers or administration as many offices have been created with the use of acoustic walls and conversations leak between the 'offices.' Doors on offices were not normally shut during interviews. As they accompanied the worker to an interview a common side remark was "Can't get enough of this place eh?" The implication was clear, the prospective resident had again failed to improve his position in life and this was the occasion to reaffirm his dependency and failure. The intake workers review the activities of the client since his last visit with a particular emphasis on whether steps have been taken to deal with what the worker perceives to be their 'problem.' If, as in most cases, the client has done nothing or very little the worker admonishes him, again reinforcing his condition as a dependent person. He is literally reduced to a childlike state. One worker prefaced this portion of the reprimand thusly, "When you gonna WAKE UP...?" This analogy is particularly potent for it reflects the disjuncture most homeless feel with the rest of the world. The conditioning of our society has broken down. They are neither connected nor 'awake' in terms of our ideas concerning the proper use of time. One observer, Gerald Fisk, has commented that the homeless subvert the meaning of time. After this process of status reinforcement is completed and the client makes a token gesture of agreeing to 'try harder' 'do better' or 'get (his) shit together' the worker issues a blue card good for a two week stay.

Once admitted the man must now wait for the four o'clock 'cattle call.' Men interviewed early in the day after processing through the admittance process were often asked what they intended to do until four o'clock. The answer was always that they would wander around the streets, and in the words of one man, "do nothing, kill time. What the hell else can you do with no money?"

Sleeping arrangements in the shelter for the men consist of bunk beds in large, bare rooms sleeping thirty to forty men. There is considerable competition for upper bunks due to the erratic behaviour of chronic drunks and the mentally ill, "The first time I came here, to Seaton like, they let this old guy in at seven. He was a fuckin' wino. The next thing I know he's pissin into a cup and then, can you believe this, he drank it! The he pissed all over his bunk. That's why you go for the top bunk."

Although overt violence appears to be a relatively rare occurrence given that several hundred men share the shelter there is considerable concern expressed around the subject of theft of personal items. Reports of items being stolen were commonplace amongst current and former clients. Younger men who had stayed at Seaton House were most critical of it. Stories of intimidation for money and personal items were commonplace in their accounts of the shelter. It was common for many to express a strong dislike of the shelter. Don, put it this way, "We all call it Satan House. It's a fuckin nightmare. Shit, old guys shittin' in their pants, fuckin' psychos screamin' at you. A lot of guys get fucked in their . . ., young guys when they come in cause there's no one around at night. A lot of cons go there when they hit the streets. Young kids shouldn't be in there. I didn't sleep at all. I've never been back." While it is difficult to validate the stories of the teens interviewed theirs was a consistent negative reaction to the mention of the facility in comparison to positive comments about shelters for teens which are typically housed in small houses and where only six or eight people sleep in a room. The sheer scale of Seaton House is intimidating. Many ex-residents compared it to a prison or mental asylum, and certainly there are a fair number of parallels.

As homeless men tend to own very little aside from the clothing on their back, personal possessions have great significance. They represent some form of status in the street world and are their last symbol of material accumulation. In the tribal world of the street, shoes, socks, warm outer clothing, hats, and mitts are the necessities of life; without them dignity is again damaged as one has to beg for more from staff or do without. Doing without can lead to physical injury very quickly as body extremities become frostbitten, or one develops blisters due to ill-fitting shoes. "Pretty well you have to tie things down in here. Shit, they'll steal your shoes, socks, anything they can get their hands on. You have to sleep with everything rolled up under your pillow." Few of the men indicated that these conditions allowed for restful sleep. At night the bunk rooms are a cacophony of coughs, belches, moans, grunts, screams and noise. The drunks who are not sufficiently inebriated to require staff medical interventions are free to disturb the sleep of others. Those on drugs or suffering from various mental disorders also contribute to an atmosphere that provides fitful sleep. This is why it is common to see men lounging on their beds from the time they enter the facility in order to gain as much rest as possible. As Frank commented, "Life on the street is tiring man, **damn** tiring."

Men are provided with breakfast and dinner at the shelter and are given a bag lunch for the day. The food is of excellent quality. A typical lunch included quiches, salad, yogurt, fruit and beverage. Aside from ever-vigilant staff who watch for signs of trouble to provide pre-emptive intervention, and the dishevelled presentation of a few men, the scene might well be one from a staff cafeteria at any Canadian factory. One significant difference was noted however. None of the men engaged in discussion with their companions. There was a sense throughout the building, echoed in the non-communication of residents, of personal isolations reflecting perhaps the felt isolation from society in general. Rather than comraderie amongst the men there was in their faces and actions the unmistakable mark of the beaten down, powerless to reject their own rejection.

In many shelters of this type there is a common television room in which a large screen TV is switched on constantly. The volume is turned on low and the men sit, lounge and sleep on the cast off furniture that typically adorns the room. There is a great deal of symbolism in this form of decoration which the poor across Canada are familiar with. The homeless exist as societal castoffs marooned in a world of material possessions thrown away by society much in the way we delegate the homeless to the position of a throwaway person. Again, few men in any of the 'lounges' I visited spoke to one another. There are few attempts to change the channel and men content themselves with whatever program happens by chance to appear.

Seaton House also has a long-term residence for over three hundred men. Here men who have developed what may be termed a chronic dependency in the shelter system are housed. Men pay rents that are linked to income, so that a person with no means of support does not contribute to his upkeep, while those with a variety of income (pensions, disability payments etc.) pay up to $600 per month. In this residence men receive a bed and all meals. If a man has no income then he receives $105 per month to cover his personal needs. This is supplemented somewhat through a tuck shop that sells toiletries and personal items at wholesale cost to residents. Tobacco is a major item of expenditure for many residents.

The conditions in the residence are a source of some contradiction. Much attention is paid to the cleanliness of halls and living spaces, which are immaculately clean. The appearance is one reminiscent of Canadian hospitals from my youth or many of the mental institutions in contemporary Britain. The building is tired, the walls painted alternatively institutional green or yellow. Long-term residents live for the most part in rooms with six to eight men. There they are provided with a stark bunk, locker and lock and a grey metal night table. Conditions are far more crowded than in a hospital ward and conditions far more stark. There are virtually no decorations in any of the rooms. There is no sense that one is in a place that is 'homey' in any real way.

Men lounge on their beds in this facility as they are not required to leave the premises during the day. Residents sit lining the halls, lounge on their beds, or lay sleeping with the covers pulled over their heads at mid-day. There is absolutely no privacy in the building and all but a few doors are constantly open. Men linger in the doors of the room like phantoms in some menacing human cuckoo clock. Readers familiar with the movie **Awakenings** would not feel out of place walking the halls of this museum of human alienation. Disabled men share one large room with ten beds. Again, men lingered in their wheelchairs, few, if any, conversing, many with absolutely nothing to occupy their time.

What is more disturbing is the realization that many of the men who are resident have been at Seaton House for many years. One resident I encountered had lived there continuously for twenty years. While it is obvious that many of the men have developed institutional syndrome and would find it difficult if not impossible to function in the outside world, a visit to the residence is a profoundly disturbing experience even for a writer who has visited many such places internationally. Men who reside at Seaton for long periods may become staff trustees. They are then accorded a position of some authority whether it is running welfare applications to the downtown office or manning the resident's laundry facility. For these contributions they are paid approximately $60 every two weeks in addition to the $105 they normally receive. The jobs bring a sense of self-worth to men although little renumeration for what often amounts to a full day's work.

There are real attempts made by the staff to make life more tolerable for the men. There is a billiards room and a new recreation room is being installed. There is a doctor who visits regularly, an on-staff nurse, and a staff who co-ordinate recreational activities. Men are encouraged to participate in the monthly field outing, and busing is provided to get the men out into the community.

Although many of the residents are senior citizens they are not transferred to seniors' residences. This reflects the stigma attached to persons who have been admitted to Seaton House. "The seniors homes don't want to look at our men. They want guys who've worked for twenty years, lived in the suburbs, good citizens. The guys in here have some kind of problem, some behaviours that can't be tolerated in most of these places. So, once a man is brought to our door, that's it, no other place will touch him."

Seaton House meets many of the immediate needs of homeless men for food and shelter but its mandate stretches little beyond this due to a lack of adequate funding. The lives of the men who come through its doors are often filled with despair, personal failures and rejection by society-at-large. Despite its imposing and impersonal character, it has not been able to dull the essential worth of the majority of its residents.

Teen Shelters

Teen shelters serve a specific age category of homeless young people. Although the term teen shelter is one that is most commonly applied by workers and clients, this type of shelter services adolescents and young adults age 16 to 24 years. Children under the age of 16 are the responsibility of the Children's Aid Societies. Legally in Canada one becomes an adult at the age of 18 for the purposes of the Criminal Code and voting. The age range covered in this mandate reflects solely the funding criteria of social service departments that will not fund on a per diem basis after the age of 24. One might argue that this effectively extends the age of dependency by six years. Throughout the research for this book I could find no reasonable explanation for this cut-off point. How crucial an issue is this? For the homeless it means the difference between accommodation in small scale shelters with groups of six to eight people in one room (and in the case of shelters for young women 2 or 3 persons) or a bed in a large scale institution.

Teen shelters are for the most part located in downtown areas of cities, which reflects their connection to the demands of street life. Some shelters, such as Toronto's **Youth Without Shelter** have located purposely in the suburbs of the city more than an hour's ride by public transport away from the downtown area. It is argued that removal from the core may offer an opportunity for asylum from the streets, away from the influence and demands of street culture, a chance to 'break the cycle' of homelessness. Others such as **Mercury House, Stop 86** and **Covenant House** are located in the heart of the city.

The quality of accommodation offered in teen shelters is comfortable, and the majority of shelters also offer a wide variety of counselling-life skills, employment advice, help in finding housing, vocational and educational referrals, family reconciliation and medical services in addition to a bed and food. However, like their 'adult' counterparts much of the day of those in the teen shelter is spent for the most part out on the street in disconnected activities, or when permitted, idly sitting and chatting with other residents. The teen group is more active than their older male counterparts but despite the show of energy very little seems to get accomplished on a daily basis. As most co-operative shelters are two-week-stay residences it means that teens are, once again, hardly settled before the task of finding the next shelter lifeline occurs. The kinds of problems that this population exhibits are hardly conducive to resolution in a matter of days, and so staff, despite their best efforts, express an inground apathy tempered by the day-to-day experience of attempting to motivate their charges.

Their efforts are futile in the area of counselling; streetwise kids of only a few months experience are far more skilled at manipulation and gameplaying than their young staff counterparts. At one of the shelters I visited there were severe rules regarding physical contact between any residents. This however proved to be of little impediment to the residents. As Polly commented, "When me and Terry want to get it on we just sneak upstairs to the bedroom. Someone looks out for the staff so we don't get into trouble." Despite the rules prohibiting sexual relations or even touching, which would result in immediate discharge, Polly and Terry had formed a relationship, regularly engaged in sexual liaisons on the premises, and were planning to move into a basement apartment together. Polly, despite her street experience, had also been the victim of manipulation by Terry. Another resident, well aware of their relationship, pointed this out: "Terry, he's a pimp man. He's just lookin' to turn that chick out and in a few weeks she'll be workin' the street for him."

Most teen shelters reflect the rigid rules that parents impose on their children despite the fact that their clientele are often well past the age of majority, plus several that reflect the violence which can pervade street interaction. Here are a list of infractions from one shelter that result in the immediate removal of the individual:

1. Having alcohol or non-prescription drugs on the person.
2. Use of drugs or alcohol in the building.
3. Being caught with a weapon on the premises.
4. Smoking in the shelter.
5. Sexual interaction.
6. Involvement in violence or threats.
7. Vandalism.
8. Involvement in behaviour that necessitates the calling of police.
9. Noisy or disturbing behaviour in the neighbourhood.

These rules **may** be necessary. However, there is a list of a further sixteen offences which are "warnable." Any person who accumulates two warnings is subject to immediate discharge. These 'offences' consist of:

1. Being late by 1/2 hour for curfew.
2. Being 1/2 hour late for supper.
3. Refusing to obey staff instructions.
4. Verbal abuse of staff or clients.
5. Being in someone's bedroom or standing in the door of the bedroom.
6. Minor vandalism.
7. Entering unauthorized areas without staff supervision (with malicious intent; i.e., reading a file on a desk, using a phone).
8. Kissing, hand holding, hugging, massages, lap sitting.
9. Behaving as a lookout for others.
10. Guilt by association.
11. Horseplay.
12. Leaving facility after curfew.
13. Excessive noise.
14. Absence from supper and curfew.
15. Absent overnight (which results in an immediate discharge).
16. Obscene language.

Street kids find shelters of this type to be intolerable since administration staff set up middle-class rules of behaviour that are entirely foreign to the lifestyle they lead. It is as though, through the construction of overly repressive rules, the shelter hopes to accomplish the task of remaking the 'bent' homeless teen. While adult hostels generally rely on only three rules; no drinking, drugs or violence, teen shelters are often characterized by an attempt to overcontrol their clients behaviour. This generally results in the teens rebelling within a short period of time. "The rules in this place. All it is is fuckin' rules. Who can remember it all? You can't have a smoke and I'd get kicked out for what I just said to you. Even if someone's had a bad day and you put your arm around them, you're warned and then booted. You can't even be human." This approach is an attempt to imbue habits of 'good' behaviour but is misplaced for it represents no more than institutional management, which can do little to alter behaviour for its effects are temporary. Residents stay only briefly and they recognize that such rules are related only to a normalized existence that has been conceived by the operators of the shelter. They are cogniscent that within the space of a few days or hours they will once again be on the street, or on their way to another shelter. Incidentally, there are a further 25 behaviours in this shelter that can result in 'cautions' or 'final cautions.' These range from possession of a lighter to not making one's bed, and three of these will result in eviction.

Most teens rate shelters with simple rules of behaviour much more favourably than those that try to impose multiplicities of rules that are often forgotten inadvertently and then lead to dismissal. The location of one such shelter in the periphery of the city means that eviction late in the evening literally strands the individual in the middle of suburbia with no means of getting back downtown.

Families with Children in Converted-Use Motels

A new and highly innovative program is currently being implemented for families with children in the Toronto area. This unit is an attempt to provide families with a longer-term residence that they can use to re-establish themselves in employment and eventually in long-term housing. Located in a modern, well-equipped former motel in the extreme east end of the city, the building is well situated and impressive, much like any other low-rise office building in the area. Commencing in the fall of 1991 families were admitted to the motel unit and reside in rooms during their stay. Each room contains a double bed, microwave, fridge, washroom, television, telephone, and bunk beds for children. Although such arrangements are crowded the units are clean and spacious and many look out onto a grassy area that is being converted for use as a playground. There is a central kitchen area with large freezers for those cooking chores that cannot be accomplished in the rooms. A daycare centre was planned to open in the spring of 1992 to provide assistance so that parents have a fair chance of seeking, securing and retaining employment.

Unlike previous facilities food is not provided for the residents, rather they are given a per diem related to family size. A family of two parents and two children would be allotted thirty dollars per day for food. Children attend local schools during their residence. Caseworkers provide assistance with applications and counselling for families having marital problems. There are simple rules of behavioUr which centre on abuse of alcohol, drugs, or the perpetration of violence. As it is a living unit, visitors are permitted in the rooms until a reasonable hour given that children live in the building. The former director took a flexible approach, reflecting his many years of experience in the field of homelessness. The clientele are broken down into several distinct groups generally; those who have a long history of involvement with the welfare system; refugees; and those who have become homeless as a result of marital dissolution. There are several families waiting for placement in the residence's larger suites that have eight or more children.

The type of program represented by this final type is in a sense an ideal. The approach of the director is to provide a humane shelter for those who have been battered by life. Families are accorded their dignity and self-esteem in the process, a factor often missing from our dealings with the homeless. Individuals are given the responsibility of handling their own food shopping and preparation so they do not become institutionalized. Children may receive daycare so that parents can have time to sort out their lives and make a new start.[10]

Despite community opposition to the establishment of shelters for the homeless, the director was able to find a new way of looking at the problem of homeless families. A crew of workmen installing telephones, upon discovery that the motel was to house homeless people, become angered and complained bitterly that it would lower housing prices in the area. Bernie thought for a moment and said, "This is a shelter for homeless children, some of whom have parents." "Homeless kids," the workman smiled, "Well that's okay, what can I do to help."

CHAPTER FOUR

Life on the Streets

People on the street need a place to go,
People on the street need a place to go,
Walkin' through the night up and
down the avenue,
Lookin' for a place, a place to
go, a place to go,
There's a muffled scream from the
alley scene,
From the alley scene comes a
muffled scream,
And the siren wails while the
system fails,
In the steaming heat people
walk in the street,
People can't run and hide,
If you want to feel good then
you gotta feel good inside.

Neil Young[1]

One of the central problems of our attempts to understand the homeless resides in explaining why they have been cast off by the mainstream of society. When I interviewed homeless people throughout this country two questions were the focus of much of the discussion that took place. First, why do people become trapped within the cycles of homelessness for months or even years? Secondly, what is it about the life course of this individual that has locked them into a cycle of despair? The answers to both these questions were neither simple nor easily explored with homeless people. In a sense one is asking how a person constructs reality, and to reflect more deeply upon the forces, both personal and structural, that have brought them to this position as a social pariah. While it is not possible in the constraints of a book such as this to record every life story of homeless persons it is possible to provide accounts of lives that reflect broader themes in the construction of a homeless identity in Canadian society. From these accounts it has been possible to construct images of the process of being homeless and the role played by the homeless and various social service agencies in either ameliorating and/or perpetuating the homeless condition.

While no single explanation of either the causes or the realities of homeless existence would be fair to the variety of individual life courses developed by homeless people, there are commonalities which link their experiences. Further, this chapter will proceed first to present the experience of homelessness from the viewpoint of various homeless 'groups' and social service personnel and then move on to an analysis of the core problems that predominate in relegating, and keeping, homeless people in the position of societal misfits. Finally, the lifeworks of the homeless will be put into perspective by a critical examination of the various forms of legal control that regulate their lives, from municipal by-laws through to welfare regulations.

Just Getting By

To the average observer Joe is a typical 24-year-old. He is well groomed and dressed in neat blue jeans, a striped clean shirt, running shoes and a pale blue windbreaker. He has a pleasant personality and a direct manner of speaking. He talks in an animated style, is intelligent and able to contemplate his life with insight and directness. Joe is homeless. Joe has not always been homeless. Neither is he a victim of a child welfare system that cannot cope with its all too many charges. He does not have a problem with alcohol or drugs, although he has used 'coke.' His behaviour is not pathological. Joe's story is one that tells us much about the series of contingencies that can move one from full status in our society to its farthest margins. As we begin our interview I tell him what we will be exploring. He immediately blurted out the following summary of his life, "I left home at sixteen, got myself a job working for a cleaner, pretty soon I had my own contacts and started a company. I got married at eighteen, had two kids, and had a house and a mortgage. My wife left me and after that I couldn't take it and started using cocaine. Pretty soon I couldn't pay the bills and I didn't care anymore. I lost everything and now I'm here."

Joe is used to telling his story to social workers and has developed a one minute travelogue to guide them through his life. It is a symptom that is prevalent amongst the homeless, tired of talking about the same 'sad' story to worker after worker who is either looking for the root cause of their homelessness or simply going through the motions of filling out the forms. Front line workers and those that do intakes with the homeless at shelters and hostels often explain the behaviour of the homeless in terms of one overriding problem. For teens this is most often abuse whether physical or sexual; for men it is frequently a problem with booze or drugs; for families the problem is one characterized by social dependency handed down from generation to generation. The real dimensions of the problems of the homeless like Joe may lay hidden in much more complex contingencies that effect their life, but are less amenable to quick diagnoses and quick fixes. In this workers fall prey to the process of labelling people, an approach that sociologists have long explored. Labels, while they may simplify the world, are often constructed at the expense of some loss to those labelled. Howard Becker, a well known sociologist, instructs us that, "Deviance is behavior that is so labelled." In other words, the labelling of a person as 'someone with a booze problem' or 'the product of an abused home' has the effect of transforming them into a deviant individual. In this characterization their current position in society as a homeless person reflects some personal failing, inadequacy or lack of effort.[2] Persons in our society who are so labelled are therefore seen as being the authors of their own problems. Although on one level we may have some sympathy for the homeless person, the refusal to look more deeply into the roots of homelessness as a structural problem in society has had immediate consequences for both the treatment of the homeless person as a dependent in the social welfare network, and in their view of themselves. One feature of labelling is that persons may, after countless interactions in which this label is reaffirmed, begin to self-label themselves as having a problem that is largely beyond their control.[3] At the same time they are constantly confronted with it by social workers and other agency staff. The homeless person develops what has been termed a **master status**, which means that once one learns about their problem one knows all one needs to in order to interact with the individual.

Joe is viewed as a young man with intelligence and potential by the staff. In his own words, "I can do the job of the staff when you come right down to it. They all know it. I had my own business for several years, so this is nothing." Joe is also seen as a man whose homelessness is related to his 'drug problem.' A further analysis of Joe's story is instructive in terms of both the factors that lead to homelessness and the reasons that persons often remain stuck in a homeless situation for long periods of time.

During his marriage, relations with his wife were good according to Joe. He and his wife were well off financially and enjoyed each other's company. Joe enjoyed drinking occasionally at a local bar, and there a young woman, a friend of his brother's, became infatuated with him. She often joined him, his brother and his brother's girlfriend for a drink. She asked Joe to have sex with her on several occasions but he refused telling her he was happily married with children. One evening Joe returned to his home to find that his wife was extremely upset and was packing to leave with the children. Apparently, the young woman who desired his sexual attention had gone to his home and told his wife that she had been having an affair with her husband, "and went into all of the details of having sex and how I didn't love her anymore." His wife did not believe his story regarding the other woman despite the support of others who had seen him interact with her. His wife left him and soon after he "slumped into a deep, deep depression." As Joe describes it, "Nothing meant anything to me anymore. I loved my wife and children and it just didn't make any sense. I hadn't done anything and here I was being punished." Soon Joe was drinking constantly and began to take cocaine to dull the pain of the loss of his family. "I just didn't care about anything anymore, like if the world can be that cruel when you're a good guy, work hard, give your family a good life, what's the point?" In the end Joe lost his business, then his house, and within a few months of his wife's departure he was homeless.

Now after almost a year in various homeless shelters in several cities he is able to reflect on his fall from 'normalcy.' "A lot of the staff think my problem is cocaine, but I haven't done any since I became homeless. My problem is I get overwhelmed by thinking about starting out again. I guess I've earned some time off to think and get a new start. I don't want to get back into the mainstream of society right away, I've got to get my head straight. I can do it again easily, that's not the hard part (getting a job) it's knowing that I've found out what I need, then I'll be outta here." So for Joe, homelessness presents somewhat of a resting place from some of the pressures of society. What he is as a person cannot be taken away from him; he is one of the small number of homeless who can understand the label accorded them, but has the personal resources to reject this label and remain optimistic about the future. Joe observes, "Look, just because a guy loses some money that doesn't mean he's stupid. Look at Donald Trump. He lost millions. Do you hear anyone saying he's stupid, that he won't climb back again. It's all relative to where you are in society and how much you can afford to lose without sinking into a hole. I'll be back, but when it's right for me." Far from being simple bragging, Joe's comments are based in his belief in his own abilities and his assessment of his current state of mind. Like many homeless interviewed Joe had lost his connections or bonds to society when, as a good citizen doing what he felt were the right things, his world was wrongfully demolished. This was a world, then, that he could no longer simply continue to invest in. His adaptations through alcohol and cocaine resulted in his demise as a person with a stake in society, but it was precisely because he did not want a stake in a society that he saw as having betrayed him.

Going Down Slow

Jake is a native Canadian who is 26 years of age. Born on a Saskatchewan farm he is currently living in a men's shelter in Vancouver. He is immaculately dressed in clean deep blue jogging shorts, running shoes and a crisp white shirt. He does not have a dishevelled appearance traditionally, and mistakenly today, accorded to the homeless. Jake has short neat black hair that is clean. He is well groomed and could easily be mistaken for one of the social workers in the local shelter. He is pleasant and his perceptions of his own situation are clear and unwashed. Jake left the family farm when he was sixteen years old. He had been adopted from the reserve into a white farm family, and completed a high school education. "After that I met my wife. I married her when she was sixteen; I was nineteen at the time. That was the bad thing, at that time coming off of the farm and and I guess the stress of a new child in the family. I guess if I looked hard enough . . . it was wham, bam thank you ma'am and you find yourself in a predicament that you totally don't need to." He describes his adoptive parents as "the most supportive people I know. See, in Saskatchewan they distinguish between the Indian and white people whatever." Jake loved school and said in the interview, "I'd loved to go back to school."

Jake finally got work just before birth of his first child. He feels that his daughter, "changed his life quite a bit." He was employed as a farm labourer, and had a natural knack with engines. "I could run anything, I still can run any tractor and combine, you name it I can run it. I know how to weld . . . "

What happened in Jake's life to bring him to the margins of existence? "Everything was going great..like before I came out here in

February of last year I was incarcerated for eighteen months. At that time I was drinking and it was a violent crime you know. Took a baseball bat, fought with a guy over a hundred dollars, took his knees out, its just as simple as that, and obviously the courts didn't think too much of it." Previously he had spent five years in prison in Saskatchewan for committing an armed robbery. "I guess, I don't know maybe I wanted to prove something. I don't know what it was. I could see that upsetting the marriage, I mean, wouldn't you?"

Jake spent the time after prison working in a well-known restaurant bar. "Its great. The thing that happened to me I got burnt out, burn out syndrome. . like six days a week and when you're on a management team and you're working on salary it doesn't matter how many hours you put in." Jake made $500 a week at the job take home pay and had an apartment that cost $460 a month. "I just don't know what went wrong really."Jake had no savings when he quit his job in July of 1991. "I don't know, I bought a lot of things. I don't know, I'm a material person. I like to buy a t.v., everything, you see, you know that you may want later . . . like I've still got all of this in storage." Jake had worked for almost eighteen months full time six days a week in a progressively more responsible position, finally achieving the status of kitchen manager. He suddenly found one day that his will to work had left him. For him, homelessness was an oasis away from the responsibilities he was being asked to perform to survive. "Its not that I'm lazy or anything. I just want to get my head clear. I've only been off work for a couple of months." Although he is entitled to unemployment he does not collect it, a view of welfare support that is widely espoused by homeless people. Welfare of any kind places a person in a position of perceived dependency. As psychopaths I researched in a hospital in Britain put it, "Don't give me a gift, then I'm in debt to you." The homeless do not want to accumulate any more social debts than possible and often view various forms of welfare above the minimum required to survive with a jaundiced eye. As Jake put it, "Yes, I'm entitled to it but if I wanted to abuse the system I could go ahead and abuse the system up and down and left and centre and without paying anything but I don't want to do it. That's not what I'm after. I just want to get my head cleared."

The Loner

Dave is twenty-seven years old and comes from a foster parent background. He left home at 16 and has been living in the shelter system and on the street ever since. He displays the signs of complete dependence on the system and has resigned himself to shelter life. He rarely breaks the cycle of dependency:

> I'll meet somebody like a friend or a girl. I may stay there for a couple of weeks just for the hell of it depending on the situation. I'm basically here though because I don't like livin' with other people. ..its not right, I'm not used to it. Well, its a matter of pride and dignity you know, you feel weird you know like, I'm just not used to it . I don't like the idea, I'm uh, like a loner.

Dave is indeed an outcast from society. He has no friends and his only forms of social communication come with social workers and drinking buddies in the parks. He lives hedonistically enjoying the moment since the future is unreal for him:

> Some people have their own style of living, my style just happens to be have a good time . . . you're limited to the amount of friends you have (in the shelter). The hostel's full of all kinds of people, grubby people, ignorant people, people who have no brains, ignorant people, people who have no ambition, people who drink and they can't do anything like they're idiots so I meet the odd person I can get along with.

While he accepts his own limitations as a fully functioning human being he does not place blame for the predicament which besets homeless people on the system. He voices a common view that the homeless are the source of their own problems:

> Yah either drugs or they just screwed up . . . (Is it the system that screwed up?) No, no I don't believe that for one minute. Well okay, it's hard to get work but there's a lot of people here that complain about work but they don't even try get up and look. They don't even know how to comb their hair. They don't even know how to present themselves so how are they gonna get a job? They stay out all night drinkin, they wake up with a hangover, it's just that they're abusing the system.

For Dave his current homeless condition is explained as a temporary state of affairs though it has lasted over six months now:

> I'm not rushin nothin. I'm just gonna reconstruct my life
> slowly. I'm not gonna rush nothin cause I've got enough
> gray hair. I'm just gonna do it, but do it slowly and
> casually, and be happy that's all. I wanna take care of the
> mind. No stress, no nothin.'

While Dave portrays his homelessness as being relatively free of stress, in actual fact he is constantly under pressure by the front line workers to seek employment, is constantly searching for a place to stay, and is subject to the rigours of street life. While being interviewed he sported deep healing cuts on his face, the result of a brawl in a local bar. Such wounds are common in the sample interviewed for this book, as violence in many forms is endemic to homeless life.

Dave in concert with many of his fellow homeless views his current state of affairs as a form of relative freedom, having exchanged the pressures of the workplace for the problems of the street. He sees himself as having:

> Lots of freedom . . . in respect of somebody telling me
> where to go, how to do it, or you know, what to do.

Fighting Docility: Social Control Agencies Versus the Homeless

For homeless Canadians, social service, welfare and helping agencies are often viewed in a negative context as more likely to hurt them than help them. Despite the best and worst intentions of each of these types of agencies, homeless people have instinctively and through numerous encounters with the therapeutic enterprise come to realize that they are often better off with a minimum of recourse to the state for assistance. Sociologists, like Stan Cohen, have described the 'net' of control that extends throughout society.[4] He argues that all social service functions are either implicitly themselves, or are tied to institutions that control the behaviour of those considered 'different' in society. Canadian civil rights activist Alan Borovoy has written about our society's limited ability to tolerate behaviour of others that we find even mildly irritating.[5] Whether it is a group of picketers trying to protest to protect their jobs, or a homeless person asking for assistance, we often expect someone to remove them from view, in essence, to control them.

The homeless do not have a single identity in the world of helping agencies. As I argued earlier, homeless persons are often assigned a master status that helps social service personnel to 'get a fix' on them, and explain their present and previous behaviours. Various agencies assign the homeless to differing categories to fit the mandate of their organization. A homeless person may be an alcohol abuser for one agency, an unemployable person for another group, and a person with mental problems at another facility. Although these may form either significant or minor facets of their personality the point is that they face a constant stripping down of self and categorization into multiple deviant selves as they move from agency to agency. The homeless also become 'known' on their trek through various shelters and hostels. Their thick accumulating files become less of an aid to assisting them and more of a means of denigrating their lack of success in altering their life circumstances, and of providing material for cutting personal criticisms. At the same time, the homeless represent fodder for the various agencies' struggle to assert "ownership" over the homeless problem. The homeless, like other marginalized groups, such as criminals, make possible the existence of a wide variety of 'helping' agencies, who besides assisting the homeless, 'help' themselves to substantial salaries.

The homeless sense, and are the victims of, this inter-connectedness of agencies. The homeless are reduced to a state of childlike dependency. Critics of the welfare system have long been aware of the inadequacies of a system of assistance that is characterized by over-bureaucratization, inhumanity and mistrust. Ben Carniol, a professor and social worker at Ryerson Polytechnic, has written scathingly of this system. He writes what we commonly understand but is often disputed: "It has become commonplace for people in need to desperately try to **avoid getting into the welfare system in the first place.**"[6] Tied in with this concept of attempting to remain above the dark and forbidding waters of the welfare ocean is the recurring myth of capitalist culture, "the belief that each individual has both the responsibility and the opportunity to 'make it.'" Echoing the words of persons interviewed across Canada for this book Carniol's sample of welfare recipients found that there was "most often a debilitating sense of dehumanization in being on welfare."[7] In fact, most homeless persons, as with the overwhelming majority of welfare recipients, go to great lengths to avoid being on welfare. Being 'on the pogey' even for the homeless means that one has hit bottom, has sunk to a state of total dependency with no resources left to draw upon. Many contemplating the status of welfare recipients will starve themselves, commit petty crimes, beg, take the most menial of underpaid jobs or even prostitute themselves, to stay off the dole.

The medicalization of the problems of the homeless is a common approach taken by social agencies in Canada. Although all homeless are subject to categorization as somehow being slightly less than whole, women are far more commonly the brunt of such approaches. While viewing the homeless problem as emanating most centrally from some form of 'sickness' in the form of depression or some other form of mental malady has a certain appeal in that ill health may be attacked by medical intervention, a more sinister interpretation is that the illness is chronic. Again, by shifting the blame onto the victim, in this case often of family violence, oppressed by a male partner, and in the wider realms of society, as well as by asserting that the problem is largely psychological, the burden for recovery lands once again in the lap of the downtrodden. These strategic interventions put social workers in the position of reinforcing and adding to the negative images of their supposed clients. The woman is now not only homeless, but suffering from some form of mental illness! How reassuring to be a single mother thrust out from the security of one's home only to be declared essentially insane by a helpful social worker! One woman interviewed in Vancouver put it this way, "My husband left and it was a couple of months until everything fell apart. No one could help me anymore or they didn't want to, and so I had to go on welfare. Jesus, the first thing they told me was that I was sick and needed help, as if I didn't have enough worries. So I told the worker, 'Who the fuck wouldn't be depressed, no husband, no money, no place to live, no job and now I have to listen to this.'" Helen Levine wrote compellingly about the impotency of women in modern social relations who are encouraged to be the authors of their own destruction. Levine wrote it "is an insidious tool used to contain women's rage and despair to invalidate our experience of the world". Eventually, usually sooner than later, it results in "guilt, anxiety and depression" keeping women "docile and fearful, unable to act on our own behalf."[8] More destructive than this process, Levine argues, and more damnable, is the collusion that is exercised by the so-called helping professions who "in practice as in theory, collude with and reinforce the self-destruct mechanism in women."[9]

Through twenty years of reports on welfare by federal and provincial governments, two constant themes have emerged. One is that of alienation of the recipients within the process who feel lessened by the treatment they receive attempting to collect what is essentially a social right. Secondly, those who look after the welfare system, and its many manifestations through the shelters and hostels of the country, are disenchanted with the system and its recipients.

Throughout the system of social services across this country humanity is in short supply as recipients of any form of benefit are forced to act as beggars in order to receive their due, supplicating at the altar of the welfare agent. Doyle and Visano's report on social welfare services underscores the constant barrage of intimidation and humiliation that awaits those who must queue in the lengthening welfare lines in this country, the longest now in history.[10] The very position that the homeless find themselves in, asking for assistance, provides reinforcement that these are people who are not part of the 'deserving poor,' that is, those who are not personally responsible for their own sorrows. The systematic inferiorization of the homeless, the constant reminding of this status, and its continual reaffirmation in consultations between agents and agencies informs the homeless person that they are branded and stigmatized wherever they turn.

Little wonder that in a few months the homeless person has often slid into a state of dependency unable to see any means of altering their station in life. Workers that are in a position to assist them are also in an equal position to withhold services, finances, shelter, and advice. My overwhelming impression of the interviews between social workers and the homeless during some four years of research was that the worker has certain ideas about the character and problems of the individual. The worker ideally is supposed to work with the client on strategies for achieving certain goals, most generally, obtaining employment. However, the worker generally winds up lecturing the client on his/her inadequacies and lack of personal effort. The exchange is not one of equals working to solve a problem but is more accurately characterized as an exercise in control on the part of the worker. Workers often do not consciously realize that they are engaged in this process. Many genuinely wish to help their clients. A greater number, however, have grown tired of "the whining" and "laziness" of their charges. With staggering caseloads and the demand for shelter space constant, and growing, they are faced with a unending stream of anxious would-be shelter residents throughout the day. As a young female worker at one shelter put it, "I see fifteen or more every day here wanting to get in. They've usually got files several inches thick and they're hopeless. You go through the same routine you did last time and they still don't do a thing to help themselves. I'm leaving this job in two months and going to. . . . After two years in welfare and two years here I've had it. You tell these people, 'Yes there's welfare, but you've got to do something for yourself.' They have no idea, no idea at all." The homeless person is not in a position to seek other alternatives if they don't like the service they are receiving. The immediate concerns of getting a place to stay are paramount and realistically they understand that they are without the power to complain. Who would listen to a complaint by a homeless person? The homeless made their complaints over and over again to the writer in the course of interviews and conversations, but they remain secret and whispered for fear of losing even the little they have managed to wrangle from the welfare system.

Few homeless people will admit to ever being physically ill, ill enough that is to require medical treatment. Few of the homeless trust doctors or hospitals to treat them without some other obligation on their part being involved. Many fear that seeking treatment for an illness or injury will result in them being institutionalized as mentally ill. As one 25-year-old put it, "If you go to an emergency room looking this bad they'll think you've lost your marbles and try to lock you up as crazy." Medical personnel are also viewed as having links to the police and other social agencies, which they certainly do. Many of the homeless do not want any involvement with the police and so avoid doctors. Going to a physician also requires that a person give their name, address if available, and a health insurance number. There are many homeless who do not want to make this kind of information available to others, whether they are inmates on parole seeking to avoid possible trouble, persons who do not want to be found for a variety of reasons, or simply those who harbour unfounded fears. Some shelters have developed a relationship with a local doctor and/or nurse to provide on-site treatment on a weekly basis without the necessity of patients divulging information they would not be comfortable giving. In Toronto, two nurses run a drop-in clinic where homeless men and women can have their afflictions tended to without giving any information on themselves. Most commonly they are treated for ailments related to their feet or hands—exposure, hypothermia and breathing disorders. Their clinic has been operating successfully for over two years and has been able to avoid the intrusion of the medical establishment and the paraphernalia of paranoia that over-formalization seems to bring in the minds of the homeless.

"Laws are for Rich People"

Laws have particular functions in our society. The homeless being both without accommodation and hence visible on the street are subject to an inordinate amount of attention on the part of the police and other agents of control in our society. Previously in this chapter it was argued that society organizes its control institutions into a form of network. The social analyst Michel Foucault referred to the ability of these institutions to exert power over the lives of individuals in society, to make them into docile citizens, as the 'micropolitics of control.'[11] Of any group in Canada, the homeless are most subject to the ministrations of these control measures and their lives are largely circumscribed by both formal and informal regulation by welfare rules, by-laws and criminal laws. In this section the impact of these various legal sanctions on the lives of homeless people will be explored.

Welfare Regulation: The Politics of Exclusion

While social assistance is intended as a safety net for those who become most vulnerable in society, the rules surrounding the acquisition of entitlement to welfare are questionable at best.[12] It may reasonably be argued that the current welfare system does much to perpetuate the problems of the homeless by short-circuiting their attempts to re-establish themselves in the mainstream of society. The first and most significant problem with the welfare system is the ridiculous requirement that persons must have a place of residence in order to receive a welfare cheque. Without a place to stay that has an identifiable address, a homeless person is not permitted any form of assistance. Many of the homeless do not, and will perhaps never, have any address other than an abandoned car, a neglected dumpster, or a park bench. Are they any less deserving of help? Obviously, it is these individuals who are most in need of sustenance, but are rendered ineligible because they do not have a place to stay. It is the great Catch-22 of homelessness; in order to get welfare you have to have a home, if you don't have a home you can't collect welfare. Although some jurisdictions, most notably in Montreal, have developed innovative schemes to counter this inequity in our welfare system, few homeless people in this country can collect assistance without first getting enmeshed in the social control system. In other words, most homeless have to seek residence at a shelter or hostel, which then becomes their address for the purposes of welfare.

In many provinces persons are entitled to 'emergency' welfare cheques when they first present themselves to a shelter. In Ontario, they may collect slightly more than $300 under this scheme. However, one of the further problems with the residence requirements is the transient nature of the homeless population. There are, again, a not insignificant number of homeless persons who leave the shelter before a cheque can arrive. While this behaviour strikes the uninformed as incredible, one must put it in the context of life in degrading, threatening, and sometimes violent lodgings. Whether one is threatened, gets fed up with being treated badly or simply wanders off because of a lack of investment in life, cheques are often undeliverable because the intended recipient has left the address given.

While there are many critics of public assistance for the needy, few would want to change places with the homeless despite their criticisms of them as lazy and shiftless. This attitude was expressed by Mike Harris the leader of the Ontario Progressive Conservative party. Harris argued before a business luncheon at The Canadian Club that welfare recipients abuse the system. He stated, "I'm suggesting that we should not be paying out all that money to stay home and do nothing."[13] While Harris argues that the majority on welfare can be trained or educated for jobs, and suggests timing welfare payments to compliance with these initiatives he demonstrated a complete ignorance of the plight of homeless Canadians. If one considers a single mother of one child as a homeless person who will collect social assistance then how will she accomplish retraining? If she has a pre-school child it is expected that somehow she will arrange for the care of the child during her retraining. While this may seem a practical idea any cursory examination of child care in this country leads one to the simple conclusion that it is in short supply and high demand. Even if the mother were to be able to secure a place in a childcare setting for her child it is unlikely she will be able to afford it while retraining herself for employment that is going to yield a wage **insufficient** to meet her childcare expenses. The alternative is to leave her child in suspect care, spending her working days worrying constantly about her child's welfare. Women with children suffer more greatly than any other group amongst our homeless population for there is little societal comprehension of the impossibilities associated with trying to provide a decent life on a meagre allowance while juggling several disparate roles. Welfare remains for the most part as a form of indentured pauperism.

City By-Laws: Sweeping the Streets Clean of Refuse

In many cities across Canada there is a building problem with regard to attempts to control the homeless in public places. The sheer numbers of homeless in Canada's largest population centres, Toronto, Montreal and Vancouver mean that they are a growing source of 'trouble' in urban centres. The majority of the problems remain confined in the downtown cores of these cities where the homeless cluster around shelters, soup kitchens and the entertainment, business and shopping districts where passersby are more likely to have money to spare. In practical terms the homeless must remain in areas where they have some reasonable expectation of walking to and from various services. But this clustering of the homeless is seen by some as an eyesore in the community, as frightening, or as simply "bad for business". In Oshawa, a small city located 30-minutes-drive from Toronto, local businessmen complained of the homeless using the local park and walking on the main shopping street of the city. The attitude was that the homeless should be "rounded up" and prohibited by by-law from lounging in the park.[14]

Many city dwellers find the homeless frightening, particularly those who are dishevelled. "They're a nuisance" said one young woman I interviewed on the street in Vancouver. "They stink and they get on your nerves, always asking for money." The homeless remind us of the potential for failure in our own lives. Their pleas for money are generally left unanswered by most who walk by them. This is the case even when the homeless person begging is a woman with a baby. In one instance, this writer observed a young woman begging with a baby in her arms. She held out a card which said, "Ladies and gentlemen please help me. I have three children, no job and no money for food." As I observed her for over an hour begging, pleading with passing students entering a college, professors and business people who almost without exception not only ignored her, but refused to make any form of contact with her, I realized the depth of our intolerance of the weak and helpless in our society. I approached the woman and gave her some money and she showed me a Tylenol bottle. "The baby is sick. Can you help me anymore?" As a refugee she was afraid to go to the authorities for help. In her country, authorities torture and imprison you. She pleaded with me to help her with more money and continued to beg for several more hours in the cold of the Vancouver streets.

Public begging is a crime in Canada. It is referred to as panhandling. The term originated with the process of panning for gold in the goldrushes of the last century in North America. But the homeless are rarely able to make much money on the streets. Canadians are not as generous as many might like to think. On an average day begging for four hours a homeless person would be happy to walk away with $10, the price of a meal in a cheap restaurant with something left over for a coffee and a chocolate bar to ward off the cold. Myths swirl about in terms of the money to be made begging from strangers. One popular one, often repeated to the researcher over the past three years, concerns beggars who are picked up each evening by chauffeur-driven limousines to be taken to their mansions. Common sense tells us that the rewards of begging are rarely sufficient to satisfy even the most meagre of appetites. When one considers that most people will not even as much as look at a homeless woman in distress, the likelihood they will voluntarily give them money is far more remote. More inventive homeless beggars are able to use humour as a tool for opening the pocketbooks of their audience. One homeless man uses the following lines to elicit money from the street: "Help a hopeless drunk?"; "Can you help me to buy a coffin for my mother?" or "Make your day and mine, give me a looney." This man was the most successful beggar interviewed for the book. He often made $20 an hour, but just as quickly used it for food and alcohol.

While the homeless may be perceived of as beggars, few of those interviewed by this author resorted to begging as a constant source of income. Most interviewees were candid in admitting that they may have begged on occasion, particularly during the holiday season, when they could play on the conscience of city dwellers, but few viewed it as a regular source of income. It was much more likely that they would resort to situational crime, that is crime that they would not commit were they not destitute, to live. Many readers will no doubt be surprised to learn that begging is illegal.

We have already learned that begging is not a lucrative pastime. One should also be cogniscent that it carries with it a penalty which far outweighs its potential benefit to the beggar. Panhandling under many municipal by-law codes is an offence which carries a fine of $50 or more. The homeless are therefore harassed and ticketed, for the crime of having no money. They are not likely to be able to pay any fine that may be imposed at court, and are just as unlikely to show up at court for their hearing. This generally results, in cases where charges are laid, of a warrant being sworn for their arrest. Most who are finally apprehended serve a short jail term to atone for their transgression. The police also enforce loitering and vagrancy statutes against the homeless as a means of moving them from disputed public areas. When businesses complain the police approach is to simply shift the problem of homelessness to a less visible area. This is a tactic often employed with prostitutes. It does not eliminate the problem just simply temporarily moves it out of the view of those who are offended, those who have more political and economic clout and respectability in the eyes of the police and thus are entitled to protection of their sensibilities. In several U.S. jurisdictions the 'war' between the homeless and business has escalated and resulted in the passage of by-laws forbidding loitering, begging, and the pitching of tents by the homeless. While we have, in Canada, to the present been largely spared the spectacle of tent cities (although the use of campgrounds by the homeless is frequent) American cities like Detroit have been faced with overwhelming problems of homelessness. When in October of 1991 the state cut general welfare assistance to tens of thousands of Michigan residents, the effect was immediate and dramatic. Thousands of homeless began to overflow the available shelter space and filled church basements and community halls. On December 1, a symbolic tent for the homeless pitched on private church land was torn down by the Detroit police, (then re-erected the next day) in a symbolic gesture that underscored our intolerance of the homeless. The voice of the homeless is difficult to raise as one. The crisis in Detroit provided a rallying point that was viewed as a potential threat to social order. What if the tens of thousands of homeless in Detroit had had enough and organized on mass to protest their maltreatment by the state? When enough docile bodies are enraged by their oppression the potential for social insurrection and cries for accountability may be quickly raised.[15]

Loitering is another form of social regulation that directly effects the lives of the homeless. Let us consider some of the places in which edicts against resting idly for more than an ambiguous period of time are enforced. The Toronto Transit Commission has a by-law which strictly prohibits loitering on or in T.T.C. property. This is intended to be used to prevent homeless persons from riding the subway, bus or streetcar system over a lengthy period of time solely in the interests of keeping warm. Shopping malls, contrary to the beliefs of many, are not public places but rather private property. Large scale malls like Edmonton's West Edmonton Mall or Toronto's Eaton's Centre are virtually small contained cities. They also employ large private security forces who patrol the mall ostensibly to guard against theft but also to prevent 'trouble.' Homeless people often reported discriminatory treatment by mall security personnel. "Okay, so you go in to get warm, you're hangin' out not botherin' anyone and suddenly this security guards on your ass. 'Get movin.' Get the hell out of here before we charge you with trespass.'" The homeless sense they are the victims of a double standard based on visible signs of money, class and status. On a tour of The Eaton Centre, Paul pointed out the discrepancy in the actions of mall staff, "Look at those people over there! Do you think they're gonna go up to them and tell them to move? No way! They pick on us because we haven't got much. That isn't fair." Malls also eject persons who appear to be disruptive in any way. The case of a resident of London, Ontario who has a heavily tattooed face bears witness to this. He was unsuccessful in a legal attempt to force mall owners to lift a ban on his entrance to the mall because they argued that he was constantly ejected because of his failure to buy anything within a certain set period of time. One wonders how many 'window shoppers' who are not obviously without

.

means or do not display a physical anomaly are asked to leave malls because of their failure to buy something?

The Homeless as Criminals: Criminalization of the Homeless

In May of 1990 a thirty-six-year-old man described in news reports as a 'drifter' dragged a young woman to a secluded location near a railway spur where he savagely beat her to death. Her face had been beaten and identification proved difficult due to the intensity of the assault on her face with a piece of wood used as a blunt instrument. The murderer spit and urinated on the body before leaving the scene. When he returned home to a converted warehouse owned by Metropolitan Toronto, and used as an innovative shelter for homeless people, he told fellow residents the blood that covered his jeans resulted from his having to beat a girl. The homeless man was apprehended when an acquaintance saw a composite picture in the paper and reported it to police.[16] While homicide remains an atypical event according to Elliott Leyton and other Canadian homicide researchers, violence and crime are hardly strangers to the homeless who roam our cities.[17] The homeless are vulnerable, more likely to be victimized than any of us who enjoy the comforts of a home. While the home has become, according to researchers, a stage for violent scenes played out by males and enacted on females, the constant barrage of violence which creeps into the lives of the homeless is worthy of closer attention. Criminological studies of policing have demonstrated consistently in Canada, Britain and the United States that socially and economically marginal persons are the lowest priority on policing initiatives. The attitude of many of the public, which places the blame for the homeless condition of our street citizens squarely in their own laps, can be expected to have little sympathy when the homeless are victims of criminal acts. I suspect that, like prostitutes, the homeless are viewed as having to expect some measure of violence and victimization in their lives by the general public even though they are not voluntary recruits, in the main, to the life of the drifter.

Homeless people live with daily fears of being the victims of crime. Most are forced to carry some form of weapon, not by choice but simply because they must be in a position to protect themselves should trouble arise. Trouble in the form of threats, intimidating gestures, requests for money or cigarettes from threatening characters, and attacks by the deranged, stoned or drunk confront people who must not only walk but sleep on the streets. A park bench makes neither a comfortable nor a peaceful substitute for a bed, particularly when the temperatures start to drop in cold weather. Sleep is an impossibility when the stranger lurking in the shadows may be waiting for you to sleep only to steal your shoes, socks, coat or other belongings. Women, who experience victimization in the home and workplace in our society at epidemic rates, continue their vulnerability in a more exaggerated form as homeless castoffs. The horrors of the street are many, and few of us can even begin to imagine what a night sleeping in the doorway of an office building must be like. Young women who predominate as hookers are doubly prey to violence from men. The majority of young women on the street, as we learned earlier in this book, have experienced either physical or sexual abuse in the home. The street holds the promise of being beaten by a dissatisfied or 'sicko' john, being pumelled by an unhappy pimp, or being victimized by those who are sworn to protect women. When you consider that the number of homeless Canadians at any one time numbers in the tens of thousands, then this is certainly an unacceptable state of affairs. Put another way, we might wish to consider a rethinking of the problem of homelessness and crime. Since only about 25% of homeless people engage in any form of criminal behaviour according to research conducted across North America,[18] we might wish to consider the crimes committed against the homeless by virtue of their very condition. What structures in society have forced tens of thousands of its citizens—men, women, children, families—to be abandoned to a life on the streets or in the shelters of Canada? Does not the real issue of crime reside in the very existence of homelessness on such a grand scale, the failure of society to provide 'justice for all'?

A constantly recurring theme of critics of the homeless who do not want to face the severity of the problem or attempt to deny it altogether, is that the homeless number far less than their advocates would claim. While accurate counts are difficult as I discussed in Chapter One, it is interesting to note that government counts conducted through census collections invariably arrive at far lower numbers than do the agencies and groups that work with the homeless on a daily basis, year in and year out. Governments of course, at both the federal, provincial and municipal levels, adopt grossly conservative estimates of the numbers of homeless because they do not wish the true depth of the problem to be ingrained within the public conscience. The failure of governments to provide for the homeless, to prevent their even being amongst the multitude who arrive at the doors of hostels, churches, social services and shelters is an indictment of their lack of commitment to attacking the wider structural problems in the economy, housing sector, family unit and in the broader spectrum of public attitudes. **Herein** lies the true **criminality** associated with homelessness. It requires we turn our ideas around to move from blaming the victim to placing the blame squarely in the lap of governmental programs that pursue policies that impact most harshly upon certain segments of society—the poor and lower classes—and bolster the fortunes of the already fortunate.

The true violence of homelessness may be traced to the fundamental failure to provide for the needs of people who wind up homeless. While academic studies of the psychological states of the homeless, the problems of counting their numbers or their life chances may serve some higher academic function, they ignore the gravity of the problem. The essential kernel of the numbers debate concerning homelessness is this: it is rather like trying to count the drops of water while the dam is bursting, an interesting problem, but irrelevant and unlikely to prevent the flood. Academics have remained largely trapped in the role of apologists for government policies because of their inattention to the wider picture. In reviewing literally hundreds of studies conducted in America and Britain, while preparing this book, it was noted that a constant focus was not upon the victimization of the homeless by state policies but rather time and again (with some notable exceptions) that the situational and symptomatic problems of homelessness have been the focus of attention. The issue of failure to address needs is rarely analysed so that homelessness remains portrayed to us rather as a stage play in which we see the homeless as actors, but do not view the larger mechanisms that make the play possible. While the homeless suffer innumerable forms of violence in the forms of psychological suffering, emotional abuse, physical assaults, medical traumas and blows to personal dignity, their suffering is not placed within the larger context of societal failures but rather within situational contingencies.

In the next section, we shall explore in detail the roots of crimes against the homeless as well as the crime of homelessness itself. Both of these broader themes can be traced to roots within the political economy of our nation during the past decade, and more surely during the past several years. Homelessness, crime and crimes by the homeless, and against the homeless, must be placed within the broader framework of their interconnectedness with both public and private policies within the developing Canadian free trade state, the economic policies of government, housing policy, and the development of welfare systems in this country.

Rethinking Crimes Against and By the Homeless

We currently live in a country where from 'sea to shining sea' the glow of a Canada that remains immune from the influence of broader criminal forces is fading rapidly in the wake of increasing violence on our streets and in our homes. The number of murders in Toronto by October of 1992 had surpassed all of those counted in the previous year. In 1991, the Chief of Detectives reported that police were called to incidents involving handguns at a rate of one per hour. In 1991, by November, over 500 convenience stores had been robbed in Toronto with the offender using a weapon to effect the robbery. The introduction of crack as a cheap, available, and deadly drug has intensified the level of street violence in our cities from coast to coast, as some individuals fight to control the trade, while others resort to crime to feed their addiction. While violence escalates at an unprecedented rate we are also aware of a growing research literature and political awareness of the violence that is perpetrated against women and children in homes of our nation on a daily basis. Violence against women has been recognized as a problem of national significance with significant spending on research initiatives, the building of shelters for battered women and their children, and public education campaigns. It is important for readers to recognize that the violence of homelessness is both immediate for those who are on the receiving end, but also is constant and unending twenty-four hours a day. There is no place of rest for the homeless simply because, as we discovered in Chapter One, they are without homes.

Survival on the streets often means resorting to petty crimes in order to get by on a day-to-day basis. While various forms of social assistance are offered to the homeless, these are inadequate to meet the basic needs of most people. More to the point, how many of us would want to live simply having our basic needs satisfied? While food and shelter are basic to survival they are not sufficient to feed the soul of people. We have all heard the phrase, "Man does not live by bread alone." So it is that the homeless of both genders often come into conflict with the law because of the very fact that they are homeless. Recent research by McCarthy and Hagan, two Canadian sociologists with homeless street youth in Toronto, found that homelessness was criminogenic, that is, it was a direct cause of the crimes committed by the 130 youths that McCarthy studied.[19] Previous episodes of homelessness had no significant effect on the current criminality of the young people that were surveyed. This conforms with the information reported by the persons interviewed for this book.

Criminal activities are reported almost exclusively by young men who fall within the 16 to 25-year age range. None of the women interviewed for this book reported engaging in criminal pursuits for survival other than those who had been arrested under solicitation laws that govern the behaviour of prostitutes. Some had begged or shoplifted but this was reported infrequently. While it would be a mistake to infer that a large percentage of the young homeless are engaged in crime on an ongoing basis, it is true to assert that many commit either of two forms of crime. First, simple crimes of survival are often resorted to by the homeless either in order to eat or put warm clothing on their back or to attain some small luxury that is constantly denied them. For young men the crime of break and enter predominates as the means of acquiring stolen items, which can then be sold for cash. Studies of youthful offending in Canada have consistently found that such crime is the most common form of offending amongst young men. For impoverished adolescents and young men, homeless or not, their marginalization in economic terms often means that the only way of acquiring funds is through this straightforward criminal activity.[20] Break and entry or shoplifting does not require a great deal of skill on the part of the perpetrator, and yields a sufficient reward by the fencing of the goods to raise funds for a desired purpose . Since homeless youths have few means of storing items, other than occasionally in 'party houses' (abandoned buildings where drug and alcohol parties are held), they almost immediately fence the item(s). While there are established fences who will handle stolen goods, it is much more likely that the thief will sell his goods to a person walking on the street. Stolen items generally fetch only about one-fifth to one-third of their normal value. Therefore a $100 radio is likely to fetch only twenty or so dollars on the street.[21]

The overwhelming majority of crimes of the homeless are petty offences such as theft of a wallet or purse, stealing of small items from unlocked parked cars, and shoplifting. These petty larcenies, along with gambling to pass the time and begging, are the main crimes or 'vices' engaged in by the homeless. All of these activities have no greater purpose than to secure the necessities of survival. But the homeless reside in a world where drug deals are an everyday part of existence and no one on the street can avoid walking into trouble occasionally. Assaults are frequent on the street where homeless persons argue over food, alcohol, clothes, drugs or some perceived slight of character. In one incident witnessed by the researcher, a homeless woman downed a homeless man by breaking a bottle over his head and opening up a gaping wound. She continued to kick at him until police arrived to pull her off. The argument had started as a dispute over whether one person had taken more than their share of the contents of the bottle. On numerous occasions the researcher witnessed assaults of one homeless person by another in the late evening and night as finances began to wane while the need for alcohol, drugs, or food remained. Homeless persons 'stoned' on crack or cocaine, or a combination of alcohol and drugs, are a regular occurrence in the 'city of night' just as in the non-homeless population. On several occasions I watched as police tried to apprehend crack users who were hopelessly high. A man in his 30s who was 'up' on crack lay down in the middle of a downtown street and refused to move. Police spent some 15 minutes trying to get him to voluntarily walk to their cruiser before he had to be carried, while the sidewalk was filled with curious onlookers.

Most of the crimes of violence committed by and against the homeless are carried out by other homeless or street people. This lowers the interest that police demonstrate towards such crimes since research by Canadian criminologists has graphically demonstrated that the police place citizens into two groups: (1) solid citizens, i.e., those who work at regular jobs, keep regular hours, stay out of trouble, and who are at home most of the time, and (2) 'assholes,' a broad grouping that includes (although not exhaustively) drug users, ex-cons, prostitutes, sexual deviants, gays, and the homeless.[22] Police have little use for street people aside from their intrinsic value as informants in cases of crimes that the police are having difficulty solving. Livy Visano has documented the police practice of making informants out of the most innocuous of street people by implied threats to charge them with offences. This 'bending' of the rules in a variety of contexts by both uniformed officers and detectives has been documented by several Canadian researchers, including the highly regarded work of Richard Ericson of the Centre of Criminology[23] who conducted the most extensive study of police work ever undertaken in this country. If the police are willing to engage in illegal practices to 'get' persons with some social standing, what would prevent them from harassing the homeless at will. In Visano's research, for example, he reported that the police routinely hassled street youth. When he was present the police demanded his identification, questioned him about his 'real' intent (his assertion that he was a researcher was rejected) and searched his pockets illegally browsing through their contents.[24]   This appears to be a regular feature of homeless encounters with the police as the interviews conducted for this book underscored. The most frequently reported problems reported with the police included:

- being told to move from a resting place, or 'move along' when simply standing on the street
- requests for identification from police when they were doing nothing
- being treated with discourtesy by the police
- being searched, having pocket contents turned out for inspection
- search of belongings for no apparent reason
- being assaulted

While the homeless are in constant threat of violence against their person they are also forced to deal with constant harassment by the police for no good reason other than they are visible and vulnerable.

In Canada, the crimes of both vagrancy and loitering still form part of our Criminal Code. Vagrancy is an offence under Section 179 (1) (a) and is intended to punish anyone "who supports himself in whole or in part by gaming or crime and has no lawful profession or calling by which to maintain himself." This is an offence which carries a summary conviction where the penalties are less than that accorded for serious 'indictable' offences. A person may receive a six-month sentence and up to $500 fine for vagrancy, although penalties are likely to be much lighter. It is not hard to imagine how such a law can easily be applied either as a threat, or to punish homeless people who would be hard pressed in a court of law to prove that they were law-abiding citizens against the word of a police officer. Under Section 175 (c) anyone who "loiters in a public place and in any way obstructs persons who are in that place" is guilty of a summary offence. Of course, the life style of the homeless being not chosen, but imposed, means that they are always in jeopardy while this law is part of our way of defining wrongdoing. The definition of 'obstruction' is one that is constructed out of a simple paradigm: the homeless person is not a person with wherewithal, so therefore their presence will be easily interpreted as loitering by a magistrate. Under the same section, persons who 'cause a disturbance in or near a public place' are also subject to being charged. This disturbance can take the form of 'fighting, screaming, shouting, swearing, singing or using insulting or obscene language." Those who are drunk or impede or otherwise molest other persons are also liable to be charged with this summary offence. These are all behaviours which are common to areas where the homeless congregate and are behaviours that are often engaged in by the homeless who are deprived of a private space in which to get drunk, sing, swear or shout.

Another little known Canadian law also criminalizes the survival actions of the homeless. This section of the Criminal Code covers the crime of 'Trespassing at night.' This law states that, "Every one who, without lawful excuse, the proof of which lies on him, loiters or prowls at night on the property of another person near a dwelling-house situated on that property is guilty of an offence . . . ." The downtown terrain of the homeless is not only a collection of office buildings, but many streets are lined with aging housing or the newly gentrified houses, many of which were formerly rooming houses. Obviously, while this law is intended to dissuade prowlers from striking fear into the hearts of home-dwellers it also unintentionally impacts upon the homeless who often wander in just such a way as described in the law, searching for a place to sleep for the night.

On the roofs of abandoned or closed buildings, in secluded stairwells that offer shelter from passersby, but at the same time make the homeless vulnerable to attack, the homeless try to ease their weariness. The stench of urine, unwashed bodies and clothes, and the litter of old cigarette butts, food containers, worn blankets and clothes, discarded needles and other trappings of street people make it a grim place to recuperate. Most bedding places are soon discovered by the owners of the building or the police and are closed down. In downtown Vancouver, accompanied by my guide Sharon O'Leary, I saw a building once used by the homeless as a sleeping refuge that has been securely boarded up by the owners to prevent people from taking shelter from the elements. The boards are posted with prominent 'No Trespassing' signs, and the words "NO HOMELESS" and "HOMELESS DIE" have been spraypainted across the plywood barriers. The homeless have found that new technologies have their advantage and often cluster in the most severe forms of winter weather in bank lobbies where instant money machines are located. It is a grim irony that they huddle against the cold without resources in an anteroom designed to conveniently distribute money. Their intent is not criminal but merely survival, but their presence is soon noted and they are moved out by the police to seek another resting place. Homeless persons reported time and again that the police routinely woke them on cold winter nights when they were sleeping on a heat grating to tell them to move on. The homeless were cogniscent that there is a larger political agenda involved in their forced marching from one point to another in the city. When the homeless cluster in groups for warmth in a prominent area of the city, i.e., beside city hall or embassy buildings they are the target of police harassment. They are literally an 'eyesore' that has to be removed much like the Miami police remove homeless persons pursuant to their annual football classic. The governments of cities want the homeless to remain invisible, lost in the crush of city street crowds. The sight of homeless people sleeping on grates gives the wrong message about the city.

The second form of crime that often brings homeless youth particularly into conflict with the law is offences surrounding the use and abuse of alcohol and drugs. In the case of alcohol, the public nature of drinking engaged in by many homeless youth to escape the harshness of street life leaves them open to continuing police observation, harassment and possible arrest. There are a number of regulations that prohibit the drinking of alcohol in public parks, the 'living room' of the homeless. Although as a society we struck down laws which made it a criminal offence to be drunk in public almost a decade ago, we still harass the homeless who drink in parks. While we would not want the homeless to take over public parks and intimidate other users while they engage in drinking behaviours, this is an unlikely scenario. The homeless congregate only in central downtown parks that, while during the day provide a multi-use park for all citizens, often in the evening become a human jungle. They provide a place for drinking, drug sales and consumption, sexual liaisons between gay men who cruise the park looking for partners, hookers who seek customers, the deranged who have been cast off by our society and the homeless sleeping on benches.

Similarly there are many homeless young people who try to escape reality through the use of a variety of illegal non-prescription and illegally obtained prescription drugs. The most common form of street drug is cocaine either in powder form or in the cheaper, and more deadly form of crack. Cocaine in Canada's major cities retails on the street for $20 a matchhead. An enterprising homeless youth can purchase this 'hit' for $20 and split it in half, selling both halves for $20 to an interloping suburban youth out for a good time, and not likely to ask questions about price or quantity. This sales transaction generally takes only 15 minutes at which time the homeless youth can now buy two matchheads, split them into four, take one, and sell the other three for sixty dollars.

The criminal enterprise they are engaged in is both transitory in nature, and does not produce any long-term benefit for them. They do it because they lack the money of the 'suburban' kids to pay up front for their drugs, and therefore must resort to sales in order to attain the desired effect from their comforting chemicals. They do not accumulate money from the transactions as most simply get 'high' and wander into the parks or some other area to enjoy their drug induced euphoria 'trip' up and down the main street of the city, or try to find a party house where there are more drugs and alcohol available.

Their behaviour, aside from the necessity of having to sell drugs, is no different from a great number of young Canadians who want to 'party' on weekend nights. The major difference is that their party generally takes place in a public place, both winter and summer, and so is more amenable to police actions. In terms of their dreams, ambitions, and ideas about the future in fact, homeless youth are very little different from the average teenager once the hard veneer of their street persona is broached in an interview situation. However, as the incidence of violence and homicide continues its upward spiral in our major urban cores, the lives of homeless people become increasingly more difficult. The dreams of young and older homeless of escaping the street become increasingly less realistic as predatory violence and the necessity of illegal behaviours surround them.

Street people also engage in the use of illegally obtained prescription drugs. The predominant drug of choice is talwin, a medication that has often been associated with hyperactive children. The drug is sold in hits for roughly $10 and then is prepared in a solution, heated and injected. It produces a 'rush' effect and a high that street youth call 'poor man's heroin.' Qualudes or 'ludes' are less frequently used but are mixed with alcohol to produce a deepened state of relaxation for the user.

Few of the homeless escape interaction with the police. Their presence in public areas at odd times of the day arouses police suspicion, and will often result in a questioning of the homeless person in terms of what they are doing. While Canadian citizens are not required to answer questions directed by police officers unless they are formally arrested, homeless people are co-operative with the police. It was unusual for the homeless to be severely critical of the police other than to comment on their habit of moving them on from sleeping places when they were simply trying to keep warm and get some rest. Joan, a woman in her forties, put it this way, "What harm are you doing? You're just trying to sleep, bothering no one and all of a sudden they're nudging you with their stick, 'Move along.' Why do they do that? You think they'd know how much we suffer." Others reported that the police are sympathetic to their plight although this was far more common amongst homeless persons over the age of thirty. Sam, a forty-one-year-old homeless man with a severe drinking problem commented on the humane face of policing: "One night I was down in the park drinking, and I passed out from too much booze. Two cops came to arrest me and hauled me off to jail. It was lucky they did because it was a really cold winter night, snowing and ice. I would've froze to death. I fought like hell with them because I didn't want to go but that was the booze talkin.' They really saved my life I guess." However some homeless people did report that the police had on occasion, 'shoved,' 'pushed,' or 'punched' them for no apparent reason. This has been a consistent finding of a number of studies of police-homeless interactions in North America.[25] A few of the young homeless women who were prostituting to survive mentioned that the police had initially made some effort to talk to them when they joined the ranks of the ladies of the night, but their intervention was viewed with hostility. "They want to know your name and are you legal (sixteen or older). They tell you to get off the street, its dangerous and all that shit, just like they're your father. Who needs it?"

Another group of persons that is beginning to swell the ranks of the homeless are persons with AIDS and AIDS-related syndromes. AIDs sufferers already experience extremes of stigmatization, social ostracism and abuse in their lives as they learn to cope with an ofttimes debilitating and rapidly terminal illness. Some leading American spokespersons have forecast that by the middle of the 1990s our health care system will not be able to cope with the substantial costs involved in treating and housing AIDS patients in Canadian hospitals and ancillary institutions. In several Canadian gay communities private funds raised through the activities of concerned citizens have underwritten hospices or retreats for AIDS victims who often need asylum from a hostile world as well as assistance in daily living. With increasing movement politically towards the concept of user fees and the current crisis being felt in Canadian hospitals, it is arguable that soon AIDS patients may follow mental patients into the streets, victims of deinstitutionalization policies cloaked as community benevolence. Those familiar with the deinstitutionalization literature will remember that the movement to the community was heralded as a positive step towards the creation of the **Gemeinschaft** village, wherein the community would care for the mentally ill. One expects that soon similar arguments will be made on behalf of, but not by, AIDS sufferers. Meanwhile AIDS sufferers find it increasingly difficult to keep a home as they face discrimination in the workplace often resulting in job loss. Soon they find themselves without the financial resources to keep a roof above their head, and few places willing to rent to them. Residents of homeless shelters are not welcoming of AIDS sufferers, and often share a common intolerance of those with the disease. Like many among us their ignorance of the disease leads them to conclude they will catch it if they are merely in the proximity of AIDS victims while this is scientifically impossible.[26]

Our failure as a society to act in the face of these human tragedies that are compounding daily is a telling indictment of the limits of our own humanity. We are aware that brutalized young people leave home to sell their bodies for a few dollars while risking contracting catastrophic illness; that old men and women like Drina Joubert freeze to death in the cities we call our homes; that street people are subjected to untold harassments and violence, and yet we have done very little to try to either understand the depths of their dilemma or to rectify the conditions that cause and perpetuate this deplorable condition. We are content to let children live in one room of a converted motel, who have become so immune to the process of displacement that it superficially does not seem to effect them. Under this exterior of toughness and indifference, a sure hallmark of constant degradation by society, are individuals with dignity and worth who we ignore at peril to ourselves, our own humanity, and at risk to our society. Who will be the next young person to join the ranks of those selling sex? Which of our fellow workers or classmates will suddenly find themselves without a job or means of support and will be forced into a shelter existence? How many people have to freeze to death, or be beaten to death, before we will act to do something about it?

Making the Homeless into Criminals

Our society does not provide an equal opportunity for all to succeed, despite the political rhetoric to this effect that is the constant chatter spread by politicians and societal apologists. Here is one figure to mull over. In Canada there are at least one million poor children according to The Canadian Council on Social Development.[27] Sixty percent of these children live with both parents, 36 per cent live with lone-parent mothers while the remaining 4 per cent live in other forms of unique relationships. While poor families constitute 13 percent of all families with children "they account for 23 percent of 16 and 17-year-old drop-outs."[28] These children according to the CCSD report, and common sensically, experience "many unmet needs and alienation from their classmates." For them, school is not a haven for the development of the mind but rather a demeaning experience that reinforces their isolation. "Instead of a learning environment, school becomes a place where poor children are forced to confront life's inequalities first hand." Additionally, poverty means that one does not have access to good sources of nutrition, warm clothes for cold weather, or toys and books that develop skills. Poverty, in other words, "contributes to poor mental and physical health which in turn make learning difficult." In response across Canada, many schools have begun breakfast programs to feed impoverished children. One final figure gives us a first hand impression of what poverty means in terms of life choices and chances. The average poor family with two children after paying for all of the essentials of life, shelter and food is left with $1.33 per person a day to cover all other expenses.[29] This would include "telephone, reading materials, transportation, dental care, drugs and fire insurance." Anyone with school-age children will recognize that this means that these children will not be part of many school activities that require the input of personal finances. The poor in large numbers are held in a net suspended on the edge of homelessness. As economic times worsen in our society and education becomes an increasingly central requirement for continuing employment, it is the children of the poor who will continue to become in growing numbers the homeless of tomorrow.

The behaviour of the homeless in public places is a source of true discomfort for many people. When the homeless engage in aggressive begging for money, or commit a crime or block access to public buildings they become a target for public anger. Similarly, in a growing number of public protests at the national level, the homeless have attempted to publicize the depth of their poverty. On February 18 some 100 protestors dumped hundreds of old shoes outside the office of Dan Mazankowski, the Minister of Finance. They pointed out that while 360,000 Quebeckers require social housing, the federal government had cut assistance for such housing by 67%. There is currently a debate which is ongoing in many American cities about the ways in which homelessness should be handled. Should we extend more charity to the homeless, or should we attempt to remove them from view through tough policing of their activities? One contemporary governmental response is to claim that enough is already being done, a claim made for example by Brian Mulroney with regard to public assistance. Large dollar numbers are quoted in terms of what is being done but no attempt is made to address the issue of how that money is being spent, and neither are the homeless consulted about its use. The homeless remain in this country without a voice, largely unorganized in being able to lobby for control over their lives. Empowerment remains a distant concept as the homeless drift through our social welfare streams. Jim Ward, a former homeless person and homeless organizer in Canada, found that, "Many among us view the homeless as lazy and undeserving, and despite some interest in their plight there is a general malaise which clouds our view of their predicament."[30] Few successes in helping people move from the street are readily apparent, and front line workers in the area interviewed for this book could only point to a handful of cases in which they had personally overseen a personal transformation into the mainstream for their charges. This itself is a testament to the harshness of the street and the way in which homelessness creates either anger or dependency. In the former case, homeless persons recognize their predicament and also the reluctance of society to provide other than band-aid measures to keep them poised on the edges of society, never moving to its core. Dependency, the relinquishing of hope, soon overtakes many homeless who allow themselves to give up the fight to retake their independence and autonomy, feeling that the great amount of effort required will only result in failure, or at most a brief respite from their condition.

There is obviously a need to revamp some of the existing laws that circumscribe the lives of the homeless. Laws which invoke sanctions against begging or loitering need to be reviewed in terms of their unneeded and unnecessary intrusion into the lives of the homeless. While at present we have not witnessed the kinds of animosity and violence that have characterized exchanges between the police and homeless persons in the U.S., this is surely a function of the deepening of the crisis that is growing perhaps more slowly, but just as surely, as that which has arisen to the south of us. The deepening recession in our own country, growing unemployment, worsening poverty, continue to swell the ranks of the homeless and create the ever present potential for an escalation of the problems of how to deal with the homeless, whether as deserving poor or potential criminals in our cities. These issues are dealt with in detail in the chapter which follows.

For many whose lives do not follow regular paths, periodic or sustained homelessness is a continuing way of life. The institutionalization of the homelessness into a state of dependency is part of a process of transformation from a person with a temporary accommodation problem or life crisis into chronic reliance on state assistance and subjegatation to the many laws, rules and regulations both formal and informal that circumscribe the lives of homeless persons. The pressures and victimization experienced by homeless people result in the development of highly negative self-attitudes and feelings of personal unworthiness, deep embarrassment and disgrace, which can have the effect of immobilizing the homeless individual. We know that even mild depression can produce profound psychological and physical effects in persons who are fully employed and housed. For the homeless, there is no respite from the onslaught of life lived on a moment-to-moment basis. Many become immune to the demands of the world that surrounds them as the meaning of life constructed previous to their becoming homeless begins to make no sense to them. Henry Miller described this state of consciousness in his book **Tropic of Cancer** as the effect of society robbing a person of their essential dignity and hope for a brighter future:

> Somehow the realization that nothing was to be hoped for had a salutary effect on me. . . . I decided to let myself drift with the tide, to make not the least resistance to fate, . . . I would hold on to nothing, that I would expect nothing, that henceforth I would live as an animal.[32]

Some homeless people respond to their victimization by retreating into self, viewing themselves as pitted against a world that has abandoned them. George Orwell, who spent a not inconsiderable time as a homeless person sleeping on the Victoria embankment in London, and in the streets of Paris, described this process of shielding oneself against further assaults on the self. "Under siege, the self contracts to a defensive core, armed against adversity."[33] Existence becomes provisional as the homeless person cannot live for a future that looks certain not to arrive. Drug and alcohol use can thus be better understood as a form of situational hedonism, that is, that one has to enjoy some pleasure in a life filled with pain, as the next day is likely to bring more and ofttimes deeper anguish and suffering.

Other homeless people become resigned to their fate, such as those who have spent long years living in shelters. They suffer from the classic symptoms of institutionalization associated with the behaviours of mental patients and prisoners who spend long periods incarcerated. Lesley Harman's research in Canada with homeless women reflects this problem: for to many women as well as men their hostel becomes their home.[34] The shelter may represent a kind of safety from the worst violence the street has to offer; it has routines which though repugnant, dehumanizing and stifling to most of us, assume a character of acceptability to the long-term resident. Even the jail-like environment and bunk-style sleeping arrangements are no longer criticized as the person sinks ever more deeply into a state of docility. When in interviews at various shelters the residents talked about obviously poor conditions in positive terms I was at first puzzled about their attitudes? Could this place really be better than it appeared? Perhaps I was judging it by some obscure middle-class standard. It took some considerable amount of close questioning to come to the realization that a transformative process had been effected in these people. Their standards of what they might like in terms of accommodation no longer mattered since they had accepted that they would always be in this form of intolerable living condition. Like prisoners of war they had chosen the only route of survival open to them, which was to give up all their dreams in order to be able to cope with their present and future reality. There is no use dreaming of steak dinners when you have accepted that all you will ever eat is a steady diet of macaroni. To do so only brings constant disappointment, anger and heartbreak at your own failures.

Very few homeless are in a position to criticize the arrangements that are made **for** them, but never **with** them. Seeing themselves as beggars, they are reluctant to criticize the facilities and services which are offered them in case they are simply abandoned.[35] Again, this is another form of victimization as the homeless are made to understand that they no longer have any rights as a human being and that they cannot express dissatisfaction except at the cost of peril to their survival. The absence of an organized homeless response to the inadequacies and inhumanities of the social welfare system is not surprising given the control exerted by these institutions over their lives. Few employees of a corporation volunteer to criticize their work conditions at the risk of losing their jobs.

In conclusion, it is time that our society began to move away from policing policies that criminalize the survival activities of the homeless, or that repress their normal way of living whether it be loitering in a public place or begging to buy food. The homeless should be viewed properly as victims of a variety of societal pressures and failures rather than as criminals who choose their way of life and are solely responsible for their conditions of life. Whether the homeless are engaging in mere crimes of survival or those strange behaviours that are so often associated with street people—yelling into the wind, cursing society, urinating in public (when they are denied access to so many public places), or actively begging for some spare change—their acts have to be re-evaluated by lawmakers, enforcers and policymakers. Each of these forms of behaviour carries with it a heightened chance of the homeless becoming criminalized or otherwise subject to the ministrations of the state control apparatus. The homeless are thus victimized by (1) their acts of survival, (2) by other homeless and non-homeless persons, (3) the police, and (4) by the exploitation of their forced immiseration and criminality. Forced to survive in a harsh environment by government policies that exclude them from the mainstream initially, and then further reinforce this through the dehumanizing and debilitating effects of welfare dependence, many homeless people are forced into the desperate situation of having to commit criminal acts to survive or find some momentary pleasures in an otherwise intolerable existence.

Snapshots of Homeless Life

We end this chapter with six vignettes of life as a homeless person drawn from my interviews. They are from both women and men and provide snapshots of the realities of street life. Hopefully, they illustrate the kinds of struggles that permeate the lives of homeless people in Canada and their attempts to deal with them as they live a day-to-day existence. The interviews reinforce many of the themes that I have explored in the last two chapters: the bleakness of a homeless existence, the degradation associated with shelter life, the struggles required to receive assistance and the conditions that are attached to it, the abuse that can lead to homelessness, the positive views of the homeless despite their condition.

Sherri

Sherri is a thirty-year-old woman who lives on the streets. She has been down and out for over five years. She spends most of her days sitting in the parks of the downtown core, watching the people who come to use the park, smoking, and talking with her friends. She has a normal appearance and could be an office worker on her lunch hour; the only difference is that her period of inactivity is 24 hours long. Various individuals donate food to her and visit with her throughout the day and early evening. I interviewed her on the eve of her birthday on a warm summer night. Sherri grew up in the city where she is now homeless. She has had some involvement with the mental health system after she suffered a breakdown. This central event in her life, this epiphany, signalled her rapid fall into the ranks of the homeless. Sleeping on the street is not the life that Sherri would choose but it reflects her 'unwelcome' status at several womens' shelters:

> The street hostels resist me turning up there because when they are abusive I make complaints about rapes that go on in these places, indecent assault and various forms of abuse and blaming people for crimes they did not commit, and when I make myself unpopular I am kicked out. But sometimes I am not kicked out, I am simply so sick by the abuse that I would rather sit and look at the flowers . . . then be in the opium dens of Charles Dickens.

Like most homeless persons time has lost its meaning for Sherri:

Of course, time seems very strange to me now because there's no schedule in my day. It seems to me that there is no schedule in my life. It is hard to have a time sense.

Sherri receives governmental support but it is insufficient to assist her in moving out of a homeless status:

I am on family benefit, but I'm given just enough to find that I don't have first and last month's rent and I cannot support myself. They give me $580 a month. It costs $600 for first and last month's rent alone, plus I have to have food and new clothing each month. My clothing gets stolen, some of it gets soiled. I have to have shampoo, I have to have soap, I have to have carfare, toothpaste, etc.

There have been few employment opportunities for Sherri in Toronto, so a few months ago she left the city looking for a job:

I travelled Ontario because I was hoping to settle in a place if I could find a place that would hire me. Actually if I'd had the money I would have been to as there were farms that were interested and things. I was hoping to settle in a smaller community where my skills would be appreciated, where I was not known as well, where I would be able to use skills such as crocheting, maybe contribute to a gift shop or work on a farm or something. So I travelled Ontario looking for work because there were no jobs in Toronto, but I didn't make it, I had to come back here. I didn't have enough money to travel with.

Sherri feels that social workers and street people alike view street women in a jaundiced way, encouraging them to form liaisons with casual acquaintances and strangers so that they will have a place to stay:

. . . I wouldn't just take anybody and no one understood it. They all understood that if I was out here in the street, they'd invite me for one cup of coffee and I should take the man. I wouldn't do this.

This young woman on the edge of our society feels that one form of solution to homelessness may lie in government's investing in the homeless to provide solid employment coupled with accommodation. Sherri felt that one solution would be a restaurant/gift shop run and owned by homeless people

> ... opening up a cafe, a business where we would take in street people and make an investment in them in terms of business. We would listen to the people and support them until they were rested and help the person to find out what their skill was and then help train them ... and then as they became a success business-wise they would make contributions back. As you made money for the place you would support people to go into business and courses. If they were successful in their businesses they would pay so much money back to your centre, help new people out.

This form of movement towards independence and autonomy would have the effect of short-circuiting the control exercised by social services over the lives of the homeless:

> To me, you would abort the attempt of social services to lay down restrictions on how you can treat people because it's not a social services situation. It's purely voluntary and it would be a business. My personal opinion is that I've never met anyone, who wanted life, that was alive that lacked something to offer people even if all they can do was listen ... There would not be a single person that I had ever met that would not be profitable to somebody. It's an investment to give a return investment.

The park is home for Sherri throughout even the winter months:

> I sleep on the park bench. A friend of mine is staying in a hostel near by. She keeps sort of edging me to go into a hostel but I don't want to. There are people who will buy me coffees. I sit on the park bench in the freezing cold, I have no money.

When Sherri exhausts her money each month there are periods of days when she has no funds for food:

> People bring me charity. I also give charity. Like when I get money my friends and we will all go 'out on the

town' and have coffees and sandwiches and anybody who's hungry has something.

Sherri is proud of her appearance but finds it difficult to maintain her appearance. She shops in 'bargain' stores for her clothes:

I have found skirts, tops, pants and things . . . they are very inexpensive . . . sometimes they are in style and sometimes they are not. When I am able to dress nicely it's better for looking for work. When I go to a job interview and I'm dressed up they're more likely to hire me if I'm in a skirt as opposed to jeans. But there is a lot of trouble with keeping clean. There is a place in this area, the womens showers, you can go in there and take a shower. They serve dinners, if you're hungry you can have a meal. But the trouble is keeping clean, like if I don't have pocket money at night I have to rely on someone to take me out for coffee in a restaurant because there's no washrooms available. They keep the park buildings all locked up.

Bill

Bill is thirty-seven years old. He is divorced from his wife of four years and has two children. He is a skilled worker, a machinist who worked steadily for sixteen to eighteen years until the effects of the recession hit some four years ago. Bill became homeless because of his use of drugs:

I used drugs on weekends. It just got to the point where I couldn't pay bills or anything. I used to blow my whole cheque on it (cocaine), six or seven hundred bucks. It went on for years. I got kicked out, had no money.

Bill has been a regular in the shelter since he lost his job four years ago. He has been able to get away from shelter life now and again when he gets short-term employment in the construction industry:

Well I was doin' the route; Seaton House, Good Sheppard, Sally Ann. You're only allowed two weeks here, two weeks at the Sheppard.

His first experience of a homeless shelter was both shocking and degrading:

It was terrible. I got lice from the place the first time I was here. The people, you gotta hide things and people steal your shoes, jacket, whatever. People are always watchin' ya. There's some really weird people in this place.

Bill refuses to seek psychiatric or therapeutic help for his drug use. He served prison time in his late teens for selling speed but has not been arrested since. He currently lives on welfare, but jobs are few and far between. He receives $361 a month on welfare.

Bill spends his days at various drop-ins for the homeless:

There's a church right down here it's open from eight to four every day. You can buy food there, it's very cheap. Fifty cents for an egg sandwich, a meat sandwich.

When I was working it seemed like I was working with family and it seemed like you just got up and went to work long hours for ten dollars an hour so it seemed like you were going nowhere.

Bill sees himself as being somewhat institutionalized to a life of dependency at this point:

What are you doin' this for goin' to work and everything? You come here get a meal free, get lodging free and not have the same kind of headaches. It's wrong way to think but I'm sure a lot of people think that way. It's hard to get away.

Bill finds that without a telephone number it is difficult to look for a job, since there is no means by which prospective employers can get in touch with him:

It's hard to get a job. How do you put down a phone number for _____ to get ahold of you? It's pretty well impossible. There are some places where they will take messages but its really for older men.

Bill doesn't panhandle but does work at 'cash corner' for money doing casual labour for ten dollars an hour when he needs 'smokes.'

Two years ago I got a job and it was on a rotating shift and I was staying here okay. Big hang-up was that I couldn't get my sleep when the shift changed right? Like I'd go to _____ this agency so they let me sleep in the hallway there, but there was no way I could sleep cause people are walking in the hallway there going back and forth. I even tried here to get them to let me sleep here in the day, like I tried to explain it but they wouldn't listen.

Scott

Scott is thirty-three years old. He was born and raised in Toronto's east end. He left home at eighteen and has a grade nine education. He soon found a job:

I was just labouring for a construction company. And then mostly moving companies, some of the best known in the business.

Scott has a drinking problem that is severe. He drinks about twenty-four bottles of beer every day. He makes his money by:

. . . panhandling on the corner of the streets, walkin' around the streets and stuff. You'd be amazed some of the stuff you find, and I sell it. I find stuff and take it to the second hand store and sell it. I make ten to twenty bucks in a day panhandling, but it takes all day. I drink beer and stomach bitters, they're forty percent alcohol.

I had a room over at the Skidders Motel but I had a fight with the owner. He tried to move me from one room to the other. I was half drunk, we started arguin,' he pushed me and then we were fightin.' See under the hotel/motel act he don't have to give you your rent money back. You're out on the street. I was payin' $360 a month for one room with a bed, single dresser. You go down the hall to use the can. It's a tavern with rooms above.

The shelters for Scott are "fine, if you're homeless". In the shelter:

You sleep with one eye open. Like the other night there was a guy pacin' up and down, up and down. You couldn't sleep cause you don't know if he's waitin' for you to go to sleep and take your stuff or whatever. Some of the men just walk around screamin' and yellin.' Like some of them talk away and you can't understand what

> they're talkin' about. They're talkin' jibberish. You just
> get fed up with them.
>
> Yah, I've been arrested for assault, vagrancy. You can't
> sleep on the street. It against the law. The cops pick up
> you and take you . . . they give you a fine. Sleepin' in the
> park. They pick you up, take you in, arrest you for four
> hours. They give you a ticket, and you appear in court,
> either that or you pay the fine. Well, you can't appear in
> court or pay the fine. Eventually they'll catch up with you
> and throw you in jail anyway. I spent seven days in jail for
> vagrancy for sleepin' in a park.

The thrust of the law is unclear to those who break it:

> Well, you're not harmin' nobody other than yourself. But
> I guess what it is too, they don't want to see you out
> there in mid-December, lyin' in a snowstorm or
> something like that. I guess they figure, "Either we'll pick
> you up now, or we'll come and pick you up later for the
> coroner." They figure you'll freeze to death.

Dennis

Dennis is twenty-eight years old. He was a foster child from the
age of four and lived in six different foster homes separated from his
siblings:

> I was adopted at ten, left at thirteen and then I lived in a
> shack for awhile. I got a job working midnights in a
> doughnut shop. I was working illegally and got paid
> cash. I slept in an abandoned building two doors down
> from the doughnut shop. The police knew I was there,
> but they didn't do anything about it since I was a good
> kid. I worked there four years.

Like many of the homeless Dennis found that his skills were not
in demand:

> I hit Toronto and I looked for work. But there was no
> work for bakers. So I went to Georgian College and I
> tried to get a degree in culinary sciences but I only went
> two years and didn't graduate. Then I met a girl and she
> had our son. We lived together four and a half years. I

left her. We had been living in a basement apartment. It was a mutual agreement.

Shelters only provide a temporary respite and there are limitations placed upon individuals that make it difficult to get established. Men like Dennis are subject to Catch-22; those who collect welfare cheques are supposed to rent rooms, but the amount given for welfare is insufficient to rent a room:

> I've been in Toronto five years. I'm trying to stay in the shelters. But they won't let you stay here if you're collectin' a welfare cheque. They say go pay for a room with your welfare cheque, but even the rooms around here, there's not that many rooms. You pay eighty, ninety and hundred a week for a room. The most that welfare will give you is $600, but I get $361.

So, when they are ejected from the shelter men roam the streets or try to impose on street acquaintances:

> Since I got kicked out of here last Monday I've been stayin' with friends, stayin' awake in all night doughnut shops.

The shelters are difficult to sleep in and most men get little rest:

> There are seventy-five beds in each room. It's like sleeping with a pack of bears, thirty-five out of seventy snoring. Other people want to stay awake all night and talk.

Guy

Guy is 26 and has been living in the shelters off and on for three years. He is from Canada's east coast and has travelled to several cities looking for work:

> There was no work back home and it's hard to get a place here to get started. They just don't give you enough money really. Everywhere you go they want first and last and you have to buy some stuff. You have to get a place downtown so you can travel to work. They want you to get a place first before you can get some work, and you can't get work without a permanent address cause they

wanna be able to phone you to verify that's where you
live so . . . .

Infrequently, Guy is able to get seasonal or part-time work, but
the offers are few and far between:

I worked at Calgary for the Stampede last summer, then I
came back here. Usually I just walk the streets and stay
awake at night. I've slept a few times under park
benches. I do some odd labour work here and there
when it's around.

Street life is punctuated by violence and Guy gets depressed
about why he is homeless:

I just mind my own business on the street and keep my
nose out of other peoples' business. Other people get
jumped, they get beat up. This is the worst
neighbourhood in the city.

A lot of times I say to myself, "How did I get here? What
did I do wrong?" Nothing you can do.

The shelters seem to have little interest in men doing better and
getting on in life. Guy believes that men who are genuinely interested
in getting out of the homeless life should be given the chance in
shelters where they are not surrounded by those who have become
accustomed to street and shelter life and have no desire to leave it:

They really screw you around at the shelters. See, like I
was booked in here last week. I told them I was going to
visit my uncle. I'm back after three days and they say I'm
booked out. So I won't know if I have a bed till tonight. It
stinks in the shelters. If they notice a guys trying to keep
himself, to look for some work they should at least try to
treat him a little bit better. They shouldn't mix the bums
who don't want to look for work in with us.

I spent five dollars a night for a room at _____ hostel
and when I woke up in the morning my jacket was gone,
and my sandals and my t-shirt.

Some of the staff here are pretty cruel but no worse than
the people on the streets. Like I said they treat you like
you're nobody. You're here, you're a bum, you need us,

we don't need you. Insensitive attitude, but then again there are some here that are okay.

I wouldn't be here if I didn't have to be. Hopefully, I'll get off the cycle of shelters but like I said, it's hard. You try to get yourself ahead but you just can't get yourself ahead. To live here you'd have to have at least a thousand dollars in your pocket.

Guy finds that the homeless have to overcome a double stigma, that of being homeless and of being dependent on welfare. Although welfare does provide for limited housing assistance, unfortunately landlords do not view recipients as ideal tenants and so feel free to discriminate against them:

If you're on welfare they'll give you this sheet of paper saying they'll guarantee the person pays but a lot of people won't even look at you. "You're on welfare we don't even want you living here."

I hate going to welfare. I hate asking for money. If there's a soup kitchen I'll go to a soup kitchen. Last time I went, I went home cause my dad had died and came back here and had to get started over again. I said to this woman is there any way I can get an emergency cheque so I can get started over? She looks at me and says, "You don't deserve one. If you don't leave here I'll call the police cause you're tryin' to rip us off." I said, "I was away, my dad had died and I need to get started again." She said, "Well we need to see a death certificate." I said, "The hell with you, I don't need this shit," and I walked out.

The few jobs that are available at the employment centre are ones that pay so little that they will not move the individual out of a homeless condition, being neither enough to live or eat on:

There's jobs that pay $5 a hour but you can't live on that, it's not enough. You want a good job and people want a place where they can get ahold of you.

How does Guy now think of the concept of home?

My mom and dad are both dead so there's no home for me. I just try to get by day to day. You don't trust anybody on the street. It's just too dangerous.

Nicki

Nicki is 23 years old. He has been living on the street since he was thirteen years old. Like many street children he was the subject of abuse in his parental home. Like many abused children he was not believed when he complained, and his mother did nothing to prevent the abuse being inflicted:

I came from an abusive family. My stepfather beat me cause I wasn't his real son and my mother let it happen. He came into my life when I was six and left when I was eleven. He went to jail.

After enduring five years of abuse Nicki tried to commit suicide in a desperate bid to draw attention to his condition:

I went to a psychiatric hospital when I left home at eleven. My step-father had stabbed me, and no one would believe I was being abused till he stabbed me. I then tried to kill myself to get some attention. I was in hospital for thirty days. I was then accepted into a group home and I was there four and a half years.

Finally, after seven years Nicki moved out and became a prostitute to support himself:

I moved out in 1984. I quit school and I came to Vancouver and became a prostitute. I've been doing it now for seven years.

Nicki shows little concern about the threat of A.I.D.S. and of both the ways in which it is transmitted and its prognosis:

I'm personally not concerned about AIDS. I know about precautions, I know what to take, I know how to get it. I'm homosexual so I have to be very, very safe. I needed money for my drugs, I needed money for my booze, I needed money for a place to stay.

Like most street hookers Nicki took drugs to dull the pain of reality but recently stopped:

I quit drinking and drugs over seven months ago. I was a heavy liquor drinker so I used to spend a lot on liquor. I always manage to sabotage things, money burns a hole in my pocket. I used to make $10,000 a month. My boyfriend also lives here. We're going to move to the country. I'm willing to give it a try.

Street life is viewed as both frightening and dangerous, underscoring the remarks made by all homeless people:

Life on the streets is scary. The lights are glamorous and it's an all night party place but it's addictive, it's like doing drugs and alcohol. But finally you don't want anything that you wanted before and it brings you down.

Young and underage boys work the street according to Nicki. He sees himself as straddling two worlds, that of streetlife and that of the professionals who constantly attempt to help him. Nicki feels that the workers assigned to him are not qualified to help him as they have little or no knowledge of street life. His current worker is a mother of two whom he describes as "ignorant of my life". He would like to see workers in place who have lived through street experiences and thus can speak with knowledge and experience and relate to kids:

I know a couple of thirteen-year-olds that work the street, but its' really sixteen and up. Customers are judges, lawyers, I've even had undercover policemen. They drive big fancy cars.

Well, it's there. I know I'm street smart and I'm also professional smart. I've got the best of worlds. I have friends out there if I need money I know I can go there.

Nicki sees the downtown areas of cities as both exciting for young children but fraught with danger. His own life experience is a testimony to this and the decline that street violence can precipitate in one's life:

I was eleven and I used to be downtown walking the streets and I was raped when I was eleven and my mom turned around and said I deserved everything I got. They didn't care. I went through six months of surgery.

132 ... DOWN AND OUT IN CANADA

Nicki sees more and more children on the street and feels that the government and the public are not responding appropriately to the problems of homeless children, preferring to fund agencies rather than direct intervention services:

> I think we have all the agencies we need. But there's no funding for more street workers, for more of what we need, more hostels for youth, needle exchanges. We need more Winnebagos driving around feeding the hungry that are out there prostituting, that are out there sleeping on park benches. We need the money, we don't need any more agencies.

While he is not entirely negative on efforts being made on behalf of, rather than with, the homeless, Nicki views the problem as one that is growing rapidly and little is being done in terms of short-circuiting children into more rewarding lives at the point of entry:

> We're getting somewhere but it's going at such a pace that there's more and more kids coming on the streets nowadays and for sure they're not getting it in time enough. When's it gonna end? Most of it's because they've got no one to love them, no one to take care of them, no one to say, "I care."

In the next Chapter we explore the deeper structural roots of homelessness in the Canadian family, the economy and various political and social policies that have contributed to the manufacture of the human misery that is homelessness. The argument being followed, in concert with the ideas expressed here, is that a critical rethinking of the problem of homelessness is long overdue in our society. There is a real sense that there is a lack of political willpower on the part of all levels of government to address the problems of suffering Canadians. If we are to achieve a just society then it is incumbent upon us to consider the ways and means to address this serious and worsening social problem.

CHAPTER FIVE

Another Night in Paradise

They used to tell me I was building a dream,
And so I followed the mob,
Where there was earth to plough or guns to bear,
I was always there, right there,
on the job.

They used to tell me, I was building a dream
with peace and glory ahead,
Why should I be standing in line,
Just waiting for bread?

Once I built a railroad, made it run,
Made it race against time,
Once I built a railroad, now it's done,
Brother, can you spare a dime?

The Political Economy of Homelessness

Poverty is the handmaiden of homelessness. In the 1960s and 1970s Canadians enjoyed relative prosperity, while by the 1980s the cycle of prosperity had moved on. Throughout the 1980s conditions worsened on a variety of economic fronts as unemployment figures began a gradual climb that had avalanched by 1991 to the point where 15,000 jobs a month were being lost in Canada.[1] The value of real wages has also sunk correspondingly.[2] Quite commonly social analysts compare the current economic climate in our nation with the Great Depression of the 1930s, which left tens of thousands of Canadians out of work. One significant difference between the 'new' homelessness of the 1990s, and that of the 1930s is that men no longer are the sole, visible victims of homelessness. Increasingly, as we learned earlier in this book, women, children and families make up a significant and growing number of the homeless in our society. In fact, it is a telling sign that during the 1980s our modern version of the food kitchen and the food lines, so often associated with the 1930s, appeared as food banks, which grew at an alarming rate throughout the last decade.[3] Hostels and shelters also enjoyed a significant growth during this period as governments scrambled to put together piecemeal emergency solutions to the large number of disenfranchised citizens that came forward for aid.[4]

By 1993, there are many significant signs that lead us to the conclusion that the grip of the recession has hit extremely deep in Canadian society. In fact, it is by analysing both the symptoms and the causes of the failures within our political and economic system that we can develop a more informed analysis of the structural causes of homelessness. While it may be comforting to presume that homeless persons are somehow solely responsible for their own misfortunes, this approach gives us only a distorted idea of why persons lose their 'homes.' A political economy approach allows us to integrate the understandings we have developed concerning the more personalized factors that can contribute to or sustain someone in homelessness (family disintegration, personal troubles, alcohol problems, etc.), within the larger framework of the societal conditions that contribute to the production of homelessness. By moving from the personal to the societal we are expanding our understanding, stepping back, as it were, from the lives of the homeless to the life of the nation.[5] If you consider the feelings of powerlessness which are common to all of us with regard to larger political and economic forces (free trade, government policies, etc.), it seems obvious that this larger dimension is crucial to analysing the wider roots of homelessness.

To fully understand homelessness one cannot separate the condition from the political processes that shape our capitalist economy. Several analysts have suggested that we are entering a period of de-industrialization in our economy. Our federal government has propagated private sector profiteering over the past decade, an approach that takes as its model the policies of the Reagan/Bush administration and the Thatcher/Major emphasis on privatization at the cost of social programs in the United Kingdom. This is a strategy that has decimated the economic health of our country, the U.S.A., and Britain. Bill Clinton's campaign for the presidency (and that of Ross Perot) took as its main thrust the 'gutting' of the domestic economy, social programs, and education under Bush/Reagan 'trickle down' or 'voodoo' economics. Bush's demise was also reflected in Britain by October 1992 as plans by John Major's Tories to put 90,000 miners and ancillary workers out of work gave clear signs of the collapse of this approach, which increased the wealth of the wealthiest at the expense of those on the lower end of the economic scale. Similarly, the effects of Mulroney's approach are explored throughout this chapter.[6] The central assertion of this approach is that government acquiescence to private entrepreneurs will lead to increased jobs as part of the benefits of free enterprise. Not surprisingly, the thrust of private enterprise is not towards social programming but emphasizes the opposite tack, that is, the elimination of welfare programs that are portrayed as 'subsidies'. Welfare, unemployment and universal medicare schemes are viewed as unfair advantages under the Canada-U.S. free trade agreement, to be eliminated in the interest of lower production costs. Workers are viewed as so much 'surplus labour' to be exploited at the minimum wage possible. This process of de-industrialization has proceeded at an ever more rapid pace in the free trade era in Canada, as numerous manufacturers head to locations in the southern U.S.A. and Mexico to avoid workers' rights, unions, benefit schemes, taxes, stringent environmental standards, and higher labour costs.[7] The increasing decline in real wage levels in Canada, and the increasing impoverishment of working people through both declining employment opportunities, the disappearance of well paid employment (across the unskilled, semi-skilled, and professional classes), and escalating taxation rates demarcates an ever-widening gap between the well-to-do and those who are struggling to survive in our country. This includes both the erosion of the middle-class and the creation of forced dependency amongst the ranks of the ever increasing army of labour that is kept in abeyance.[8]

Economic developments in Canada, as in the United States, reflect a diversity of problems of competition within the new global economy as well as the internal contradictions of conservative economic policies. Underlying these developments have been a series of ongoing class struggles, ideological debates over the nature of welfare provision, and a proliferation of factors that have impacted upon the production of homelessness. However, traditional forms of explanation of homelessness have not proven up to the task of providing understandings but rather have served to obfuscate this social problem in a manner that both assuages our public conscience (or lack of it) or trivializes the suffering of the homeless.[9] Conservative accounts do little more than follow the approach of 'blaming the victim,' that is, ascribing homelessness to one or more social failings of the individual, holding them personally and morally responsible for their condition. In the United States, this approach was typified by Ronald Reagan's famous speech in which he fantasized that there were "10,000 points of light" for the poor to gravitate to.[10] Unfortunately, someone has normally turned off the lights before the homeless person has arrived, or even begun their journey.

While this attitude in its most inane form shows a callous disregard for the plight of the poor and homeless, in its more insidious forms it holds severe consequences for the homeless. The darker side of this concept is one that paints the homeless as 'dangerous', 'unpredictable' or 'disordered', in other words as persons to be feared, or as I argued in the last chapter, fitting as subjects of criminalization.[11] This idea separates the homeless person from full civil status, and much like the ideas of an earlier age in criminological inquiry, provides comforting reassurance for the affluent classes in our society. Lombroso, an Italian criminologist, became famous for his idea that some individuals were 'born criminal,' that is, that they were somehow biologically less advanced than the law abiding in any society.[12] The conservative viewpoint on the homeless is no less foreboding for in its false reassurance of the difference of the homeless it lulls us into believing that homelessness has no chance of becoming **our** plight, when this is not only far from the truth, but as all of us realize in the deepening grips of the current recession, is a possibility that we see like some vague nightmare that we hope does not become a waking reality.

Following Hopper I wish to argue that current views on the homeless produce four distinct typologies that are all equally as ridiculous in the pictures they paint.[13] All of them help to illustrate quite graphically the 'knowledge gap' that exists between the reality of street behaviour and our experience of it.[14] In the absence of good information, the natural human tendency is to invent, and in this process of invention our fantasies are given free flight.[15] **First**, there is the homeless person who is the crazed, psychotic street vagabond either mentally ill, or, alternatively, has a mind soaked in illicit drugs or is addicted to alcohol. **Secondly**, there are those individuals who are descendent from long lines of the chronic poor in our society, a group of ne'er-do-wells who have sprung from the ranks of those ungrateful welfare recipients who take great pleasure in spending their cheques on beer which they retrieve from the store in taxicabs. **Thirdly,** there are many on the street who are the outcasts of our society, the product of broken homes, unwanted children or who have been manufactured by our inadequate welfare strategies. **Finally,** there are a small group of free-wheeling soldiers of street fortune who see in homelessness a way to get something for nothing. As Barak has argued these explanations have one commonality in an approach that "locates the cause of homelessness within the individual."[16]

Like many social problems before it, the study of homelessness has been the subject of attempts at what Rock termed, 'ownership of the problem,' that is, to define homeless people in terms of a particular model of human behaviour.[17] The few attempts in Canada in this field have largely arisen from the psychiatric and social work fields.[18] Both take an approach that prefers to 'medicalize' the behaviour of the homeless, as reflecting mental illness, or some other form of personality defect. While the medical model arguably has had some positive effects in the field of alcohol dependency it will, without doubt, produce dire consequences for the homeless. While it may be useful to think of some of the homeless in terms of personal pathologies, it is unwarranted to assign the majority of them to the ranks of the walking wounded. According to a variety of large scale studies in the United States, under 20% of the homeless suffer from, or have received treatment for, mental illness, including drug and alcohol abuse.[19] While the medical model does not have a utility for understanding the homeless, it certainly does have considerable advantages as a tool of social control. When someone is deemed to be suffering from a medical disease, particularly one which involves a psychiatric condition, or drug or alcohol dependency, we adopt an attitude that they are more childlike and less responsible for their actions, at least in terms of their entitlement to assistance from the state. They are therefore likely candidates for control. They require discipline to be imposed.[20]

No Sweet Home

The Canadian family, as we have already discovered, is undergoing a rapid transformation from the 'ideal' of the nuclear family that predominated our vision of domestic bliss following the Second World War. Now, blended families, a union of previously married partners form a significant and growing part of our family structures. Single-parent families led predominantly by women also account for a large percentage of families in Canada.[21] Not only are Canadian women and men marrying at a later age (27.2 and 28.2 years respectively) but they are also choosing to have far fewer children, a reflection of the harsh economic realities of a society that in most major urban centres requires two working adults to carry a mortgage.[22] Families are under increasing pressures not just in terms of the economic struggle to survive with a reasonable standard of living, but to withstand a variety of societal pressures which seem, from a plethora of sociological and other sources, to be mounting a relentless attack on the fabric of modern living.

Family violence has become, since the mid-1970s, the subject of both academic research and much later, public and political attention. Before this period, women were seen to be the property of men who had exclusive rights to them sexually as well as the right to 'discipline' them.[23] In a 1975 study I conducted of wife assault in Oshawa the remarks of one offender underscored this attitude. Asked why he had shot at his wife with a shotgun while she was lying in bed he replied, "She's my wife and I'll shoot her if I want to."[24] Under Canadian law, in concert with most Western nations, a man could not be found guilty of sexually assaulting his wife until the 1980s. Wife abuse is certainly not a new phenomenon as sociologists like Walter DeKeseredy and Ronald Hinch have informed us, in fact, "violence against wives has existed for centuries."[25] The home, rather than being a sanctuary is the most probable site for a woman to suffer an assault. Contrary to public beliefs, woman abuse is a phenomenon which cuts across all social and economic barriers. It has been suggested that the over-representation of lower socio/economic families in reported cases reflects several factors including styles of conflict resolution, willingness to call police, willingness to proceed with a charge, and the higher 'stakes' involved as one proceeds up the social ladder.

A major problem of woman assault is that often those who are victims do not wish to have their assailant charged. There are several reasons why this occurs including fear of reprisal from the perpetrator, lack of belief in the effectiveness of the criminal justice system, and embarrassment that authorities and others will become aware of the crime.[26] The most overwhelming reason for non-reporting though is related to the feminization of poverty in Canadian society. Women in our society have long been in a position of economic inferiority.[27] Not only are they likely to receive less pay for a job of equal responsibility when compared to a man, but they are more likely to have a lower paying, part-time, or underemployed position.[28] This explains that while the majority of women with children work outside the home, few are in an economic position to provide themselves and their children with anything approaching their normal living conditions if their husband or partner's income is lost. Thus while their own safety, physical and psychological well-being may often be threatened, it is quite common for women to endure abuse in order to provide what they consider to be an acceptable environment for their children.

Women may have little information about the alternatives to suffering abuse in their own homes. The contemplation of a future in a shelter for battered women, followed by possible dependency on welfare, is for many women too much of a sacrifice to ask their children to make. In this protective role, women sacrifice their own selves in order to mistakenly preserve a 'home' environment for their children.[29]

While woman abuse is a problem that has received a great deal of academic, governmental and interest group attention, child abuse is another social problem which is having a significant impact upon the life of the Canadian family. Child abuse is reported in increasing numbers in every province of the country.[30] Since the dark figure of crime in the case of child abuse, that is, the number of unreported crimes, is estimated to be substantially higher than all reported cases, reported statistics represent only a fraction of all abuse committed against children. Child abuse may consist of negligence, physical and/or verbal abuse, psychological abuse, or sexual assault taking a variety of forms. In 1981, **The Badgley Report on Sexual Offences Against Children and Youth** found that amongst the children they interviewed that one in three boys and one in two girls had at some time in their lives been sexually victimized.[31] Males are responsible for 70 to 85% of all abuse against children committed in Canada.[32] Beyond this, one must also consider the overall system of patriarchy and male domination that has left women and children to predominate overwhelmingly as victims in every sphere of criminal activity. But the more significant crimes, it has been argued by critical criminologists, lie within the manipulation of economic and legal structures by males who thus ensure the continuance of female subjugation.[33]

Economic pressures have also been a major force in the production not only of discord within the Canadian family, but in the direct creation of homelessness. Throughout the 1990s economic conditions have deteriorated rapidly under the conservative federal government's approach to fiscal management. Let us consider some of the indicators that provide a reflection of the economic state of our nation. Incomes fell 1.6% for the average Canadian family in 1990 as compared to 1989 according to Statistics Canada figures.[34] Average family incomes ranged from a low of $39,701 in P.E.I. to a high of

$57,027 in Ontario.[35] More disturbingly, the number of Canadians who had to subsist on low incomes, that is, in which food, shelter and clothing accounted for more than 56% of their income, was the position that 3.8 million Canadians found themselves in.[36] More than 1,000,000 of the poor of this nation in 1990 were children![37] Between 1989 and 1990 the number of children living in poverty jumped 15 percent in Canada.[38] According to Ken Battle of the National Council on Welfare, this trend is a direct result of rising unemployment. He suggested that, "there's been no progress in reducing poverty."[39] Financially, it simply does not make sense to relegate so many of our children to a future that will simply increase the probability that they will be dependent upon welfare services. All of the things that Canadians desire for their children are routinely denied to these young people, and there are a number of other problems that spring naturally from poverty. Children in poverty are a growing burden on our provincial and national purse. In 1991-92 Ontario and its umbrella municipalities spent $5.45 billion dollars on welfare, an amount that puts it almost on a par with education as a mainstay of expenditure.[40] A House of Commons Subcommittee on Poverty reported in December of 1991 that the costs of child poverty are astronomical.[41] Early school leaving amongst poverty-stricken children will cost us $1.3 billion over the next twenty years in unemployment benefits, $23 billion in income that they will be unable to earn, and $7.2 billion in taxes that will not be collected from them since they will be sentenced to unproductive lives.[42]

A closer examination of the trends underlying these figures also reveals that it is becoming increasingly difficult for family heads to find full-time employment as only 58.4% of family heads were able to work full-time.[43] The average number of earners per family also dropped to 1.75 in 1990 which was a fall from a figure of 1.8 in 1989.[44] These figures also reveal that women, particularly as single parents, suffered the greatest decline in income during this fall. "More than 60 percent of female lone-parent families were low income, a jump from 53% in 1989. The average income for such families was $21,961, 7.3% less than in 1989."[46] There were a variety of other family groupings that suffered declines in income level ranging from 7 to 10 percent including single-parent families headed by females, two-parent families with no income, and families headed by males under the age of 25. Many millions of families remain below the artificial low-income ceiling devised by Statistics Canada which is $28,081 for a family of four living in a city with over 500,000 residents.[47]

Unemployment has grown substantially in the 1990s so much so that by April 1992 more Canadians were out of work than at any time in the nation's history according to Statistics Canada. Their numbers continue to rise at a rate of 500 per month.[48] But this is not a new trend; in fact, a report by The Economic Council of Canada concluded that, "Unemployment in Canada has shown a steadily rising trend in the three decades since 1960, with the average for each decade surpassing the average for the previous decade."[49] An examination of the unadjusted jobless rate for March 1992 reveals that 1,695,000 Canadians were out of work.[50] This figure does not reveal the true extent of unemployment in Canada for hidden within it are several other additions to unemployment figures that are conveniently not taken into account in government calculations: the number of persons who have simply given up looking for work, who in other words is now without hope of finding a job. The number of these individuals are impossible to estimate accurately but it is certain they number in the hundreds of thousands, comprised of a variety of workers. Consider for a moment the plight of thousands of workers who are losing their jobs in Canada each month as factories close and employers relocate to the U.S.A. or Mexico. A worker in his fifties may find that he/she has become redundant, and is considered too old to be suitable for retraining. Young workers with limited education and skills find that there are jobs for which there are fewer and fewer retraining schemes.[51] The new catchphrase of conservative economics in this regard is termed 'restructuring,' a word that is synonymous with eliminating not only legal impediments to profit making and the international transfer of capital, but the elimination of workers and their rights.[52] Unions, unemployment benefits, and social security schemes are viewed as expendable. So it is that each month more Canadians are out of work despite rhetoric from the Federal government that the 'recession' is over, a declaration they made **three times during 1991 alone!**[53] The economic reality is that the recession is over for the wealthy and factory owners as many have fled from Canada in anticipation of a North American/Mexico duty-free zone. This dismantling of the Canadian economy was presaged by sociologist Gordon Laxer, as I have already argued in his brilliant book **Open for Business** that documented the selling off of not only our national resources, but the ability of the average Canadian to make a reasonable living.[54] Several major economic analysts have publicly declared the obvious: "Canada is certainly in a protracted recession."[55]

In smaller cities across Canada, particularly those which have been dependent upon manufacturing for the employment of their populace, the situation is extremely grave. In Windsor, the downtown area became a virtual ghostown during 1991-95 as stores closed weekly, succumbing to the pressures of unemployment as well as cross-border shopping as cash-strapped and overtaxed Ontarians tried to stretch their dollars. The Mayor, Mike Hurst, commented that the number of people who are unemployed or on welfare was "horrifying".[56] The most disturbing part of this scenario in Windsor, which is repeated across Canada, is the depth to which the current unemployment has cut. Like the homeless they may become, the unemployed are increasingly, " middle-class, people-next-door types who have exhausted their unemployment benefits, are in hock to their families and have nowhere else to turn."[57] Welfare assistance by January 1992 in Windsor had hit record levels as in a city of 191,000, with a workforce determined by the Canada Employment Centre to be 137,000, roughly 10,000 were unemployed, a rate which is approximately 25%.[58] This figure does not account for the number of children who are dependent upon these individuals. The Economic Council of Canada's conclusions on this issue are informative for our discussion, for it clearly demonstrates that "there are already a number of disturbing signs that unemployment will remain a serious problem for some time to come."[59] Their research, which looked at three decades of rising unemployment in Canada, found that "rising and persistent unemployment" were constant factors in the nation's ill health. In other words, Canadians workers can expect little relief from the problems of unemployment. Further, the report found that increasing long-term unemployment has become a mainstay of the Canadian economic picture. There also have been substantial increases in the number of older workers who find themselves permanently unemployed as employers attempt to sidestep payment of long-term benefits to workers approaching retirement age. Encouragement to both permanent and semi-permanent retirement has been a leading economic strategy in the 1980s and now continues at an accelerated pace in the 1990s as both industry and government attempt to trim budgets. This has also been accompanied in 1993 by suggestions that the age of eligibility for government pension schemes should be raised beyond the current 65-years floor. This is important in any consideration of homelessness for Canada has an aging population that will fall within the scope of this problem within this decade, and the first decade of the new century.

Another central indicator of the financial health of the nation is the number of businesses that run into trouble and have to declare bankruptcy. For the latest year of available figures, 1991, the figures reveal that bankruptcies are occurring at record numbers that amount to no less than a crisis. In the first eleven months of 1991 there were 69,947 bankruptcies in Canada, a 42% increase over the same period in 1990.[60] During the first ten months of 1990 the Canadian government paid out a record $15 billion in unemployment benefits or 37% more than the same period in the previous year.[61] The government's fears over a possible inability to cover the costs of unemployment accounted for a 24% increase in premiums during the first half of 1991 and a further 7% increase that came into effect on January 1, 1992.[62] Tightened rules and decreased benefit periods are also impacting, like all of the above factors, in the production of homelessness. More than this, the current crisis has been softened by many of the unemployed drawing upon assets and family resource networks to remain solvent. However, these alternative resources are scarcely unlimited, and it often means that seniors are further subsidizing the current economic downturn.

Throughout 1991, 1992, and 1993 Canadians have been watching as large retail chains fold up shop and retreat into bankruptcy. Among the list of casualties has been the Cotton Ginny clothing chain, Birks, Peoples' Credit Jewellers, Dalmys for Children, Bata Shoes, Bargain Harolds, Foot Locker, Tip Top Tailors, Dofasco, and a variety of manufacturing firms including the well known Sklar-Pepplar furniture makers. The Canadian Manufacturers' Association feels that, contrary to government pronouncements that these firms are simply victims of economic restructuring, industry may soon tailspin into "triple-dip" recession (if it has not already), predicting that it is possible that more than 1,000 manufacturers will close their doors during 1992.[63] While interest rates have fallen substantially over the past year, this has not brought the necessary relief to provide business owners with choices regarding their futures. As unemployment soars there are few customers buying big ticket items, and despite the fall in interest rates, mortgage rates remain relatively unaffected with five-year terms still pegged at 9 1/2% when the prime has been set at record lows for the past two decades. Interest rates on most credit cards still remain at 18 to 21% (and in some cases more).

Dependence on welfare is another indicator of the economic well-being or ill health of a nation. Welfare is for many the net between homefulness and homelessness. In Ontario, Canada's largest and wealthiest province, 13.9% of its citizens were dependent on welfare by June of 1991. Comparatively, during the 1981-82 recession the rate for those on welfare was only 5%. In June of 1989, that rate was only 6.8%.[64] In fact, in Canada only New Brunswick has a higher proportion of its population on welfare, some 10.1%.[65] By February of 1992 1,151,000 people in Ontario received welfare assistance compared to 644,100 only two years previously.[66] Again, if any trend is consistent with economic developments in the 1990s it is the slipping of greater numbers of low- and middle-income families into the ranks of the poor and impoverished across the country. Another disturbing trend is the manner in which the rich in Canada have fared increasingly better during this period while increasing numbers of Canadians form lines at food banks in order to eat each month.

Across the country those who are on social assistance make up an increasing percentage of the population. In June of 1991 the following figures were released from Statistics Canada that show this trend. As a percentage of the total population the rates were: Newfoundland (9.1%); P.E.I. (8%); Nova Scotia (9.4%); New Brunswick (10.1%); Quebec (8.9%); Ontario (9.7%); Manitoba (6.5%); Saskatchewan (5.5%); Alberta (6.4%); British Columbia (7.0%); The Yukon (4.5%); and The Northwest Territories (18.5%).[67]

Municipal governments are faced with declining revenues as unemployment rapidly rises, businesses fold, and lower interest rates bring them a lower margin of return on investment. Budget cuts coupled with tax increases that outstrip wage rises are now beginning to target massive welfare programs at the federal, provincial and municipal levels as governments struggle with growing deficits. The federal government chopped its budget to provide adequate housing by $150 million over the last four years at precisely the time when the mayors of Canada's sixteen major cities called for a renewed commitment at the federal level to subsidized housing.[68] The response of the Federal Minister of Housing was to suggest that the mayors devise "solutions which don't involve money. We can't just throw money at a problem like this and hope it will go away."[69] That, in the case of all levels of government, has not become a problem to date! In December of 1991 the province of Ontario cut a variety of services to welfare recipients that particularly affected single mothers and the disabled, the two most vulnerable groups amongst welfare recipients.[70] Wheelchairs, colostomy bags, artificial limbs, oxygen tanks and children's summer camps were cut from the welfare budget. In fact the Metropolitan Toronto City Council voted in April 1992 to cut a variety of 'non-emergency' items from its general welfare budget.[71] The items cut included: Christmas allowance, non-emergency dental care, beds, bedding, and last month rent deposits. Without the latter allowance it is impossible to rent accommodation in the Toronto area and so more are added to the list of the homeless by this type of policy. The conclusion of scientific studies on the effects of welfare on children is clear: childrens' life chances are severely diminished when their families become dependent on welfare. They suffer from increased risks to health (both physical and mental), achieve lower educational standards, and develop behavioural problems at a rate far greater than that amongst children of non-welfare-dependent parents. To this must be added the dangers of living in areas that are more crime intensive, where drugs are dealt and used in the neighbourhood, where violence is seen as an acceptable means of conflict resolution and where there are few avenues to success that open to the future. As one homeless mother I interviewed lamented, the temptations of a life of crime are often difficult to resist for teens subsisting on welfare: "My son was fourteen and they caught him dealing crack. He was making $400 a night. I told him, 'You've got to get an education and get out of this crime.' He turned to me and said, 'What job am I ever gonna get that pays $400 a night?'"

Finally, an old phenomenon renewed provides a window on the depth of the economic woes of the country, foodbanks. While Canadians who lived throughout the Great Depression of the 1930s are familiar with the sight of line-ups for soup kitchens, the foodbank, as a social institution, has reached a level of usage that disturbs those who manage their resources. While food banks began as a stopgap measure in the early 1980s, by the end of the decade they had become a needed source of sustenance for hundreds of thousands of Canadians each month.[72] Foodbanks exist in every major city in the country with the total number at some 1,100 institutions. In Metropolitan Toronto, 120,000 people of which 51,000 are children depend upon the foodbank each month to eat. Foodbank usage is estimated to have jumped some 50% over 1991 levels across the country, as more join the ranks of the unemployed and exhaust their financial and familial resources.[73] Even on university campuses throughout Canada foodbanks have become common as students attempt to make fewer dollars stretch across their school year.[74] There are clear signs though that the ability and will of the community to provide the necessary food to keep the banks operational is waning. In 1992 foodbank drives continue to fall short of their expected goals by ever-increasing margins.

In the remainder of this chapter I present the life histories of three women and their children to illustrate several predominate themes in the process of becoming and being homeless.

Women, Children and Homelessness

Sally is a 29-year-old woman who is living with her eight-year-old son Sean in the Toronto motels program. She is extremely overweight, the result not of a generous diet but rather of poor nutrition. Her childhood was not a happy one, "Well, my mom and dad separated but it was for the best. They fought too much and my

Dad raised myself and all my brothers." Sally and her four brothers did not do well in school. Sally received a grade 10 education before dropping out and was married at 19 to another high school dropout. She was married for five years in a relationship she describes as "good, real good." Eventually the relationship began to fall apart when she moved up to a home they purchased in a rural area while her husband stayed behind in Toronto commuting up on the weekends. "My husband was a very good provider . . . he made $600 a week and our mortgage was only $300." Sally did not work during the marriage, "My husband never wanted me to work; he wanted me to stay home and raise our son because he, uh, he didn't have a good childhood himself, and his mom was never home, too busy runnin' around and his parents were split up so he said, 'I want our son to have a good home life.' He worked for a construction company and was a boss, a foreman."

By the time I interviewed Sally she had been separated from her husband for five years. She describes the events leading up to her "kicking him out" in the following way, "Well we decided to move up north so he was stayin' down here with my mom; she never charged him nothin' and then it got to the point that he wasn't comin' home on weekends at all. It got to the point where Sean and I would be up north alone but he'd wire the money up. He wouldn't be home for three months at a time. Then I found out he was running around with my cousin so...my best cousin... my favourite cousin. Oh we were close, real close. We more or less treated her as our own sister. I just asked him one night he came home and I said to him, I says, 'Are you, is it true you're foolin' around with my cousin?' He says, 'Sally' he says, 'It is true.' So I just says, I threw his dinner in the garbage and I said, 'Get out.' But he didn't think that I was really serious until I threw most of his clothes in the yard there. On our marriage day I told him, I said to him right before I said 'I do' I said, 'If you ever fool around I'll leave you even if it's once . . . I did.'"

Sally was not without resources. She sold her home and had $65,000 profit to her credit. However, by this time she was living with another man, a native Canadian who promised to build her and her son a home on his reserve in the country that she and her son liked living in. "I didn't want no guy but then he stopped his support payments ($300 a month) because he met another girl. Then I met this native guy and it was . . . that was the nightmare. I lost my home. Well, uh, he promised me he said, Sally lets move up north to his reserve. He was good to me. But my friends and family were tellin' me Sally he's no good, he's an alcoholic and I wouldn't, I don't know, I was just so stupid I wouldn't believe it. Yet I would see him drinkin' eh, every day.

He could drink, uhm, a twenty-sixer and then some. It didn't matter to him. He'd pick up a two-four (of beer) drink it then pass out or whatever but then he told me to sell the home, this was in the middle of winter. He said, We'll go further up north to his reserve. So I sold the home.

Sally moved to an apartment in Toronto with her son and her boyfriend where she began to pay $1,150 a month for an apartment, living on the profits from her house. She describes in a few words how she lost her money, "I gave it all to him." Sally continued, "I bought myself and Sean a few things, not expensive. He wanted a pool table, a $4,000 pool table. I said, 'I need this to buy a house up north.' He said, 'Don't worry, don't worry. I'm getting you a house.' His demands for money accelerated, 'Sally go the bank and get me two grand out. Buy me a car.' I just spent the money on him. It went down, down, down. Then when I came to the last twenty thousand, I said to him, 'Phil, when are we going to get this house?' 'Don't worry about it' he said. I told him, 'This has got to stop, I'm goin' down hill.' Eventually Phil got an application for a home site from his reserve but didn't bother to send it back. Sally confronted him, I said to him, 'Phil you always told me you were gonna pay me back. You don't pay me back a dime.' I lost everything and I blame myself. It was my own fault. I was blind. Within four months all of her savings were gone. 'Then I was broke. I got in touch with welfare. Welfare would just cover the rent, that's because it was expensive rent and I think I only had like $50 left over. So I lost the place.' Sally was able to find a home to rent in the suburbs. The effects on her were profound but were even more pronounced on her child. 'Sean, my son, suffered a lot through this, like his grades have gone way down.' I said to Sean, 'I'll get you another house.' He's not used to this. So I got another house, but I couldn't again afford the rent. I'd only have $125 left over, and for a job, it was so hard to get job. I don't know how many applications I filled out and then here I am. I said to the landlord, 'I'm not gonna see my son starve, my son comes first, even before me.'"

Sally and her son moved in with her mother. "But my mom's got boarders, too many actually, she's overcrowded, and then also she's getting put into a one bedroom. See she's not supposed to have anyone living with her where she is so I had to come here. It's a public housing apartment."

Life in the motel is hard for both Sally and her son. "He just hates it. He's not used to living like this. My son always had the best of everything, now from the best of everything he's got nothing, he's got nothing." Living in a crowded motel room has had more serious effects on Sean's behaviour. "My son was so well behaved before. I'd just tell him to do something and he'd do it. Now if I ask Sean to do something he gets mad, upset, or 'Why do I have to do it? Why don't you do it?' or stuff like that and he'd never been like that and my friends even said to me they noticed a change in Sean since all this happened. Sean feels the sense of difference from his classmates, "Like he says to me, 'Mom, all my friends go to a home, like they go home. I have to come back to this motel every night.' He hates it."

Sally describes the living conditions in the motel room as "very cramped" partially because she has entered a survival relationship with another native man who lives with her and her son in the room. The room is a 12 by 12 typical motel room with an extra single bed for her son. Sean is also exposed to various forms of deviant behaviour in the motel concourse including wife abuse, violence and the two most commonly reported problems, prostitution and drug abuse. "Sean sees it too and that's why I'm really upset. Sean said to me, 'Mom, that's a hooker.' He sees it all the time. I mean you go out here on the street and you see all kinds of girls and that you know, and he sees that." Sean has friends at the motel, "but then they come and go," explains Sally.

Sally has only one friend left that she sees on occasion. Her friend upset her with her observations on her decline into homelessness, "Sally you know at one time you were young and you had all this, you were young. You had more than all of us, all of our friends put together. Now look at you. Now you got nothin!"

Sally gets $17.50 a day for food. "We manage. I always make sure Sean has, like I just won't go out and buy . . . like I'll even do without. There's like two slices of luncheon meat left I'm gonna give it to my son before I give it to myself. I always make sure Sean has his supper regardless. Like daily I have to go shoppin' daily." Sally often goes without food during the day so her son will have enough to eat. Even the food she can buy is of questionable nutritional value. Few homeless families can afford to buy fruit or vegetables and so survive on the staples of most poor families in Canada: pasta, canned foods, sandwiches, hot dogs, powdered milk and hamburger. Local supermarkets do not help matters for as Theodore Caplovitz pointed out many years ago, the poor pay **more**. Take a sign posted in 1991 on a Windsor A&P store. It stated that persons cashing social assistance cheques to pay for goods must take 10% as 'gift certificates.' Local merchants are aware that poor people do not have any choice in where they shop. They do not have the means to transport themselves and their children, and so are forced to shop close to their motel rooms. Like 'convenience' stores these merchants artificially inflate the price of their goods so further limiting the choice that the homeless have in terms of food varieties.

Sally is concerned about their life in the motel. "This is no place for a child at all," she told me. "There's prostitutes. I hear a lot of fights." Sean is frightened by the constant fighting of the neighbours. "Sometimes he says, 'Mom, he says, one of these days like his fist is gonna come through our wall because when he gets mad he always hits our wall at two in the morning.'" Sally 'lost everything' and the only possessions that she and her son retain are their clothes and "things of my son's that are sentimental like you know stuff that he had when he was in kindergarten. I keep everything of Sean's everything, baby pictures and stuff like that. I sold everything."

Sally suffers from periodic depressions but tries to put on a brave face for her son, "Everytime I look at Sean I think no, I can't let myself get down or this kid's even gonna suffer more. This kid's seen more in his eight years. At his age I'd never seen half of this. I look at myself and Sean and I think at eight years old I'd had no worries." Sally maintains that her mother's leaving the family when she was five had no effect on her although this is unlikely, "My mother it didn't bother me that she left." Sally feels sorry for her son. She and her son depend on Goodwill stores for secondhand clothes. "You only get $17.50 and if Sean needs a pair of shoes or boots, well I got him a pair of boots for $4 over there and a jacket." These purchases even further deplete their food budget as Sally explained, "I had to say, 'Well Sean you need your winter coat, your winter boots so like no I can't buy this kind of meat or no I can't buy jam 'cause we need that for your winter boots.'" When Sally bought the coat her son complained, "He said 'Mommy this smells,' and it did. It smelt like puke and it did. So I really had to wash it three times." Sally has only used a food bank once but it was not a pleasant experience for her. "It was my fault, but I had to bring Sean down there. I couldn't leave him in the motel alone. I brought him down there and Sean just looked at me like he was disgusted in me, for the first time I really saw disgust in that kid's face. I didn't say anything to him 'cause I knew exactly how he was feeling."

Sally spends her day cleaning the room, or looking through the paper for jobs. In the evening she and her son go for walks, when the weather is good, to pass the time. As the reader has discovered, in common with many other women who fall into the cycle of poverty and homelessness, Sally has accepted the attitude of social workers, friends and others that it is **her** failings that have made her homeless. Like battered women who blame themselves for their own victimization, Sally is herself a victim of society's labelling of the out-of-role behaviour of women as "deviant."

Battered But Not Beaten

Family violence according to a variety of sociological researchers in Canada is pervasive, cutting across socioeconomic boundaries. Violence against women takes many forms from child abuse through spouse abuse through to sexual assault. In all of these forms of violence the relationship of women to men, and particularly our patriarchal society, provides a framework for the subjugation and victimization of women. Battered women are forming an ever-increasing number of our homeless population. Some use shelters as a temporary means of escaping violence and regrouping for self-sufficency.[75] Programs for these women are often seen as transitional from a status of financial dependency towards independent self-hood. A significant number of these women however have neither the educational skills or history to enter the workforce easily. Many require lifeskills training, education in languages, or skills upgrading in order to find and keep employment. Though the majority of women desire employment in terms of the self-sufficiency, status, and independence from welfare dependency it brings when children are with the woman, this generally proves to be an impossible goal to attain. When a woman has more than one child to provide for, and they are not of school age, the difficulties become insurmountable. Daycare arrangements often are so expensive that they would effectively reduce the family income of women to a point below social assistance payments that are, in themselves, insufficient to cover living expenses. So women become caught in the Catch-22 of homelessness. Their unwillingness to consider work options is seen as a sign of laziness while they are criticized at the same time for remaining dependent on various forms of assistance.

Martha exemplifies the problems that confront battered mothers who must seek refuge from the men in their lives. A thirty-three-year-old woman, she has resided in Canada for nineteen years. She was married for ten years and has two children, a five-year-old boy and a seven-year-old girl. Martha and her husband had enjoyed a marriage that was relatively free from either arguments or problems. They had their 'ups and downs' but nothing out of the ordinary. A year previously her husband, who had worked steadily as a carpenter, had suddenly stopped working and spent long days doing nothing. Six months before she became homeless another significant event in their lives changed the nature of their relationship. "My husband's sister passed away earlier this year and he became very depressed. There was no . . . everything was blamed on me. We couldn't even enjoy a good day because his sister was dead. If I didn't go to the cemetery disgrace, a bad wife and no respect for his family and everything became so tangled up with the death he wasn't livin' a real life he was just relating everything to his brother and then he became abusive. He hurt me physically and mentally and it came to the point that he was threatening me, and giving my death into detail. Like I had three ways that I was gonna die."

Martha endured beatings from her husband for over half a year. Her husband's sister had not been close to her husband before her death, but after the funeral her husband's behaviour became even more bizarre. "We had to have a big picture of his sister blown up to have in our house with flowers next to it. He would talk to his sister to the picture and he wanted the children to kiss the picture every day. I thought that was abnormal. He would go out to our balcony windows and scream for his sister 'Please come and help me, come and help me I can't live anymore.' Previous to the death they hated each other, they fought constantly. He was never close to her."

The behaviour that finally forced Martha to flee with her children to shelter was a threat against her life. "I left on the Wednesday. On the Monday he picked them up from school and told them I was dead and I wasn't aware of that. The whole night he kept telling them he was going to go to Florida with them. On Tuesday he did the same thing but into more detail with them." Martha took his threats seriously: "I guess I could only figure out that I was trying my best to pretend that everything was going to be okay and that I could manage on my own saying that I could put up with this, you don't give up. I have very strong religious beliefs and I didn't want to leave my home. But then when I drove the children to school and they cried and hung onto my neck and said they don't wanna go 'cause I wouldn't be there after school for them 'cause I'll be dead, and that really put the knife through my heart. My son even asked me if I'll remember them after I was dead. He couldn't come to my funeral because they'll be going to Florida."

Martha had sought counselling after the death of her husband's sister but her husband refused, a common theme with most women in crisis as men see counselling as an admission of weakness. "I tried to persuade him to go for counselling together for so long and he would always put it off. He said only crazy people go to that. So I went on my own, and I never told him because I was afraid too 'cause I knew he would stop that 'cause he had told me that once he knew I would go for counselling and tell them all sorts of lies that we would be through." Her husband began to control all aspects of her interaction with the outside world attempting to isolate her further in the home: "I couldn't phone anybody 'cause he would get on the other side of the phone and wanted to know what was going on and then he would finish the conversations without telling me. He says, 'Okay fine, I'll take it from here.' He used to call me names all the time. The worst things on earth. He always said that I was a bad mother."

Martha had held a job for ten years at a hospital before the birth of her children and had worked herself up through increasingly responsible jobs. "I worked very hard to get to that position. I knew everybody in the hospital including doctors. He hated the attention that I was getting at the hospital. So when I had the two children I finally had to quit because it was too expensive to go back to work. All of a sudden you're just like bang-bang with these two children at home twenty-four hours, gettin' up in the middle of the nights. You know everything was all mixed up all of sudden but I was still doing it. And if I got upset at night and said you wanna go out or do something, 'lets go for a drive,' he'd get very upset because he was tired from work and I was askin' too much of him." He also 'didn't like the idea' of her escaping from the house to mothers and tots or volunteering at the local school.

Soon her husband began a pattern of physical abuse. "He choked me and he loved to grab me by my shoulders and my neck and throw me against walls. He would do this in front of the kids too and my daughter would be in between us." Her husband did not want her to seek employment as a teacher's aide despite job offers from friends in the schools. "I just love being with the kids. My husband hated that because he said, 'You have to get dressed up. You're gonna be talkin' to all the male teachers and the principals and you're gonna be flirting with them.' He hated that." When Martha tried to earn an income to prevent having to collect welfare her husband objected, "I was going for interviews just before I left because my husband was just sitting at home, sleeping, watchin' Oprah and Donahue and everything. He would just lie on the couch all day long and just wait for me to come home and start arguing with me." Her husband at the same time refused to look for work, "Why should I work, he would say, just to give you money?"

Her husband refused to look for work. When she arrived at the shelter her parents tried to help but were victims of the economic recession themselves. "On the weekends they bring me canned goods and things like that. My father worked nineteen years in the same company, now they closed the doors. He's out of work. He's fifty-six. There's nothing. He's just waiting around."

The children mirrored the father's behaviour during the first few weeks in the shelter. "They were very agitated. They would be hitting each other. They'd be doing things that my husband and I were doing. Talking to each other exactly. My daughter was using the same words and that used to make me cry inside."

Martha still lives in fear of her husband. She has only let her parents know where she is staying. "He might really hurt me," she explained.

Giving up Your Children

For some homeless women the escape from male violence does not end with their impoverishment in the limbo of shelter life. Jan and Jim are both twenty years of age. When I interviewed them they brought Jan's five-year-old daughter to the interview, a seemingly happy, bright child. Jan looks much younger than her 20 years and has the physical appearance of a teenager. Her interactions are punctuated by expressions common to adolescent culture. She was dressed in a white shirt and jeans and had long black hair. Her 'boyfriend' was similarly dressed but looked drawn and tired. Underneath his eyes large black marks, signs of fatigue and malnourishment, punctuated his face. His posture in the chair was one of someone who was extremely tired and his speech was slow as though it required some effort to speak. Jan on the other hand was very eager to be interviewed and smiled throughout.

Jan left home at the age of fifteen because of her pregnancy and began to live common-law with a male friend. Her daughter Kate was born early in this relationship and the girl's father left soon thereafter. Jan then entered into another common-law relationship which produced identical twin boys who are two years old. Jan and Jim have lived together for two years. Both have Grade 10 educations. Jan has never worked since leaving home and has survived exclusively on social welfare support. They became homeless in the fall of 1991, the first time either of them had been without shelter in their lives. They had been living in a basement apartment in the home where Jim's mother rented the first floor until she asked them to leave following a 'big argument'. "We got into an argument, a heated argument and we just left. The police were involved and they told us, for the benefit of the kids, because especially for her, they've been around some major violence. So when my mom started freakin' out, she's addicted to prescription drugs, so she got a little haywire and she called the police and the police came. The police said we could have stayed, but it wasn't safe for us to do. Like I paid my own rent, me and her, like we have our own rent receipts and everything. We were entitled to stay." They paid a rent of $600 a month and both were receiving social assistance, Jan's family benefits and Jim's welfare. They received $17 a day for food.

When they first moved out of their basement apartment they were not aware of the motels program, but found themselves in one of the motels used to house the homeless along with regular paying customers. "Originally in the beginning of October we went to the Lido. We had a little bit of money. We pawned our T.V. off to a friend of ours and we stayed as long as could around in motels because we didn't know of any place we could go. Then we found out about this place and then we phoned them. We were stranded in a restaurant for like four hours tryin' to find a place to stay and uhm we phoned them and they said we'd have to get the police that came to the incident at the house to phone them and all this stuff. Finally we were able to come. We just showed up here and they sent us to a motel over here."

For the past year Jan and Jim have been involved in a complicated battle with Jan's "ex" over custody of the children. This resulted in a series of kidnappings of various of the children several times by Jan's "ex" and by Jim to retrieve them. The expulsion of Jan and Jim from their apartment was also related to this ongoing battle. "There was an ongoing court case for around a year-and-a-half or so. He had the twins. The only time he's ever let the twins out of his sight is just before we came to the Lido. He phoned her up and said that he had a bad headache. He thought he was gonna hurt the kids 'cause he couldn't get an aspirin and he has no money and this and that, the whiney sort. So we went and picked up one of the twins and the other one had already been sent to his ex-girlfriend's and he told us to pick him up the next day. The night we picked up the one twin was the night my mother freaked out."

Jan's "ex" wanted custody of the twins according to Jan so that he could collect increased welfare benefits. "He got another girlfriend after we split up. She got pregnant and had his child and then she was looking after the twins. He just had the income 'cause in Ontario the welfare comes in the man's name so he just collected the cheques and she just lived there with my kids and then she had her baby and she took her baby and she left him. So now he's there by himself with the twins." Jan's "ex" showed up at the motel in the early morning hours to retrieve the boy. It was the third occasion on which he had kidnapped the child. The police did not respond to her call for almost an hour: "One cruiser showed up and they didn't do nothing. So I said, How come he can come here and kick in the door and take the children from a sleeping bed at quarter to midnight and you guys aren't going to do nothing?'" Jan was told that because she did not have a custody order there was nothing that could be done. Assuming that this was also true of her husband, Jan, Jim and some other members of the motel community went to Jan's "ex's" house to retrieve the children the next day. The police told Jim he could not be charged. "I went down the next day with a couple of friends, he opened the door, I pushed the door open, I grabbed the kid, handed one to her, she walked to the car, I had the other kid in my arms. I started walkin' off the porch, the guy tackles me and wipes me out on the cement. The two-year-old kid smashes his head on the concrete. I got the other kid in the car, he grabs the other kid and runs into a neighbour's house. We got in the car and started driving back. We were three doors away from here and we got surrounded by about 25 police cars and they held me for a month on an assault charge. They gave me $2,000 bail the day after they charged me, and I don't have any family except my mom so I ended up doing thirty days in the detention centre and they dropped the charges."

While Jim was in detention Jan's "ex" showed up once again at the motel, this time with the police to serve an interim custody order without notice. "He went to court and got custody of Kate and I was even't notified. The police are there. They're ready to arrest me but there's no way I'm gonna hand her over. She's sobbing, she's clinging to me and he's standing out front smirking away, thinking 'ha ha ha, I got ya.' But then I phoned him later on that night to make sure she's arrived there and he gets on the phone and tells me how he's doing this to hurt me." After 11 days she was able to go court: "As soon as the judge found out this was a government program and I wasn't staying in 'a Lido motel' he awarded me interim custody of Kate." Although she was also awarded visiting rights for the twins her husband did not comply with the court order. Soon tired of battling her "ex" she gave up custody of the twins to her husband. Survival as a homeless family has meant that two of her children have been lost to Jan.

You Can't Afford to Live Here Anymore

Another factor that has made a significant contribution to the increasing number of homeless in our society is the spiralling cost of housing in Canada. One of the primary causes of homelessness is the economic development trends that have surfaced within our urban centres. Research has clearly demonstrated that the number of households in Canada that pay over 30% of their income in rent has increased dramatically in the 1980s and 1990s.[76] In fact, government statistics show that between 1976 and 1981, 23% of households were in this category, while by 1985 this number had risen to 27.8% of all households. In large cities, welfare recipients find that the situation is intolerable and that the thirty percent figure is often grossly exceeded.[77] Some, according to research, pay 64% of their allowances on housing each month. One homeless man I met who was begging for food on a street corner in Vancouver typified this unacceptable state of affairs. "After paying for my rent I've got about $50 a month for food, so I have to use the food banks or beg here each day to eat." A study conducted in 1984 that examined women renters found that some 38% of female renters exceeded the 30% mark in their rent bills. Further evidence of the feminization of poverty, if any was needed, was provided by a 1985 Canada Mortgage and Housing Report which revealed that fully 40% of families headed by a single female lived in housing that was crowded and/or in need of serious maintenance, and/or cost more than 30% of their income.[78]

Throughout the 1980s another disturbing trend evolved in Canadian cities, the process now termed gentrification.[79] This process involves the renovation of inner city housing stocks in the downtown core, or zone of transition as Burgess referred to it. This is an area immediately adjacent to the downtown core that would have been composed, until the mid-1970s, of a variety of old housing stock in poor and deteriorating condition given over to low income families, boarding houses, and some commercial uses. During the latter half of the 1970s there was a movement of middle- and high-income families into this core area, and the remaking of deteriorating inner-city neighbourhoods began a gradual, then accelerated pace of change. These areas in Canadian cities like Montreal, Vancouver, Halifax and Toronto have undergone a process of transformation into middle-class enclaves. There is a variety of examples that one can cite across the country: Toronto's Cabbagetown, Centretown in Ottawa, Halifax's South End; Mount Royal in Montreal, and Kitsilano in Vancouver. This development has not been restricted to the Canadian scene for similar developments can be easily located in the Lewisham and New Cross Gate areas of London, England, in various cities across the United States and in a number of the countries of the European Economic Community. The process then is not specific to Canada, and this suggests that there are larger social and economic forces at work in this development.[80]

There are certainly some positive aspects of inner city restructuring: (1) the renovation process preserves traditional housing stocks and heritage housing; (2) renovated properties provide a source of tax revenue for city councils; (3) there are spin-off effects that are felt in the downtown areas in terms of revitalization of businesses, and a reversion to pedestrian and people-centred streets. However, the major drawback of these developments is that they remove low cost housing from the housing market in the core area of the city that provides accessible services for low-income individuals and families. There are a number of feasible explanations of gentrification that have been developed by housing and social analysts. Two central features are:

1. Drastic increases in housing demand as a result of the baby boom of the post-war era and the decline in average household size. Between 1976 and 1986 the overall number of Canadian households increased by 29 percent, there was a 38% increase in the number of households with heads 25-34 years of age; and a 47% increase in households headed by those aged 35-44. During this same period the total population of the country increased only 11%.[8]

2. There are a number of social trends which have impacted to increase the demand for these forms of housing. As Marlene Mackie, a noted sociologist has pointed out, these include: a substantial increase in Canadians who do not marry; increases in the average age at which both males and females do marry; increased divorce rates that create housing demands; and decreases in the number of children couples are having within both traditional and new forms of relationships.[82] This type of family unit has shown a demonstrated preference for inner-city housing, which they are in a position to afford given dual income earning power. The inner city is a place devoid of the sterility of suburban living now associated with seniors, immigrant populations and commuting problems. Disparate groups including gays, artists, students, political activists, and those who preferred a cosmopolitan lifestyle compete for space in the downtown core. As George Fallis has pointed out, gentrification reflects the shift that has occurred within urban economic arrangements as manufacturing jobs have been replaced by service and a variety of managerial, professional, administrative and technical forms of employment that cluster in the downtown area.[83]

There are a number of factors associated with gentrification that directly contribute to the production of homelessness. We have already found that low rental housing disappears rapidly in the face of renovation and renewal. This means that rooming houses that were capable of providing rooms for a dozen people or more suddenly are converted into space that is occupied by one or two individuals. Landlords and property owners are motivated in this process to attempt to convert aging apartment buildings and hotel properties into condominiums for sale at staggering profits or to renovate once affordable apartments into units that are only affordable to the wealthy in society.

The extent of the loss can be readily appreciated when a review of Canadian studies of the housing market is reviewed. In the City of Toronto between 1975 and 1985 the number of private rental units declined by 11,000, with the majority of this loss accounted for by low-cost housing and rental units in core areas of the city.[84] Between 1982 and 1986 **The Ontario Task Force on Roomers, Boarders and Lodgers** estimated that 1,700 rooming houses were lost each year to demolition or conversion.[85] In Ottawa the loss was even greater as 40 percent of the rooming house units disappeared between the years of 1976 and 1979.[86] These losses were largely confined to the Centretown and Sandy Hill areas of the city. But when one considers that this occurred only at the onset of the gentrification process, one can estimate that this loss has accelerated appreciably in the past decade-and-a-half. Finally, the city of Vancouver provides one of the more startling examples of this decline, moved not only by the forces of renovation but, as I discussed in an earlier chapter, by the push to displace low-income persons from hotels where they were permanently lodged, to accommodate tourists for Expo. During the years 1973 to 1976, a collection of inner city neighbourhoods lost over 2400 rental units, which accelerated to a rate of 1,000 units per year during the 1976 to 1981 period.[87] Ley informs us that from 1976 to 1981 there was a pronounced elimination of low rental residential hotels from Vancouver's zone of transition effectively reducing the number from 1200 to 450.[88]

In Calgary the vacancy rate reflects that of most of our other urban centres. The effective vacancy rate during the latter half of the 1980s and early 1990s was a mere 1%. Athough considered in isolation this is a major contributor to homelessness, one must also weigh in two additional factors, soaring rents and the cost of real estate, which has experienced a steady rise through the past decade. These factors have all made a substantial contribution to the rising rate of homelessness in Calgary, and on the prairies generally. A 1990 report that received input from 36 agencies estimates that there are, at a minimum, 7,000 Calgarians with no 'fixed address' and this number is growing at an alarming rate.[89]

Seniors are a specific group in our society that are being hit hard by the disappearing stock of affordable housing. The Council of Aging in the Ottawa-Carleton area recently carried out a study that concluded that there was a lack of affordable housing for seniors in their catchment area.[90] Women seniors, as we might expect given the discussion in this chapter, were the most likely victims of this shortage, particularly those who had incomes in the $10,000 to $30,000 range. Examining data from the 1986 census the Council found that 83% of the elderly population in Ontario is composed of women seniors over the age of 65, and further that 85% of these women live in rented rather than owned accommodation. This reflects our earlier analysis of the feminization of poverty which mirrors womens' limited time spent in the full-time work force during the past four decades and their subsequent lack of private pension incomes from employment sources.[91]

The rise in rents during the 1980s was not only unprecedented but accelerated at a rate unheard of in previous decades. In Toronto, for example, rents increased some $562 for a three-bedroom apartment in 1984 to $738 in 1988, or roughly a 32% increase.[92] However, most apartments were renting for well above this as demand outstripped supply, and landlords exceeded rent control increases in a variety of ways. "Finders fees" of several thousand dollars were not uncommon for quality apartments as renters struggled to find good accommodation that was in severely limited supply. This practice though illegal became part of the standard practice of renting for several years and still continues today. In St. John, rents for a similar apartment increased from $342 to $427 a month, a rise of 24.8%.[93]

What has been the extent of federal investment in affordable housing during this time of increasing crisis? It is reliably estimated that since the mid-1970s successive federal governments have spent a total of $5 billion to support the construction of rental housing. During 1982 and 1983 it initiated programs to support first-time home-buyers through grant programs that cost $1.5 billion. However, in 1984 the government's expenditures in the area of direct housing were a mere $942 million.[94] Its own research was a direct comment on the gravity of the situation and on its own unwillingness to address the area of homelessness. In one 1985 consultation paper it was discovered that there were in excess of 500,000 rental households that were not living in adequate accommodation, that is, that was physically adequate for their needs and uncrowded.[95] A further

200,000 persons who were homeowners were in serious difficulties in terms of being able to afford their houses. It was during this period, of course, that thousands of Albertans walked away from their homes, selling their rights in their properties to "dollar dealers" who paid them $1 dollar for their homes and then rented them until foreclosure proceedings were finalized and the house was seized.[96] Government estimates found that in all owned and rented properties that only 1.4% lacked basic facilities (running water, bathrooms, etc.) and 12.5% needed major repairs in order to bring them up to an acceptable livable standard.[97] All of these figures are estimates and therefore open to some scrutiny. I would suggest that given the other evidence on the decline of low income housing that we have already examined that these estimates are conservative accountings of the depth of the homelessness crisis in the mid-1980s. The full effects of this acceleration in the lack of affordable housing and the gentrification of our cities began to be fully felt in the 1990s. Combined with rising record unemployment across the country, declining incomes and standards of living, decreasing tax bases for the support of welfare programs, and lack of government investment, the full effect of the homelessness problem has only begun to be felt in the first two years of the 1990s. Given all the indicators these problems are not going to disappear in the near future. As Canada adjusts to "new global economic realities", the transformation of our work into service-based jobs, the effects of "Free Trade", and long-term unemployment for millions of Canadians, homelessness has not only assumed a central place in our societal social ills, but without a fundamental shift in the approaches we have assumed towards this problem it will become a problem without solution.

Greg Barak has argued that we can take one of two general societal approaches to homelessness. Either we can approach the homeless with understanding, working with them to find new alternatives to the present limitations on a variety of our fundamental economic and social policies, or we can continue to attack the homeless as different and undeserving, making them into deviants and criminals. This is a major juncture in our society that I argue will have far reaching ramifications for the type of society we **enjoy** or **endure** in the near future.

What is to be Done?

The Federal government in announcing a recent $500 million initiative for 'children at risk'[98] has acknowledged, if begrudgingly, the depth of the problem. The problem is that the terminology they are using waters down the problems faced by millions of our children. The federal government's actions in this regard are not only not beneficial but are patently patriarchal. These children, as the reader will have understood by this point, are not "at risk," they have been risked, and the futures they should have enjoyed, irrevocably damaged by the federal government's economic and social policies that have put them in this position in the first place.[99] As Sheila Copps commented in the House, "What good does it do to send out meal guidelines to mothers when they have no food to give their children?"[100] The image of Benoit Bouchard holding babies and giving out handouts, of funds that should have been available years ago to assure these personal tragedies should not have happened, reflects the attempt by all levels of government to deny responsibility for the production of the problems of homelessness, and to largely ignore them.

In the final chapter of the book we explore alternatives to our current societal approaches to homelessness analysing innovative policies and ideas in the areas of government spending and housing.

CHAPTER SIX

Ending Homelessness

I must be invisible,
No one knows me,
I have crawled down dead end streets,
On my hands and knees.

Cause I'm a lonely stranger here
Well beyond my days
And I don't know what's goin' on
I'll be on my way.

Some will say, that I'm no good,
Maybe I agree,
Take a look,
Then walk away,
That's alright with me.[1]

Helping the Homeless

Throughout this book the problem of homelessness in Canada has been examined through both the individual perspective of those who are suffering a homeless condition, and in a broader analysis of the societal forces that produce homelessness. The overwhelming majority of the homeless are not only deserving of renewed and redirected efforts to ameliorate their conditions of living in the short run, but of radical alternatives to eradicate homelessness for all but that small minority who cannot, or will not, be helped by our efforts. There are those who have lived through a variety of institutional identities, often for many years, who have become socialized to a life characterized by dependence, hopelessness, victimization on the street, and in some cases the pathology of drugs, alcohol abuse or mental illness. Whether it is the case of they have become accustomed to life in a shelter, or the street and its relative freedoms, they do not wish us to intervene in their lives and certainly this would not be conscionable. They will not be converted or corrected to either individual integration or some larger social purpose and will likely remain dependent upon society for survival throughout their lives. But these people we must remember only represent perhaps 3% of all our homeless.

In this chapter I explore various means by which we as a society can develop alternative ways of dealing with the homelessness crisis. Since the evidence presented in the book thus far underscores the failures of our current approaches I will attempt to consider ways in which homelessness can be eliminated or substantially ameliorated in Canada. To adopt this position is to suggest that homelessness is not a social crisis that we have to allow to continue to grow, that we have power both as individuals and as part of a larger society to address the core problems that act as a catalyst to homelessness. This is in itself a radical suggestion for it is contrary to a myriad of public and private interests that have a vested interest in the continuation of this devastating social problem.

Homelessness as a Social Enterprise

There is no doubt that unless the federal government tackles the problems that are directly contributing to homelessness—extreme and deepening poverty, acute shortages of housing and lack of employment opportunities—that homelessness will continue to flourish as a national disgrace. One of the central contradictions of homelessness, like criminality, is that we are quite content to provide shelters for the homeless, just as we are more than willing to build prisons for the criminal in our society. But one of the clear findings of research on charitable/social control institutions is simply that once they are built we have no problem in quickly filling them. Governments are able on one hand to ignore the problem of homeless teens selling themselves in order to survive, while providing millions for the building of shelters. Concomitantly, thousands of jobs have been created for college- and university-educated social workers to minister to the needs of the homeless. Homelessness, it can be unequivocally demonstrated, creates work for many care workers, welfare workers, street workers and other associated social tinkerers and control agents in our society. However, while we have no problem committing vast sums of monies to tackling the **problems** of the homelessness, it would be unthinkable simply to give the money to the homeless so that they could purchase long-term accommodation and to create jobs for them.

Our current approach places a disproportionate amount of our resources into the provision of short-term solutions for the homeless. While the provision of shelter spaces is vital, the transition to long-term residency must be a priority of not only the funding bodies at all levels of government, but of those working directly in the field. This has been the case in several notable examples. In Oshawa, the men's hostel was successful in renovating the second floor of their building to provide private apartments for a dozen long-term chronic homeless. In the supportive atmosphere that is engendered by the dignity and privacy of one's own home, many of the men have been able to escape lives that were once characterized by daily alcohol abuse. Their lives have been invested with meaning, and they have been given back their status as full-fledged citizens of our society.

Unfortunately we have been unable to the present to develop any long-term preventative programs for the prevention of homelessness. Taking teenagers as an example we find that that government funding agencies are quite eager to fund successions of studies dealing with street prostitution, runaways and children at risk. There are several excellent researchers, including John Lowman of Simon Fraser University, Livy Visano of York University, and Gus Brannigan of The University of Calgary, who have conducted first rate studies of street prostitution. We have had two commissions, The Fraser and Badgely Reports that contributed to our knowledge in this area in the 1980s. We have, in other words, an overabundance of information on 'children at risk.' Case workers with decades of experience can tell us that child abuse and neglect directly contribute to the majority of homeless runaways in our society. Yet, despite all of this work, we have to date, not been able to put a dent in the number of children who annually join the ranks of the homeless prostitutes in our society while others disappear into oblivion. Of what use is research that simply documents these same problems over and over as if something new was being discovered. The simple truth is we often have no idea how to intervene effectively in the lives of those who live on the margins of our society, or our ideas fall more within the realm of 'tinkering' rather than fundamental change.

The level of government apathy on this problem in Canada parallels that of the experience of the United States. It is often suggested that Canada lags behind the United States by several years in the development of social ills, and this certainly would appear to be the case with homelessness. While James Wright, amongst others, has informed us that homelessness began to assume the status of a major social problem during the 1970s, it was not until the 1980s that homelessness began to assume these dimensions in Canada. It was during this period, as we learned in the discussion in Chapter 5, that the effects of a shrinking housing supply and growing long-term unemployment began to be fully felt in Canada. Politicians have been largely reluctant to make public pronouncements concerning homelessness perhaps hoping, in the conservative attitude that often typifies Canada's approach to social ills, that somehow no one would notice that something was very amiss.

A quick review of newspaper articles over the 1980s and into the 1990s will reveal that few politicians have ventured an opinion on homelessness, other than to pronounce that it was not a serious problem, or to call on public-minded citizens, in an obscure way, to help fight homelessness in their community. These calls typically occur in the Christmas holiday season hoping to use guilt to motivate the citizenry into action. This too forms part of the long standing government attempts to make homelessness into issues of charity and volunteerism. In this approach the community is seen as having a form of never-ending capacity to absorb and ameliorate all kinds of personal and social problems. Some examples that Canadians will be familiar with are: (1) police promotion of community action against crime (drug pushers, prostitutes) since authorities are "powerless to do anything," and (2) government dumping of mentally ill patients into the community when hospitals were closed as the community would help them to regain their sanity. Incidentally, while the original idea was to transfer the hospital financial resources to the community this did not happen and so ex-patients were left to fend on their own, often provoking anger in the neighbourhoods they settled in.

Homelessness can certainly be milked as a political issue for it only requires that politicians show some concern for the plight of the impoverished rather than paying attention to the roots of the problem and without pledging concommitantly to act. In fact, it can be reasonably argued that the majority of our efforts have been largely confined to treating the symptoms of homelessness rather than its causes. Our political priorities are interesting to consider. Canada has little problem in finding billions to finance its participation in the 'Gulf war' and on defence spending, but this investment has meant that the pecuniary interests of the state have not been focussed on homelessness as a pressing social challenge.

Every cut that has been made by governments in the area of social welfare spending most certainly has a devastating impact on families, many of whom hover on the edge of homelessness and for whom such cuts mean a further descent into disintegration. While there seems to be no shortage of money for investment in advanced weaponry, there are correspondingly calls for reductions in social programs so that our spiralling national, provincial, and now, municipal debts will not grow further out of control.

If politicians seem immune or indifferent to the plight of the homeless then there are certainly lessons that one can take from this book in terms of changing not only our attitudes but our approaches to the homeless. First, we must move beyond simple toleration of the homeless to a a recognition that this is a problem that cannot be hidden in doorways, abandoned buildings and alleyways of our nation. Homelessness is a problem that is taking centre stage in our society. It is a problem that effects every aspect of our national and social life in this country. The legions of the homeless and pre-homeless, and those in living in poverty, number in the millions in Canada. While the homeless have remained largely invisible in our society, their numbers make it impossible to ignore them in the urban context. Most of us are already aware that the number of people on the street, begging, crying, in pain, destitute, hungry, homeless and out of work is growing each year. It is virtually impossible in any large metropolitan area to travel in the city without encountering the homeless. They are no longer concentrated in the downtown core, but have spread out throughout the cities, partly owing to the relocation of various forms of temporary shelter accommodation in the suburbs, and in some cases due to the efforts of the homeless to escape the violence, pressures and oversaturation of the downtown areas.

Our attitudes towards the homeless reflect our own ambivalence about their condition. Sometimes we feel inclined to give a beggar money, whereas when we are confronted every half block with demands for money we 'turn off' the person. We thus make them dependent on our charity rather than asking why they are there in the first place, and how far are we from their fate. Again, in my interviews with young homeless people, it was common for them to express complete surprise at their present condition, a fate that they had never dreamed could have befallen them. The problem with charity is that it not only has limits but is never freely given. Somehow we assuage our own guilt and admit our sense of powerlessness with homelessness when we give the homeless money. It is at this moment that one is most likely to understand that homelessness for the vast majority is a product of forces well beyond their own control.

Attacking homelessness effectively will involve a radical shift in our thinking. It must move beyond mere philosophizing on the problem to action. It must move beyond the traditional conceptions of social service provision for these are not adequate to meet the needs of the homeless. This is a form of poverty that we have never experienced before in this country, which not only cuts across social and economic boundaries, but includes a widely diverse population of individuals. The new homeless are single women, teens, mothers with children, families, fathers with children, the unemployed who cannot find work, the abused adolescent, senior citizens and the elderly, refugees and illegal aliens. Within traditional approaches to homelessness our efforts are bound to fail for they make an underlying assumption that the problem is a temporary one that requires only band-aid efforts over the short term. But as the economy fails to respond, unemployment grows, welfare rolls pass the million mark and our streets are flooded with the throwaway and cast-off people of our society. There is no end in sight, nor will there be one unless dramatic efforts are made.

Foodbanks and charitable organizations have begun to realize that their organizations have been used by successive governments as a way of avoiding responsibility for the homeless. Indeed, there has been a concentrated effort to seek further involvement by religious organizations in providing shelter and food for the homeless in the rising tide of homelessness. In Michigan, the kind of scenario that could easily be played out in Canada developed when the Governor, John Engler, severely cut welfare benefits in midwinter 1991. Suddenly thousands of welfare recipients were unable to make their rent payments and were turfed onto the streets. Church basements were quickly called into use to house the homeless as shelters were filled to overflowing by a rush of homeless people. The lesson to be learned from Michigan, and other states in the U.S., is that short-term solutions will eventually exhaust the economic coffers of society, and there will still be massive numbers of homeless, and those who are poised to become homeless as soon as benefits are cut or eliminated. Existing shelter arrangements are simply not sufficient under these conditions.

The degree of disdain with which our society holds homeless people is perhaps best illustrated by the fact that at the start of the last federal election homeless people, it was recognized, were being denied the right to vote. Until a church advocacy group brought the issue to the courts in the middle of the election campaign there was no movement on the part of our government to ensure that those with 'no fixed address' could vote in elections. This ultimate denial of access to the democratic process is reminiscent of the struggles of women much earlier in this century to obtain voter rights, for without this fundamental right homeless people have no input into decision-making in Canada. The fact that we are talking about the abrogation of such a fundamental right in 1990 and not 1890 is compelling evidence of our sustained attempt to render the homeless not only invisible but powerless.

In an earlier chapter I examined the numerous laws which circumscribe the lives of homeless people, including those dealing with begging, vagrancy, and welfare entitlements and it is these laws that will form the target for attacks by homeless people in the political process. The homeless in this country, as with their contemporaries in the United States, have to cope with trying to organize in a widely disparate group of individuals who have perhaps somewhat different political agendas. One of the starting points of this organization is likely to be amongst women who may find commonalities and support within the feminist movement towards social and economic emancipation. Attempts by the homeless to gain control over their lives are also hampered by the contradictions of political gestures by our governments' leaders at all levels that lament the problem of homelessness on one hand, while at the same time failing to deliver on new programs or substantive economic initiatives. President Bush, confronted at his inauguration by a protest of several thousand homeless, promised a 'kinder, gentler America' and then proceeded to cut social service budgets in line with state governments. The homeless are, in reality, at the mercy of the state and its offshoot agencies for with little voice in the political process, except that provided by poverty advocacy groups, they are unable to change the direction of political decisions in our country. When you consider that until 1991 they possessed no ability to influence the political process at all, except by their presence on city streets, it is no wonder that they have remained invisible! While there will be advocates of a conservative view of the homeless problem that will suggest that there are far fewer homeless in this country than I have suggested (in the face of estimates by direct care givers), the average Canadians ignorance of the plight of the homeless, and the depth that the problem has assumed in this country, is no accident. But no one commentator can deny the suffering of women and children who go hungry in our society, who go to bed hungry and would do so in greater numbers were it not for charity, and have been denied fundamental rights to decent housing, work and food by unresponsive government policies and social service delivery. Disenfranchised at the voting booth and without voice at the provincial or national levels they have been simply convenient to ignore. If we believe in the old adage that the squeaky wheel gets the grease then homelessness is about to sound a shrill cry across this country that will require extraordinary efforts to deal with.

The experience of homeless organizing in the U.S.A. has taught us that not only are the homeless capable of organizing but that they can become an effective voice for change over the conditions that impinge upon their lives. The political fight of the homeless in Canada for their basic rights has more than one foe. Aside from government indifference, neglect and outright hostility, they also face communities that oppose their existence in particular neighbourhoods. The recently gentrified neighbourhoods of our downtown spaces want the homeless removed from their space to improve the quality of their lives. The homeless, as I have suggested, are viewed as a threat to person and business, and therefore attempts to construct low-cost housing, group homes and alternative forms of accommodation are met with great public furor. Put simply, most neighbourhoods do not want to accept society's marginal populations into their midst. Proposals to build a shelter for young people in a suburban area of Scarborough, Ontario were met with outrage by the local homeowners and businesses. While many support the notion that something must be done to help, particularly, the young homeless, many see the issue strictly in terms of imagined falls in property values or view the homeless as dangerous felons with an appetite for trouble. The NIMBY or "not in my backyard" movement has been not only vocal but extremely hostile to the imposition of the deviant or marginal into their urban enclave. They view the homeless in the same way as former President Reagan who saw the homeless as being homeless "by choice." Two prominent Canadian analysts of the homeless problem, George Fallis and Alex Murray, have suggested that "homelessness is not so much evidence of people falling through the cracks as it is evidence of a society less willing to help."[2] Certainly this reflects the current understanding we have of the dynamics of homelessness, but it also reflects the lack of information about homelessness and its causes that the average Canadian has been subjected to.

The homeless are looking not for a handout as many of us might surmise, but a hand-up in society. The overwhelming majority of the homeless want to work, want to lead constructive lives and want to be a part of society, not apart from it. The homeless are faced with the problem of the incredible inertia in our service delivery system and of attempting to coerce substantive changes out of it.

Creative Alternatives to Homelessness

There are three levels of input that are central to the creation of viable alternatives to homelessness, particularly in the provision of affordable housing. There are: (1) the private sector, (2) third sector organizations, and (3) municipal governments. The private sector can and will respond to the need to build low-income housing if it is a profitable venture.

Government priorities have to be redirected towards partnerships that will make it viable to build, for example, mixed income condominium and apartment units that generate substantial numbers of housing units at a reasonable return on investment. The private sector can also be encouraged to lend expertise to the design of low-cost housing, and to take an active role in communities by tying construction contracts to the provision of low-income housing by developers.

Third sector organizations, which include churches, charitable groups, self-help groups, co-operatives and non-profit groups as well as numerous voluntary organizations, grow up in response to the expressed needs of those less fortunate in our communities. The contradiction for many of these groups is that traditionally they have relied rather heavily on the government for funding of their activities. One could cite amongst organizations that assist the homeless groups who help released prisoners (John Howard Societies and Elizabeth Fry groups); ex-psychiatric patients who have been de-institutionalized (The Canadian Mental Health Association); battered and abused women and children (shelters, rape crisis centres, hostels); the physically challenged (associations for the disabled); seniors (various seniors organizations); immigrants and refugees (settlement houses and cultural associations). Third sector groups other than non-profit housing groups have not been able to make serious inroads into the problem of homelessness as they are often run by well-meaning yet inexperienced amateurs and compete against one another for limited funding or private charitable donations. The contribution they make may be seen in their provision of some 8,000 beds nationwide. Overall, when one examines permanent housing units, "all social housing in Canada makes up about 3 percent of the national stock, and the approximately 60,000 co-operative housing units underwritten by CMHC are less than 1 percent." This is clearly not a serious effort to address the needs of the homeless in other than a very temporary way. The depth of our dependency on charitable organizations to provide a wide range of services to the community is staggering with over half of all the 47,000 charitable organizations being directed towards welfare related activities. Voluntary and charity organizations are being called upon by communities to fill the gaps that governments at all levels are leaving in the field of service provision in the welfare field, although as I have already pointed out, their ability to provide these services is declining in the face of ever-increasing need. United Way Agencies, for example, saw a real decline of 10 percent in their operating budgets between 1991 and 1992, at a time when demands are far outstripping their ability to provide service at a desirable level. This has also precipitated turf wars over not only who should provide services but which of the 'needy' are truly deserving of attention. Women's organizations have argued that treatment programs for male abusers should not be funded while there is a shortage of beds for battered women and children. These are obviously issues of ownership of the problem that will become more common as both government investment and private sector contribution to charitable groups dry up.

Nationally The Urban Core Support Network, which has operated since 1974, supports numerous types of information and strategies with local municipal residents' associations across the country. At present, there are currently eighteen "regional federations of housing co-operatives." The National Anti-Poverty Organization has provided arms-length leadership since 1970 and various forms of lobbying for improved housing to low-income groups. Certainly, national and local native groups such as The Assembly of First Nations and Native Friendship Centres, particularly in the Prairies, Toronto and Vancouver, have attempted to address the specific needs of native homeless through the establishment of hostel programs and counselling.

In Toronto, organizations like the Fred Victor Mission have been able to establish long-term small-scale residences for hard-to-house single men, converting shelter space into a long-term solution. Cityscape, a non-profit housing program, recently rented and converted a large downtown warehouse facility into a residence for 50 street people, which allows them to convert open space within the warehouse into personalized living space. This alternative that allows for personal choice and freedom is one that is favoured by its residents, but is only, once again, a short-term solution owing not only to the fact that the project is limited in its funding period, but the fact that warehouses of humanity do not pose more than a temporary, yet innovative, alternative to street living. Since 1986, housing programs have been relentlessly shifted to the provinces away from federal responsibility. This according to Wolfe has engendered long, possibly unlimited delays. In Halifax, for example, non-profit organizations had so few housing starts they could not be recorded in 1986-87. This development has had the effect, they argue, of closing down many community resource groups while causing other groups like the Cooperative Housing Federation to set targets of 5,000 units per year (a target that is not being reached). In the future it is likely that we will witness co-operative efforts between public/private/third-sector groups as has been the case in the U.S. and Britain. Other possible avenues for addressing long-term homelessness may lie in innovative schemes that require the acquisition of residential properties, low-cost financing for housing projects, and coalitions between the homeless and voluntary sector organizations.[5]

The group Habitat for Humanity in the U.S. has provided an interesting and potentially useful model for Canada. Their program consists of community volunteers who donate their skills and local building suppliers who donate materials to renovate derelict properties or to build new houses in the manner of barn raisings. Given investment by university researchers in the engineering field into affordable housing alternatives it may be possible to provide some limited amount of new and reconditioned housing in this manner. The homeless have also come up with innovative mobile shelters based upon the construction of a plywood 'capsule' that can store a long-term homeless person's possessions as well as providing a bed for the night. This form of radical solution is less likely to prove viable as it does not decrease a homeless person's vulnerability to personal attack by any measurable degree.

The final sector that has the most potential to contribute to the amelioration of the homeless problem is the municipal governments of the country. In their analysis of the role of municipal governments Tom Carter and Ann McAfee correctly assert that municipalities, although pressured daily by the ever-increasing number of homeless who arrive requiring services, respond to homeless problems typically "with inappropriate tools and inadequate funds." They argue that city governments can adopt one of two strategies for dealing (or not dealing) with homelessness. First, there is the **reactor model** which involves action by the core power structures in the federal and provincial government in alliance with non-profit and co-operative groups. This occurs when the local government is unwilling to make an investment in solving their homeless problems. The second role is that which they have termed the **facilitator model** in which the city responds to demands, and through a variety of means including subsidies, action programs, lobbying with other levels of government and supportive policies at the level of permit processing and rezoning, encourages proactive enterprise. Some of our larger cities such as Toronto have large departments that deal with the development of low-cost housing. Vancouver and Regina also have delegated the authority for this form of development to a separate city department. Winnipeg, which attempted to address its housing problems through the inauguration of the Winnipeg Housing Rehabilitation Corporation, found that over a decade of work only 400 units had been completed. Overall, the more than 100 municipal non-profit housing organizations have largely operated in a reactive manner rather than taking the role of comprehensive developer associated with Toronto. Overall, one must conclude that 'municipalities are weak when it comes to ability to respond to housing need.'

The problem of homelessness in our country can only be attacked through the efforts of a variety of public and private groups and the homeless themselves. One of the central lessons of the development of widespread homelessness in the United States is that at some identifiable point the homeless begin to organize into a collective movement. The marches on Washington by the homeless in the 1980s, tent city protests, and the involvement of celebrities in bringing public attention to the plight of the homeless moved homelessness from a marginal issue to the forefront of American social consciousness. There are signs that this is beginning to happen in Canada, for there is, in any society, a given juncture at which the accumulated misery of all of the political and economic factors discussed in this book, which impact upon the creation of the homeless and their continual desperation, ignites the fires of protest in groups that are so subjugated. In October of 1992 the homeless marched in Ottawa to draw public and governmental attention to their condition.

In the short term there are a number of suggestions that emanated from the homeless people interviewed for this book. First, a priority must be to make further improvements to short-term shelter accommodation, to humanize it. This can be accomplished through a refocusing of funds into the production of a positive living environment and the provision of solid counselling, educational and job placement. Shelters, since they are short-term at any rate, must rework their current accommodations, improving both the physical structures as well as the interior environment. While staff might not wish the homeless to stay long-term it does not mean that in the short-term they have to reside in shelters that resemble correctional facilities. Neither does it mean that they have to be subjected to arbitrary and punishing rules concerning their living environment, particularly governing their rights to "lounge" if they wish to. Large shelters must be closed and give way to smaller living units that provide longer term residence rather than acting as a catalyst to the production of a wandering army of transients. Shelters must also be built that accommodate various identifiable needs groups discussed throughout this book and that allow the highest possible opportunity for the homeless person to re-establish themselves. This is particularly true in the area of shelter accommodation for women that I, since the research was concluded for this book, has been substantially altered for young women. As of 1992, only women between the ages of 16 and 18 are eligible to be funded for shelter accommodation on a per diem rate.[6] Those over 18 are now required to seek accommodation in adult women's shelters that include a wide selection of homeless women. The number and quality of these shelters in Canada are both extremely low.

There are a number of short-term band-aids that are of practical utility to the homeless that have been mentioned not only in interviews conducted for this book but by various researchers on homelessness. These have included variously: 1) more protection for roomers; 2) the building of more public toilets and drinking fountains; 3) liaison with employers to lower qualifications for jobs to give a chance to those with limited job experience; 4) converting abandoned or unused warehouse space and housing for the homeless; 5) helping the homeless to purchase co-op dwelling units that are collectively owned; 6) distributing low-income housing throughout cities so that the homeless do not continue to be stigmatized by relegation to the downtown core of 'skid row' or similar areas; 7) more security of tenure in housing for those who do have personal problems; 8) more public baths and places where street people can safely, and with dignity, clean themselves; 9) co-operation with department and other stores to provide appropriate clothing and other necessities of life to the homeless. The Homeless Persons Outreach Group in Toronto also concluded in 1989 that one of the most important steps forward in attempts to change living conditions for the homeless was the provision of forums in which to educate both the public and politicians about them, to give them a human face. Another recommendation of the group, which canvassed clients in a number of hostels and shelters, echoed the expressed desire of many of the persons with whom I spoke, and that was that the homeless themselves should be employed to help the homeless. Organizations like Beat the Street have taken this approach to tackling the challenge of homelessness as it was started by three homeless people and now has offices in several cities helping street people to become educated and providing counselling and information services.[7]

Baxter constructed another substantive list of recommendations based upon her interviews in the Vancouver area. They included: 1) educating the homeless concerning application for special housing (for HIV positive persons, natives, the mentally ill, and adolescents particularly); 2) social housing should be built on a small scale, i.e., with room for eight or ten people and some supervision available if needed, a view of positive housing expressed by many long-term homeless in my sample; 3) changing societal attitudes that it is permissible for people, including children, to "exchange sex for shelter"; 4) homeless families have the right to be placed in decent, safe accommodations suitable for children, not skid row motels and hotels; 5) there should be a loosening of by-law regulations regarding the rental of units in private homes; and 6) minimum wages and welfare need to be increased so that they provide enough to live on, not continually relegating the homeless to the "loop" of homelessness.[8]

While the above raise a number of praxis issues for immediate consideration, the prospects for serious reductions in the number of temporary, short-term, long-term, and chronic homeless will rely upon more co-operative efforts. I have argued that homelessness cannot be traced to one simple cause, often involving factors and contingencies at both the personal and the structural levels, so solutions will cut naturally across these boundaries. The personal is often related to the public as C. Wright Mills instructed us. New partnerships that move beyond current societal arrangements will be required to address this social problem. At a minimum it will involve the homeless themselves, all three levels of government, private enterprise, volunteers as well as charities, and the community in which the homeless live.

Following Baxter, it is suggested that the inalienable right to housing should be entrenched within the Canadian Charter of Rights and Freedoms. More than half a million Canadian households endure deplorable living conditions, prehomeless, while more than 100,000 are annually homeless. The central notion of this proposal is contained within the 1948 Universal Declaration of Human Rights of the United Nations of which Canada is a signatory. It states:

> Everyone has the right to a standard of living adequate
> for health and well being . . . including food, clothing,
> housing and medical care and necessary social services.

Similarly, Baxter argues that provincial governments should ensure that discrimination in housing on the basis of sex, race, creed, family composition or sexual preference, age, level or source of income, or disability is not tolerated and is punished severely. While there are clear signs that we are aware of systemic discrimination in the criminal justice system, employment and housing, we have not seen, and homeless people have been the victim of, lack of effective enforcement.

A number of proposals also emerged out of a symposium held during the United Nations International Year of Shelter for the Homeless by a number of housing experts in Canada. There conclusions called for a reallocation of existing resources and a reordering of priorities to meet the needs of the homeless. The participants argued for solutions that are local in nature, flexible and responsive to local conditions rather than anchored in national policies that do not reflect grass roots needs or desires. No one working with the homeless would argue for the creation of a ministry of homelessness. The further bureaucratization of this problem, like that evidenced in our federal government's approach to native peoples, would result in more employment created by homelessness rather than solutions that help the homeless. Fallis and Murray and their colleagues suggest that an overarching approach that teams government and the private sector will be able to address the significant challenges of providing relief for the homeless. Centrally, they cite the factors of income support, assisted housing, and social services as core elements in finding innovative solutions to homelessness. They confirm one of the central assertions of this, and other works on homelessness in Canada, namely that, " . . . the homeless simply do not have enough income to meet what all Canadians would accept as basic needs." They conclude: "The money can be found."[9]

To Annihilate The Future or Not?

I can at least say, here is the world that awaits you if you are ever penniless.[10]

In this book I have attempted to explore both the human faces of homelessness and the wider political and economic forces that create homelessness in our society. The number of homeless in this country has been growing steadily over the past decade in Canada, a process that has seen rapid acceleration in the early 1990s. No longer can we as a society ignore the homeless in our midst as they begin to crowd the streets in ever-increasing numbers, and neither can we delegate responsibility for their condition to them. While most of the homeless services in our society for food, shelter and medical assistance have improved also over the past decade so have the rising numbers of homeless exhausted the capability of our current methods of dealing with the homeless. In the end, the homeless are still on the street, they rely upon our waning charity to survive, and have little or no voice in the direction their lives are taking. Given the perilousness of much of our own existence and the thin veil between homefulness and homelessness in our society, our approach to the homeless in the future requires radical redirection. Orwell wrote that the "great redeeming feature of poverty" was "the fact it annihilates the future." This is certainly true if we choose not to intervene. The promise of The World Summit for Children held in September 1990, and co-chaired by Prime Minister Mulroney, promised children would become the nation's priority. Between that time and 1992 no new major programs were announced to help children in poverty.

There are many thousands of lives that are being unalterably damaged by the upward surge of homelessness in this country, and we ignore this social condition at our own peril in Canada. As a country that is undergoing rapid social and economic transformation it is important that we not leave the homeless out on the street awaiting our whimsical generosity. During the course of my research when I interviewed a young homeless family, their daughter, a precocious five-year-old, drew a stark depiction of three figures crowded into a tiny black box. It was her depiction of life for the homeless in a motel. She reminded me of my own daughter and the home that awaited me. Leaving the interview, to face a Christmas with no toys, no Christmas tree, and a macaroni dinner, she inquired innocently as she hugged me, "Isn't there anyone who looks after little children in Canada?" If this book accomplishes anything with you, the reader, perhaps it is to find a positive answer to that question for all homeless Canadians.

Endnotes
INTRODUCTION

[1]Jones, Maxwell. **The Therapeutic Community**. London: RKP, 1960.

[2]Egger, Steve. "Serial Killing of the Lambs in our Dreams". Paper presented at The ACJS Annual Meetings, Pittsburgh, March 1992.

[3]Ericson, R.V. et al., **Visualizing Deviance: A Study of News Organization**. University of Toronto Press, 1987 and T. Fleming, "Mad Dogs, Beasts and Raving Matters: The Presentation of The Mentally Disordered in the British Press," in T. Fleming and L. Visano (eds.) **Deviant Designations: Crime, Law and Deviance in Canada**. Toronto: Butterworths, 1983: 153-184.

[4]See Greg Barak, **Gimme Shelter**, New York: Praeger, 1991 for a review of extant literature.

[5]Figures released October 2, 1992; CBC News, Windsor.

[6]R.G. Smart, et al., **Drugs, Youth and the Street**. Toronto: ARF, 1990.

[7]D. Milovanovic and S. Henry, "Constitutive Criminology" in **Criminology**.

[8]The interview sample consisted of: Victoria, 10 interviews (8 female, 2 male); Edmonton, 10 interviews (7 male, 3 female); Vancouver, 15 interviews, (10 male, 5 female); Oshawa, 20 interviews (19 males, 1 female); Windsor, 7 interviews (4 males, 3 females); Toronto, 157 interviews (99 males, 38 females, 20 families). Families are counted as one interview although partners, and in six cases,

children, attended at the interview. One family member may have spoken about the experiences of up to six other members of the same family unit. The age of respondents varies from 16 to 62 for females; and 16 to 72 for males excluding children who were not direct interview subjects.

[9]N. Denzin, **Interpretive Interactionism**, Newburg Park: Sage, 1989, 48-49.

[10]N. Denzin, **ibid.**, 7.

[11]The Daily Bread Food Bank of Toronto, for instance, reported that the fall food drive had raised only 50% of their target goal for donations, leaving countless families without food. **The Toronto Star,** October 10, 1992. See also Graham Riches, **Food Banks and the Welfare Crisis.** Ottawa: Canadian Council on Social Development, 1986.

[12]For a review of existing literature see Thomas O'Reilly-Fleming, "No Home in Their Native Land: Homeless Canadians as Marginal Persons in the Social Order," **The Journal of Human Justice,** Vol. 2, Number 1, Autumn, 1990; 55-74.

CHAPTER ONE

[1]R. Ropers, **The Invisible Homeless**, New York: Insight, 1988.

[2]M. McLaughlin, **Homelessness in Canada—The Report of the National Inquiry**. Ottawa: Canadian Council on Social Development, 1987.

[3]See Bingham, R. et al. (eds.). **The Homeless in Contemporary Society**, Newbury Park: Sage, 1987; Hombs, M.E., and M. Snyder, **Homelessness in America—A Forced March to Nowhere**, Washington: Community for Creative Non-Violence, 1983; Hopper, K., and L.S. Cox, **Litigation in Advocacy for The Homeless: The Case of New York City**, New York: Community Service Society, 1982.

[4]Mayor Art Eggleton, New Year's Speech, City Television, January 1, 1991.

[5]Examples include: **The Fisher King, Curly Sue**, and the 48 hours documentary, **Homeless in America**.

[6]**The Gallup Report**, (by L. Bazinoff and P. MacIntosh), Monday February 18, 1991. See also **Gallup Report** (by L. Bozinoff and A. Turcotte), Monday Sept. 14, 1992, which states, "that slightly more than four-in-ten Canadian workers (41%) believe that there is a chance that they may become unemployed." **The Gallup Report** of Thursday May 7, 1992 found that, "Almost six-in-ten adult Canadians cite some aspect of the economy as the most important problem facing the country today. Fifty-nine percent of the public mention unemployment, inflation, or a related economic ailment."

[7]See the discussion in Chapters Five and Six of this book.

[8]For a discussion of the British situation see: O. Brandon, **Homelessness in London**, London: Christian Action, 1973; B. Saunders, **Homeless Young People in Britain**, London: Bedford Square Press, 1986; S. Watson and H. Austerberry, **Housing and Homelessness—A Feminist Perspective**. London: Routledge and Kegan Paul, 1986.

[9]This reflects somewhat the argument first advanced in I. Taylor, P. Walton, and J. Young, **The New Criminology**, London: RKP, 1975 for a fully human theory of social deviance. See also more recent left realist arguments that advocate praxis at the local level; M.D. Schwartz and W.S. Dekeseredy, "Left realist criminology: Strengths, weaknesses and the feminist critique." Unpublished paper.

[10]An estimate offered by the Canadian Council on Social Development in M. McLaughlin, 1987.

[11]Estimates provided by coalition of downtown shelter agencies for youth in Toronto from various interview sources; Canadian Mayor's conference 1990-91; R. Daly, **A Comparative Assessment of Programs Dealing with the Homeless Population in the U.S., Canada and Britain.** Ottawa: CMHC, 1991.

[12]By June 1990, the average cost of a single-family dwelling in Metropolitan Toronto was $265,000 according to **Real Estate News.** High inflation rates prevalent until date 1992 were a contributing factor.

[13]Daly, **ibid.,** 1991. For discussion of the changing composition of U.S. homeless populations see, Penelope L. Maza. **Homeless Children and their Families: A Preliminary Study.** Washington: Child Welfare League of America, 1988; Peter H. Rossi, **Down and Out in America: The Origins of Homelessness.** Chicago: University of Chicago, 1989.

[14]One reflection of this is that "guides" to Toronto homeless services are now given out in a variety of languages.

[15]See Barak, **ibid.,** 1991.

[16]L. Gorman, and J. McMullan, "In Defiance of the Law of the Land: Social Control and the Unemployed Movement in the Dirty Thirties in British Columbia," **Canadian Criminology Forum, 8,** 1987: 84-102; Nels Anderson, **The Hobo: The Sociology of the Homeless Man.** Chicago: University of Chicago Press, 1923; N.Anderson, **Men on the Move.** Chicago: University of Chicago Press, 1940.

[17]W. J. Chambliss, "A sociological analysis of the Law of Vagrancy." **Social Problems,** 12: 46-67. The best account of the history and application of vagrancy statutes. See also Ken Morrison, "The Control of Vagrancy: Historical Perspectives." Paper presented at the Canadian Sociology and Anthropology Association Meeting, Victoria, British Columbia, June 1991.

[18]For a praxis-based discussion of this problem see A. Borovoy, **When Freedoms Collide.** Toronto: 1987. Borovoy has, for many years, been chief legal counsel for the Canadian Civil Liberties Association.

[19]For an in-depth analysis of the hypocrisy of both formal and informal legal structures that exert control over the lives of homeless Canadians see the discussion later in this book. In the American context see G. Barak, **Gimme Shelter.** New York: Praeger, 1991.

[20]In Oshawa, Ontario business owners attempted to have

homeless people removed from the local adjoining park since their presence was deemed to scare away potential customers.

[21]For a review of the major sources see T. O'Reilly-Fleming, **ibid.**, 1990.

[22]This is a matter of considerable debate in the literature and hence of confusion and divisiveness in terms of comparative research. For a good overview of this problem see James D. Wright, **Address Unknown: The Homeless in America.** New York: New York University Press, 1989.

[23]See for example, M. Hope and J. Young, **The Faces of Homelessness,** Toronto: D.C. Heath, 1986.

[24]**Coles Concise English Dictionary.** Toronto: Coles Publishing Limited, 1979: 832.

[25]Again, **The Fisher King** is one of the best examinations of these popular images.

[26]K. Hopper et al., **Not Making It Crazy: Some Remarks on the Young Homeless Patient in New York City.** New York: Community Service Society, 1983 and K. Hopper et al., **One Year Later: The Homeless Poor in New York City.** New York: Community Service Society, 1982.

[27]Terence Morris, **The Criminal Area.** London: RKP, 1957 is the classic example of research on the effects of overcrowding and inadequate housing. See also, Robert E.L. Faris, **Chicago Sociology: 1920-1932.** San Francisco: Chandler, 1967; David I. Decker, et al., **Urban Structure and Victimization,** Lexington, Mass.: D.C. Heath, 1982; K.D. Harries, **Crime and the Environment,** Springfield, Illinois: C.C. Thomas, 1980; and Robert E. Park, et al., **The City.** Chicago: University of Chicago Press, 1928.

[28]Walter S. Dekeseredy and Ronald Hinch, **Woman Abuse: Sociological Perspectives.** Toronto: Thompson, 1991, 7-37. This is the most comprehensive survey of woman abuse in Canada and the most meticulously documented.

[29]L.A. Visano, **This Idle Trade,** Concord: Vitasana, 1987 and M. Webber, **Street Kids: The Tragedy of Canada's Runaways,** Toronto: University of Toronto Press, 1991 are both excellent sources on runaways and city street life in Canada. Another more personal source in Evelyn Lau, **Runaway: Diary of a Street Kid.** Toronto: Harper and Collins, 1989; Margaret A. Michaud, **Dead End: Homeless Teenagers, A Multi-Service Approach.** Calgary: Detselig Enterprises, 1989. Bruce Ritter, **Covenant House: Lifeline to the Street.** New York:

Doubleday, 1987 provides an interesting account of some of the innovative attempts to help runaway and homeless children.

[30]D. Roth et al., **Homelessness in Ohio: A Study of People in Need**. Columbus: Ohio Department of Mental Health, 1985.

[31]S. Watson and H. Austerberry, **Housing and Homelessness—A Feminist Perspective**. London: RKP, 1986.

[32]M.E. Hombs and M. Snyder, **ibid.**

[33]For a discussion of the gap between research and policy consult Brian Fay, **Social Theory and Political Practice**. London: George, Allan and Unwin, 1975.

[34]F.S. Redburn and T.F. Buss, **Responding to America's Homeless—Public Policy Alternatives**. New York: Praeger, 1986, 45.

[35]For a discussion of this in the American context see Edmund McGarrell and Timothy Flanagan, **Source Book of Criminal Justice Statistics, 1984**; Washington: U.S. Government Printing Office, 1985 and M. Hindelang and M. Gottfredson, "The Victim's Decision Not to Involve the Criminal Justice Process," in W. McDonald (ed.) **Criminal Justice and the Victim**. Beverly Hills: Sage, 1976, 57-74. For a Canadian source see R. Linden, (ed.) **Criminology: A Canadian Perspective**, 2nd Edition. Toronto: Harcourt, Brace, Jovanovich, 1992:68-82.

[36]G. Barak, **Gimme Shelter, ibid.**

[37]For a discussion of the medias use of "crisis" reporting see S. Hall et al., **Policing The Crisis**. London: Macmillan, 1978; and R. Ericson, et al., **Visualizing Deviance: A Study of News Organization**. Toronto: University of Toronto Press, 1987.

[38]D. S. Mallin, "Sheltering The Homeless," **Canadian Home Economics Journal**, 37(3), Summer 1987:114-116.

[39]Quoted in **The Toronto Star**, December 30, 1987: A1, A10.

[40]McLaughlin, 1987, **ibid.**, 4-6.

[41]**Ibid.**, 4.

[42]An estimate reported in numerous interviews with service personnel in Toronto: One shelter alone had more than 1,100 separate admissions over a one-year period.

[43]Visano, 1987, **ibid.** Father Bruce Ritter, the founder of Covenant House a shelter for teenagers located at the corner of Church and Gerrard Streets in Toronto, has stated that 90% of street kids sell sex in order to survive, often naively becoming entrapped in the world of prostitution. **The Toronto Star**, February 11, 1986:A12.

[44]Webber, **Street Kids, ibid.**

[45]Put in the context of several youth riots in Toronto during 1992, the resentment of youth at being treated as 'throwaways' is significant.

[46]**The Montreal Gazette,** April 1, 1987: D1.

[47]See for example, **The Halifax Chronicle Herald,** Nov. 29, 1986:1-2; **The Winnipeg Free Press,** August 10, 1987:40; **The Montreal Gazette,** May 1, 1987:A4; **The Winnipeg Free Press,** February 21, 1987:49; and **The Vancouver Sun,** Nov. 29, 1987:A1.

[48]David Bairstow, **A Place to Call Home—Housing Solutions In Low Income Singles in Ontario.** Toronto: Ministry of Housing, 1986:35.

[49]D.S. Mallin, **ibid.**

[50]D. Bairstow, 1986.

[51]United States Conference of Mayors, **A Status Report on Homeless Families in America's Cities—A29 City Survey.** Washington: U.S. Conference of Mayors, May 1987.

[52]See F. Engels, **The Condition of the Working Class in England,** Oxford: Basil Blackwell, 1958; and Charles Dickens, **Hard Times,** London: Penguin, 1978; and Charles Dickens, **Oliver Twist.** London: Penguin, 1978.

[53]A portion of the U.S. Mayor's Report, **ibid.,** 1987 describes the arrival of a family with two young children to their facility. When offered a platform surface and toys to play with, the children could not play. They were looking for a confined space that resembled the backseat of an automobile.

[54]One shelter worker commented with pride, "We make sure they're all out of here by seven (a.m.). They can't just sit all day." This reflected a general attitude in many, but not all, hostels for adult males.

[55]D. Bairstow, **ibid.,** 1986.

[56]H. Brody, **Natives on Skid Row,** Winnipeg: Social Services Publication, 1981; J. Hylton, "Locking up Indians in Saskatchewan," in T. Fleming and L. Visano (eds.) **Deviant Designations: Crime, Law and Deviance in Canada.** Toronto: Butterworths, 1983: 61-70.

[57]For a compelling account see Geoffrey York, **The Dispossessed: Life and Health in Native Canada.** London: Vintage, 1990.

[58]Verdict of Coroner's Jury: Of the jury serving on the inquest into the death of Drina Joubert, February 12-25th, 1986, aged 41

years. Ms. Joubert froze to death on December 17, 1985 in an abandoned truck parked behind a Sherbourne Street address. She was the 19th resident of Toronto to die of exposure since the beginning of 1984. See also Bairstow, 1986: 54 and **The Toronto Star**, February 12, 1986. The jury concluded, "Clearly, the bureaucracy designed to help the most disadvantaged among us has become unresponsive to the need of the people it was created to serve. It is fragmented and inefficient."

[59]A. Scull, **Decarceration: Community Treatment and the Deviant**. Englewood Cliffs: Prentice-Hall, 1977.

[60]G. Barak, **Gimme Shelter**, 1992, **ibid**.

[61]See **Streethealth, Report on Homeless Persons**, 1992.

[62]**Streethealth, ibid**. Also, Baxter and Hopper, **ibid**., 1981: 18; Wright, 1987; Hope and Young, **ibid**., 1986: 31-52; J. Sebastian, "Homeless: A State of Vulnerability," **Family and Community Health**, Vol. 8 (3) 1985: 11-24.

[63]A. Scull, **Decarceration**, 2nd Edition, 1984; 1-2, 64-75.

[64]Baxter and Hopper, **ibid**., 1981: 1.

[65]Scull, 1984, **ibid**.

[66]J. Talbott, "Cure for the Chronically Mentally Ill—Still a National Disgrace," **American Journal of Psychiatry**, 136, 688-89.

[67]R. Reich and L. Segal, "Psychiatry Under Seige: The Chronic Mentally Ill Shuffle to Oblivion," **Psychiatric Annals**, 1973, 3: 37-55.

[68]Visano, **ibid**., 1987; O'Reilly-Fleming, **ibid**., 1990.

[69]C. Krauthammer, "When Liberty Really Means Neglect," **Time**, 1985, December 2, 103-104.

[70]E. Bassuk, et al., "Is Homelessness a Mental Health Problem?" **American Journal of Psychiatry**, 1984, 141(12): 156-1550.

[71]Hope and Young, **ibid**., 1986: 20.

[72]D. Roth, **ibid**., 1985.

[73]Hope and Young, **ibid**., 1986: 21.

[74]K. Schloss and N. Giesbrecht, **Apparently Suffering from Mental Disorder**. Toronto: Centre of Criminology, 1974.

[75]G. Barak and R. Bohm, "The Crimes of the homeless or the crime of homelessness?: On the dialectics of criminalization, decriminalization, and victiminization," **Contemporary Crises**; 1989, 13: 275-288.

[76]D. Snow et al., "The Myth of Pervasive Mental Illness Among the Homeless," Social Problems, 33: 407-423.

[77]J. Wright et al., ibid., 1987: 192-184.

[78]J. Wright, "The Mentally Ill Homeless: What is Myth and What is Fact?" in Social Problems, 1988, Vol. 35, No. 2, 182-191.

[79]Wright, ibid., 1988: 184.

[80]D. Rosenhan, "On Being Sane in Insane Places," Science, 1973, Vol. 179, 205-258.

[81]R. Ropers, ibid., 1988: 81.

[82]Snow et al., ibid., 1986.

[83]J. Wright, ibid., 1988: 183.

[84]J. Wright, et al., ibid., 1987.

[85]J. Wright, et al., ibid., 1987; J. Wright, ibid., 1988.

[86]J. Wright, ibid., 1988: 85.

[87]M. Tenszen, "Union Urges Pay Hikes in 'Toronto the Costly'", The Toronto Star, May 19, 1990.

[88]Barak and Bohm, ibid., 1989; O'Reilly-Fleming, ibid., 1990.

[89]J. Stein, "Qualitative Research Techniques and Homelessness." Paper presented to the Qualitative Research Conference, Glendon College, York University, May 1991.

[90]N. Denzin, Interpretive Interactionism, ibid., 1989.

CHAPTER TWO

[1]Standing Senate Committee on Social Affairs, Science and Technology. **Children in Poverty Towards a Better Future.** Ottawa: January 1991.

[2]Mary Labatt, "Children in Poverty—Educators must be advocates for children." Federation of Women Teachers' Associations of Ontario, Newsletter, April/May 1991, Volume 9, Number 5:3.

[3]Carolyn Jack. "Children in Poverty—A Startling Profile." **Canadian Forum,** September 1990.

[4]While food banks are trying to move to a policy of closing their doors in protest against government refusal to feed the hungry in Canada this is a difficult task to accomplish in the current economic depression. Until governments agree to finance the operation of food banks they are likely to remain open. Some advocates believe however, that closing the food banks and causing widespread hunger and starvation is the only way to force the government to take over the running of them, i.e., that government officials will only respond when crises are occurring that are deeply disturbing to the general populace. See also Jack, **ibid.** at 17.

[5]Gordon Laxer, **Open for Business,** Toronto: Methuen, 1990. The finest sociological exploration of the issues of the selling of Canada to multinationals and U.S. financiers. A recent winner of the John Porter Award in sociology from the Canadian Sociology and Anthropology Association.

[6]**The Windsor Star,** May 1991.

[7]A. Mitchell et al., **The State of the Child in Ontario.** Toronto: Social Planning Council of Metropolitan Toronto, 1990.

[8]There have been only a few published attempts to look at the phenomenon of homelessness in Canada. They are: Sheila Baxter, **Under the Viaduct: Homeless in Beautiful B.C.,** Vancouver: New Star Books, 1991. This work is based upon interviews with the homeless and workers. Baxter is an experienced worker within the homeless movement and previously did research in Montreal. Her book is a valuable contribution to our knowledge. Lesley Harman, **When a Hostel Becomes a Home: Experiences of Women.** Toronto: Network Basic Series, Garamond, 1989. A field study of homeless women living in hostel accommodation and a feminist analysis of the patriarchal construction of homelessness in Canada. Marlene Webber, **Street**

Kids, Toronto: University of Toronto Press, 1991. This is primarily a look at runaway kids and their involvement in various forms of street survival. It also examines some of the causes of family dysfunction in Canadian society and the making of the street sex industry. See also R. Morris and C. Heffren, **Street People Speak.** Oakville:Mosaic, 1988.

[9]See W. DeKeseredy and R. Hinch, **Woman Abuse,** generally. Also T. Fleming, **Violent Domestic Assault.** Unpublished M.A. Thesis, University of Toronto, Centre of Criminology, 1975. For a concise review of Canadian studies see Des Ellis, **The Wrong Stuff.** Toronto: Collier MacMillan, 1987. M.D. Smith, "The incidence and prevalence of woman abuse in Toronto." **Violence and Victims,** 2 (3), 173-187.

[10]See for example, M. Spencer, **Foundations of Modern Sociology,** Toronto: Prentice Hall, 1990, Chapter 12. For an analysis of the changing nature of the Canadian family see Marlene Mackie, **Exploring Gender Relations: A Canadian Perspective.** Toronto: Butterworths, 1983.

[11]According to R. Smart et al., in their report **Drugs, Youth and the Street,** Toronto: Addiction Research Foundation, 1990 street youth in their sample (N = 145) reported using drugs for "coping and escapism." They also found that, "Drug and alcohol use among street youth was much more a coping strategy for dealing with the street life." Street youth reported that "once on the street it is difficult to escape this lifestyle."

[12]See T. Fleming, "Mad Dogs, Beasts and Raving Nutters: On the Presentation of the Mentally Disordered in the British Press," in T. Fleming and L.Visano (eds.) **Deviant Designations: Crime, Law and Deviance in Canada.** Toronto: Butterworths, 1987.

[13]While it is unusual to see under 16s on the street one should not infer that they are not among the homeless. Smart et al., **ibid.,** reported that of 86% of their sample that had lived with their biological parents that 19% had left home before the age of 11. Many of the young people interviewed for this sample indicated that they had left home before the age of 16, often when they were 10 or more years of age. Some interview subjects reported that younger homeless streetkids were often living in motel rooms where they made a living as prostitutes but avoided the streets because they would be subject to apprehension by the Childrens' Aid Society.

[14]Alan Borovoy, Address to The University of Windsor, Faculty of Law, 1990.

[15]See Webber, **ibid.,** 39-78.

[16]For sociological analysis of prostitution in the Canadian context see, L. Stevens, **The Stroll.** Toronto: New Canada Publications,

1986; R.F. Badgely, **Sexual Offences Against Children: A Report of the Committee on Sexual Offences Against Children and Youths,** Ottawa: Supply and Services, Canada, 1984; J. Lowman, "Taking Young Prostitutes Seriously," Canadian Review of Sociology and **Anthropology,** 24 (1) 1987; Tom MacDonnell, **Never Let Go: The Tragedy of Kristy McFarlane,** Toronto: MacMillan, 1987; **The Fraser Report on Prostitution and Pornography,** Ottawa: Supply and Services Canada, 1986; L.Visano, **This Idle Trade.** Concord: Vitasana, 1987.

[17]The practice of spending the last of the morning hours in johns' cars is referred to as "the breakfast club" on the street. Johns park their cars in the wide laneways of Toronto's Rosedale community and engage in sex, smoking, drinking and drug use with the street prostitutes. As the sun rises they leave the alleyways and head to one of the handful of all night cafes that welcome street people in Toronto.

[18]Phil Collins, **Another Night in Paradise,** by Phil Collins, 1989, Copyright WEA Music of Canada Ltd, Atlantic Recording Corporation from the album . . . **But Seriously.**

[19]L. Harman, **ibid.,** 15-26.

[20]Phil Collins, **ibid.,** 1989, Copyright.

[21]Labatt, **ibid.,** 3-5. Labatt notes that far fewer father-led single-parent families live in poverty, only 28.4%.

[22]National Council of Welfare. **Women and Poverty Revisited : A Report by the National Council of Welfare.** Ottawa:Supply and Services Canada, 1990. For one the best analyses of poverty effects in Canada see D. Ross and R. Shillington, **The Canadian Fact Book on Poverty—1989.** Ottawa: Canadian Council on Social Development, 1989. They cite a higher figure of 71.7%.

[23]See the discussion on mental illness and homelessness in the first chapter of this book.

[24]An estimate proffered by several shelter workers encountered during the research process.

[25]See L. MacLeod, **Battered but not Beaten: Preventing Wife Battering in Canada,** Ottawa: Canadian Advisory Council on the Status of Women, 1987, 38; W. DeKeseredy and R. Hinch, **ibid.,** for a discussion of the estimates of woman abuse provided by various researchers.

[26]L. MacLeod, **ibid.,** 30-35.

CHAPTER THREE

[1]Jimmy Cox, **Nobody Knows You When You're Down and Out.** Copyright, MEA Inc., ASCAP. Performed by E. Clapton.

[2]M. Foucualt, **Discipline and Punish—The Birth of the Prison.** New York: Vintage, 1979. 135-169.

[3]For an excellent discussion of teens and prostitution see Marlene Webber's book **Street Kids,** 79-134.

[4]Canadian Public Health Association. **Street Youth and AIDS.** Ottawa: CPHA, 1990. The result of a "comprehensive" study by Queen's University that interviewed 712 young people in ten cities across Canada aged 15-20. They were, however, defined as street kids if they had spent at least 24 hours away from home at any time during the past year. Most researchers would reject this designation as too inclusive, and not reflective of "hard core" street regulars. They found 32% of street youth never used condoms, while 42% used them "most times or always." More than 50% of the male prostitutes had engaged in anal intercourse.

[5]Walter Miller, "Lower Class Culture as a Generating Milieu of Gang Delinquency," **Journal of Social Issues,** 14 (3):5-19, 1958. The propensity of male street hookers to characterize themselves as heterosexual is also reflected in Visano's correspondents. See also Webber, **ibid.,** 114-5 for an interview that presents this point of view in a positive and non-critical manner.

[6]Robert Stebbins, **Deviance: Tolerable Differences.** Toronto: Prentice-Hall, 1987. One of the most comprehensive examinations of sexual deviance in the literature.

[7]Ibid.

[8]Henry Miller, **Tropic of Cancer.** New York: Random House, 1977.

[9]Michael Bolton, **When I'm Back on My Feet Again.** Copyright, CBS Records, 1989.

[10]See also Chapter Five in this book.

CHAPTER FOUR

[1]Neil Young, "People on the Street" 1986, Silver Fiddle Music, ASCAP.

[2]See Howard S. Becker, **Outsiders**. New York: Free Press, 1963. Ostensibly the argument is that no behaviour is deviant until it is so labelled by society. The use of L.S.D., for example, was not illegal in the U.S.A. until the late 1960s when its use became criminalized. Before that point it was one of the 'tolerable' deviances in our society as Robert Stebbins pointed out in his work, **Deviance: Tolerable Differences**. Toronto: Prentice-Hall, 1988. This process is referred to as labelling. While some labels have little effect on those to whom they are applied, others may carry significant weight in terms of evoking negative societal reactions. The label "ex-criminal" has moral, legal and social implications, while the label "lazy" carries with it more limited sanctions.

[3]Richard Ericson's early study of released delinquents in **Britain, Young Offenders and their Social Work**. Farnborough: Gower, 1975 is one the finest examples of field research on a group that engaged in self-labelling. For an exhaustive analysis of labelling theory see R. Ericson, **Criminal Reactions: The Labelling Perspective**. Farnborough: Gower, 1975.

[4]Stan Cohen, "The Punitive City: Notes on the Dispersal of Social Control," **Contemporary Crises**, Vol. 3, 1979: 339-363, and Stan Cohen, **Visions of Social Control: Crime, Punishment and Classification**. Cambridge: Polity Press, 1985. According to Cohen, the net of control is growing progressively wider in contemporary society and the mesh is becoming increasingly smaller, trapping persons who were formally of no interest to social control agencies in its web. This is, in essence, an outgrowth of the increasing size of control agencies like the police and the progress in technological invasion into privacy. This argument is very similar to that produced by Emile Durkheim on the boundary maintenance functions of deviance, that is, as the system of control swallows up all of the most visible and severe forms of deviance, new more marginal types of deviance will be scanned for infractions and be subject to criminalization. See my earlier article, "The Bawdy House Boys: Some Notes on Media, Sporadic Moral Crusades and Selective Law Enforcement," **Canadian Criminology Forum**, Vol. 3, No.2, 1981.

[5]Borovoy, **ibid.**

[6]Ben Carniol, **Case Critical: Challenging Social Work in Canada.** Second Edition. Toronto: Between the Lines, 1990:91.

[7]**Ibid.**, at 92.

[8]Helen Levine, "The Personal is Political: Feminism and the Helping Professions," in A. Miles and G. Finn (eds.) **Feminism in Canada: From Pressure to Politics.** Montreal: Black Rose, 1982.

[9]**Ibid.**, 91.

[10]Robert Doyle and L. Visano, **A Time for Action!—Access to Health and Social Services for Members of Diverse Cultural and Racial Groups in Metropolitan Toronto** (Report 1). Toronto: Social Planning Council of Metropolitan Toronto, 1987.

[11]M. Foucault, **ibid.**

[12]For a feminist analysis see J. Dale and P. Foster, **Feminists and State Welfare,** London: RKP, 1986. See also **The General Welfare Assistance Act,** Sec. 1 (i) (i) Chapter 188. R.S.C. Statutes of Canada; The Special Senate Subcommittee on Poverty, Poverty in Canada, Ottawa: Information Canada, 1971:83 found that the welfare process was degrading to all parties involved in it: "It repels both the people who depend on the hand-outs and those who administer them. Alienation on the part of welfare recipients and disenchantment on the part of welfare administrators was evident..." In Ontario, short-term benefits known as general welfare assistance typically are allocated to the jobless and those with temporary illnesses. Family benefits is a longer term form of aid and goes mainly to sole-support parents and disabled people. See also Richard Titmuss, **Commitment to Welfare,** London: Unwin, 1970.

[13]**The Windsor Star,** April 1990.

[14]Greg McDowell, "Hostel residents take pride in 'home," **The Oshawa Times,** Saturday, July 28, 1990: 3. The residents found that they had been the victim of discrimination. Neil Pare, a long-time resident of the 18 unit men's hostel, commented, "They just put everyone down instead of coming here and finding out what it is like," he said, "There are many good people living here." "It was like a Simcoe Street merchant was treated as a citizen of Oshawa and were (sic) weren't." Article courtesy of Terry Dunn, Emergency Housing Supervisor.

[15]Brenda Ingersoll, "Scrambling for Shelter" **The Detroit News,** Monday November 4, 1991. Kenneth Cole and Jim Mitzelfeld, "Homeless Protests don't move Engler," **The Detroit News,** January 1, 1992. The Governor commented that a protest by homeless persons

who set up a tent city named "Englerville" outside of his office was to be ignored since "clearly, they are here not because they are homeless but because they represent people who are homeless and in need." Engler said he believed that "many homeless people in the state have set their expectations too high."

16Tracey Nesdoly, "Drifter admits railyard killing," **The Toronto Sun**, Thursday November 26, 1991 :35.

17See Elliott Leyton, **Hunting Humans: The Rise of the Modern Multiple Murderer**, Toronto: McClelland and Stewart, 1986; and Neil Boyd, **The Last Dance: Murder in Canada**. Toronto: Prentice-Hall, 1988.

18See the review in G. Barak, **Gimme Shelter** and Barak and Bohm, **ibid.**

19B. McCarthy and J. Hagan, **British Journal of Criminology**.

20Ibid.

21For the most thorough, although somewhat dated, example see, Edwin Sutherland, **The Professional Thief**, Chicago: University of Chicago Press, 1937.

22Clifford Shearing, **Police Deviance**. Toronto: Butterworths, 1983.

23R. Ericson, **Reproducing Order: A Study of Police Patrol Work**. Toronto: University of Toronto Press, 1982; and R. Ericson, **Making Crime: A Study of Detective Work**. Toronto: Butterworths, 1981.

24Visano, **ibid.** and personal communication with the author.

25See variously Barak, **ibid.**; Barak and Bohm, **ibid.**; Streethealth, **ibid.**

26Darryl Sturtevant, "Building Community Partnerships," Ottawa: Health and Welfare Canada, 1991. "Housing is an acute problem for PLWAS (People Living With Aids), both because of their frequent inability to hold down a full-time job and the social ostracism they often experience." I am indebted to my colleague Alan Sears for his discussion of unreleased research material on this important topic.

27Canadian Council on Social Development, **Overview**, No.1, Fall 1991.

28Ibid.

29Ibid.

30Jim Ward, **Organizing the Homeless**. Ottawa: CCSD, 1987. **The Windsor Star**, February 18, 1993.

31Miller, **ibid.**

[32]Ibid.

[33]George Orwell, **Down and Out in Paris and London**. London: Penguin, 1970:15.

[34]Harman, ibid.

[35]Carniol writes, "For the many women clients who remain trapped within poverty, the impact of welfare policies and practices makes it abundantly clear that they remain subservient to and controlled by others. In the name of public assistance women clients are systematically degraded under the guise of official policy . . . The welfare department's authority to terminate payments creates profound fear and anxiety among male as well as female welfare clients. The system further propagates ideas of male hegemony as women are constantly questioned on whether males who live with them give them money, while males are never asked the same question about female live-in companions. The double standard is not only painfully evident but patently discriminatory and sexist. In many provinces single moms are "employable" even though they have children who are not of school age so they must look for paid work or be cut off welfare, presumably dragging their children behind them to the interviews": 102-105.

CHAPTER FIVE

[1]Harburg-Gorney, **Brother Can You Spare a Dime?** Harms Inc. ASCAP. Copyright.

[2]**Statistics Canada, 1992.** Press Release. Statistics on Unemployment.

[3]See Graham Riches, **Food Banks and the Welfare Crisis,** Ottawa: Canadian Council on Social Development, 1986. Also Jacks, **ibid.**, and Labatt, **ibid.**

[4]See "The Shelter Movement in Canada," in **Vis-A-Vis**, Ottawa: CCSD, Summer 1989, Vol. 7, No.2. They state that by 1979 there were 71 shelters that housed women and their children in Canada. By 1987 this number had grown to 230 shelters and by 1988 end there were 292.

[5]C. Wright Mills, "The Big City: Private Troubles and Public Issues," (edited by I. Horowitz), New York: Oxford, 1963, 395-404. I am referring here first to Mills, intertwining of the concepts of **trouble** and **issues** (the personal and the structural).

[6]See Ratner and McMullan, 1985, **ibid.**

[7]In a free trade zone that takes in these countries there is a natural market incentive for manufacturers to relocate in areas where labour costs are substantially reduced, benefits are lessened and environmental standards are not applied to production.

[8]Steven Spitzer, "Towards a Marxian Theory of Deviance," **Social Problems**, 22, 5, 1975. There is, in effect, a 'surplus army of labour' that is routinely discarded into the ranks of the unemployed and the imprisoned and recalled when society needs their labour services. There is no doubt that the numbers in this surplus army in Canada have grown substantially over the last decade. S. McBride, **Not Working: State, Unemployment and Neo-Conservatism in Canada.** Toronto: University of Toronto Press, 1991, p. 31 writes,"massive unemployment, once thought to have been banished, has returned as an apparently intractable feature of the political and economic landscape." For the relationship of this to criminal activity of the homeless see W.A. Bonger, **Criminality and Economic Conditions.** New York: Agathon, 1967.

[9]I refer here to political explanations and those academic

writings which continue to shunt the homeless into the ranks of medicalized conceptions of deviance in our society.

[10]Under Reagan the lights dimmed measurably as his approach to economics favoured further assisting the wealthy to accumulate wealth at the expense of the poor and middle class in society. Burdened with this wealth they would then benevolently create jobs for others in society, a further reinforcement of a patriarchal society. In Canada, McBride, **ibid.** at 13, concluded that during the 1980s in Canada, under Mulroney's Conservatives, quite the opposite happened; "Instead of supplying the public purse with tax funds for the state's welfare activities, business itself has become a recipient of government spending." Gordon Ternowetsky, "Who Are the Real Welfare Bums," Paper presented at The Organization for Justice Conference, Saskatoon, Saskatchewan, 1989. Ternowetsky found that Canada's five biggest banks enjoyed profits of over $8 billion dollars for a five-year period but cut their workforce by 11,119 employees. Almost one-third of those profits reflect government tax breaks, i.e., federal and provincial governments did not collect statutory taxes owing. There is some evidence that banks attempt to make these profits look smaller in various quarters by stalling reporting of profits so as not to raise public indignation.

[11]For a discussion of the production of deviant images see Fleming, 1983, **ibid.**

[12]C. Lombroso, "Criminal Man," in **The Heritage of Modern Criminology.** Cambridge: Schenkmann. See also the excellent overview by T. Caputo and R. Linden, "Early Theories of Criminology," in R. Linden (ed.) **Criminology: A Canadian Perspective.** Toronto:Harcourt, 1992: 165-181.

[13]Hopper, **ibid.**

[14]Fleming, 1983, **ibid.**

[15]Jack Levin. **Gossip.** Englewood: Sage, 1992.

[16]Barak, **ibid.** at 98.

[17]Paul Rock. "On the Ownership of Criminological Problems." Paper presented at The Centre of Criminoloy, Toronto, 1981.

[18]See Ward, **ibid.**; Baxter, **ibid.**; Webber, **ibid.**; A.D. Ross, **The Lost and the Lonely: Homeless Women in Montreal.** Montreal: McGill University; B. Farge, "Homeless Women and Freedom of Choice," in **Canadian Journal of Community Mental Health,** 8 (1) 135-145.

[19]Snow et al., **ibid.**; Wright, **ibid.**, Barak, **ibid.**

[20]Foucault, **ibid.**

[21]Mackie, **ibid.**

[22]Mackie, **ibid.**, Spencer, **ibid.**

[23]See DeKeseredy and Hinch, introductory chapter, **ibid.**

[24]Thomas Fleming, "Violent Domestic Assault." Toronto: Centre of Criminology, Unpublished M.A. Thesis, 1975.

[25]DeKeseredy and Hinch, **ibid.**, 1-2.

[26]See DeKeseredy and Hinch, **ibid.**, for a discussion of issues in non-reporting.

[27]See Spencer, **ibid.**; DeKeseredy and Hinch, **ibid.**; T. O'Reilly-Fleming, "Homeless Women and Children in Canada," in **Canadian Women's Studies**, August, 1992.

[28]See Spencer, **ibid.**

[29]This is a difficult dilemma for many women attempting to guage the seriousness of their situation in an abusive relationship as versus the other forms of economic and psychological pain that life in transition may cause them and their children.

[30]See Peter Silverman, **Who Speaks for the Children? The Plight of the Battered Child**. Toronto: General, 1978. Also McLeod, **ibid.**

[31]Badgley, **ibid.**

[32]Ibid.

[33]See for example, D. Currie, "State Intervention and the 'Liberation' of Women: A Femininst Exploration of Family Law" in T. Caputo et al., (eds.) **Law and Society: A Critical Perspective**. Toronto: Harcourt, 1989, 271-292. See generally C. Smart, **Women, Crime and Criminology**. London: RKP, 1979.

[34]**The Windsor Star**, "More feel grip of poverty," Thursday January 9, 1992:A16.

[35]Ibid., at A16.

[36]Ibid., at A16. "Statistics Canada said the drop in incomes last year was widespread."

[37]Ibid. at A16. This represents an increase of 150,000 over 1989.

[38]Ibid.

[39]Ibid.

[40]**The Globe and Mail**, "Cuts in Programs Cloud Future for Poor Children," Saturday December 28, 1991:A9.

[41]Ibid.

[42]Ibid. Quebec now spends in excess of $10 million dollars a year on school feeding programs.

43Ibid.

44Ibid.

45Ibid.

46Ibid.

47Ibid.

48Statistics Canada. Press Release, October 1992. See also, **The Globe and Mail,** "Bank rate plunges to 6.99%," April 16, 1992:A1.

50Statistics Canada. Unemployment Figures, March 1992.

51Alternatively they may find that the funding for retraining schemes has been exhausted due to rising demand. **The Windsor Star,** May 9, 1992:A1, "Rising unemployment drains job retraining fund." During the first four months of the year the $4 million dollar budget had already been spent by Windsor's Canada Employment Centre.

52Restructuring is a form of "doublespeak" for cuts that eliminate employment.

53Announced by the Federal Conservative government.

54Laxer, **ibid.**

55See **The Windsor Star,** "Latest figures continue to cloud local economy," Thursday, January 9, 1992: A1.

56Ibid.

57Ibid.

58Ibid.

59Ibid., See also McBride, **ibid.**

60**The Windsor Star,** "UI Payments soar along with bankruptcies," Saturday, December 21, 1991: A1.

61Ibid.

62Ibid.

63Ibid.

64**The Globe and Mail,** April 3, 1992.

65Ibid.

66Ibid.

67Statistics Canada. Economic Trends, June 1991.

68P. Begin, **Homelessness in Canada.** Ottawa: Research Branch, Library of Parliament, 19 April 1991. See also footnote 69.

69**The Windsor Star,** April 13, 1991: A2, "Ottawa says no to cash for poor."

[70]The Toronto Star, "Metro faces 'horrendous' budget cuts," January 7, 1992: A1.

[71]Ibid.

[72]The Toronto Star, "Public is tired of food drives, organizers fear," April 6, 1992: A3; The Windsor Star, "Food bank demands aid," August 28, 1990, "Toronto's biggest food bank has threatened to bill the Ontario government $32 million for services rendered since 1986. They estimate that by 1991 they were feeding 87,000 people a month; The Toronto Sun, "Poverty menaces our kids," November 26, 1991, Fiona Knight of Foodshare said, "51,000 children use foodbanks every month—up 80% since last year. More than 300,000 children live in poverty in Ontario; Labatt, ibid. at 3, reports that by 1991 the Daily Food Bank was giving away 140,00 pounds of food a week, the same amount they had given away in the entire year in 1984; Jack, ibid. reports that 560,000 children depended on food banks to eat in Canada in 1991 and that 1 in 7 children in Toronto are dependent on food banks. University students have also felt the crunch of a rapidly declining economy and the effects of large losses in the summer and part-time employment market. See Krishnan Ray, "Students flock to food banks as aid falls short," Excalibur, December 4, 1991; Marilyn Scott, "U of T food bank to open soon at Women's Centre," in The Varsity, February 6, 1992. See also The Globe and Mail, "Death of infant five years ago carries child-poverty message," March 30, 1992... physicians and food bank organizers cited the example of a child's death from starvation to illustrate how poverty-stricken children in Manitoba are increasingly in danger because they are often poor and ill-fed."

[73]Ibid.

[74]Ibid.

[75]Shelters may offer a period for "transition" but they rarely provide long-term residence.

[76]Begin, ibid.

[77]Ibid.

[78]Ibid.

[79]Gentrification is a process that refers to the conversion of former low-cost housing through renovation into housing for the middle and upper classes. An example of this process would be the Riverdale district of Toronto formerly a part of "Cabbagetown," a reference to the Irish poor who once inhabited the former slums of this area.

[80]George Fallis and Alex Murray, **Housing the Homeless and Poor: New Partnerships among the Private, Public and Third Sectors,** Toronto: University of Toronto Press, 1990. This is a well researched and very well written book on alternative means of tackling the problems of the homeless. See particularly Alex Murray's excellent chapter entitled, "Homelessness: The People," pp. 16-48. The book presents an excellent analysis of the process of gentrification. See also the discussion in Barak, **ibid.**

[81]Statistics Canada, 1987.

[82]Mackie, **ibid.**

[83]Fallis in Fallis and Murray, **ibid.**

[84]O'Reilly-Fleming, 1990.

[85]Ontario Task Force on Roomers, Boarders and Lodgers, **ibid.**

[86]Fallis and Murray, **ibid.** at 60

[87]Ibid., at 60. O'Reilly-Fleming, 1990, **ibid.**

[88]D. Ley, **Gentrification in Canadian Inner Cities.** Ottawa: CMHC, 1985.

[89]**On the Outside Looking In: An Examination of Homelessness in Calgary.** 1991. Research Report: Social Services.

[90]Begin, **ibid.**

[91]Begin, **ibid.**

[92]Begin, **ibid.**

[93]Begin, **ibid.**

[94]Ibid.

[95]Ibid.

[96]Ibid.

[97]Ibid.

[98]This initiative is for intervention and education.

[99]You cannot be at risk if you have already suffered the indignities associated with poverty and homelessness that have been discussed in this book. This creative use of doublespeak leads to the false conclusion that the 'risk' can be eliminated in advance of damage that has already taken its toll.

[100]Sheila Copps as reported on CBC NEWS.

CHAPTER SIX

[1]Eric Clapton, **Lonely Stranger**. Unichappell Inc., BMI, Copyright.

[2]Fallis and Murray, **ibid.**

[3]See Jack, **ibid.**; Fallis and Murray, **ibid.**

[4]Begin, **ibid.**

[5]J. Wolfe, "Some Present and Future Aspects of Housing and the Third Sector," in J. Hitchcock, et al. (eds.) **The Metropolis**. Toronto: University of Toronto Press, 1985.

[6]Personal communication by the author with front line workers, October 1992.

[7]Homeless Persons Outreach Project, **Homeless not Helpless**. Healthy City Office: Toronto, 1990.

[8]Baxter, **ibid.**

[9]Fallis and Murray, 1991: 289.

[10]George Orwell, **ibid.**, 189.